GOLDEN GATES

GOLDEN GATES

FIGHTING FOR
HOUSING IN AMERICA

CONOR DOUGHERTY

PENGUIN PRESS | NEW YORK
2020

PENGUIN PRESS
An imprint of Penguin Random House LLC
penguinrandomhouse.com

Title page graphic © 2018 *The New York Times*

LIBRARY OF CONGRESS CATALOGING-IN-PUBLICATION DATA
Names: Dougherty, Conor, author.
Title: Golden gates : fighting for housing in America / Conor Dougherty.
Description: New York : Penguin Press, 2020. | Includes bibliographical references and index. |
Identifiers: LCCN 2019039425 (print) | LCCN 2019039426 (ebook) |
ISBN 9780525560210 (hardcover) | ISBN 9780525560227 (ebook)
Subjects: LCSH: Housing—California—San Francisco. |
Working class—Housing—California—San Francisco. |
Zoning—California—San Francisco. | City planning—California—San Francisco.
Classification: LCC HD7304.S3 C68 2020 (print) |
LCC HD7304.S3 (ebook) | DDC 363.509794/61—dc23

Printed in the United States of America
1   3   5   7   9   10   8   6   4   2

BOOK DESIGN BY LUCIA BERNARD

For C⁴

It is a fresh and continuous robbery,
that goes on every day and every hour.

—HENRY GEORGE,
Progress and Poverty, 1879

The center was not holding.

—JOAN DIDION,
Slouching Towards Bethlehem, 1968

CONTENTS

PREFACE

IF YOU ASKED a stadium full of people to close their eyes and imagine what the American dream means to them, a large percentage of the crowd would be thinking of a home. Different homes, no doubt. A ranch house in the suburbs, a fortieth-floor condominium in Manhattan, a one-bedroom apartment in a new country where the kids will get a shot that the parents never had. A home is rarely just a roof over our heads. It's a roof in a bright city, or a neighborhood near work and family, close to a freeway or train stop, with parks and a stretch of water, maybe a street full of shops and restaurants. A good school, a field to plow, a welcoming church, a Sunday drum circle. Home is a private space, and yet it's the community of work and social life that determines where we want it. It's the dream of being as close as possible to the lives we wish to have.

Around the world and country, that dream is under threat. In the United States, the homeownership rate for young adults is at a multi-decade low, and about a quarter of tenant households spend more than half their income on rent. Homelessness is increasing, eviction displaces about a million households a year, and about four million people spend at least three hours commuting to and from work. One need only look out an airplane window to see that this has nothing to do with a lack of space. It's the concentration of opportunity and the rising cost of being near it. It says much about today's winner-take-all economy that many of the cities with the most glaring epidemics of homelessness are growing technology and finance centers where good-paying jobs are plentiful and industries of the future are on the rise. California, home of the nation's worst housing crisis, has the dubious distinction of having somehow managed to produce some of the highest wages in America as well as the highest state poverty rate once the cost of housing is figured in.

This didn't happen all at once. It has become a popular narrative, at least in a certain kind of high-cost city, to say that the reason housing has become so expensive is that working-class neighborhoods are being gentrified, foreign investors are parking money in U.S. condominiums, houses and apartments are being commodified by hedge funds, and companies like Airbnb are turning rental buildings into hotels. These things are all happening, and they've been exacerbated by years of federal disinvestment in affordable housing, a tax code that subsidizes wealthy homeowners at the expense of poor renters, and a building industry that hasn't had any meaningful innovation in decades.

But underneath all that is a larger disease, which is a dire shortage of available housing in places where people and companies want to live, along with tectonic changes in how today's technology-centric economy operates. Unlike in the past, when good-paying manufacturing work spread widely across the country and took middle-class wealth beyond cities into small towns, the new economy is more unequal by nature, and its companies tend to cluster around dense metropolitan areas. This has fueled a resurgence in American downtowns and tons of new jobs for people with a wide range of skill levels, but because U.S. cities don't accommodate new people or housing nearly as well or as eagerly as they used to, the growth has caused new residents and speculators to bid up prices of the not-enough housing that already exists.

For the past several decades, America has by and large solved its housing needs by building progressively cheaper neighborhoods progressively farther out. It has forever changed the landscape and upended our governance as well. In effect, we shattered urban regions into a constellation of smallish cities and reactionary single-family house neighborhoods whose influence over local land use decisions give them an astounding amount of control over how much shelter we build, where, and at what cost. These decisions have huge implications beyond housing. Rising housing costs are a main driver—arguably the main driver—of segregation, income inequality, and racial and generational wealth gaps. You can't talk about educational inequities or the shrinking middle class without talking about how much it costs to live near good schools and high-paying jobs. Transportation accounts for about a third of the nation's carbon dioxide emissions, so there's no serious plan for climate change that doesn't begin with a conversation about how to alter the urban landscape so that people can live closer to work.

One way or the other, many of the biggest challenges in America are at some level a housing problem, which is why there is now tremendous pressure on cities to abandon the old pattern of building subdivisions on distant cow pastures and instead to favor taller, denser buildings in places where people already live. The meaning of density varies, from condo towers in the urban core to triplex apartment buildings and backyard cottages in the enclaves of single-family houses beyond. Either way, as cities drive to put more housing in established neighborhoods, the result has been a furious clash over growth, class, preservation, quality of life, and the environment.

The story of modern America is the story of a nation struggling to reconcile the way things are today versus the way we think they used to be. Housing is a central narrative here as well, and like so much of contemporary society that story begins at the end of World War II. In October 1945, a month after the war ended, *Life* magazine ran a thirteen-page spread titled "The California Way of Life." The idea was to use California as a window into postwar trends—the state "may in time radically influence the pattern of life in America as a whole," the magazine wrote—and they did it by profiling three Los Angeles families who made $50,000 a year, $10,000 a year, and $3,000 a year (about $700,000, $140,000, and $42,000, respectively, in 2019 dollars).

The rich family, the Stotharts, lived in a big house in Santa Monica with a live-in cook and four cars. The middle family, the Campbells, were nearby in a West Los Angeles ranch house with a pool on a three-quarter-acre lot. No servants, two cars. The surprise was the third family, which was headed by a fireman named LeRoy Loeffler. The Loefflers lived in a six-room bungalow in Glendale that was full of modern appliances and had a backyard patio and lemon tree. "The Campbells do not live as differently from the Loefflers as might be supposed from the difference in incomes," *Life* noted.

There's plenty about this picture that we can't or don't want to go back to. All of the families were white. Women's lives are described in terms of shopping trips and social circles. *Life* made casual mention of the Stotharts' "Negro cook" and no mention of the black families across the nation who were being denied access to the federally backed loans that the Loefflers bought their house with. Circa 1945, *Life* also seemed to operate under an assumption of endless open space connected by endless open freeways. The wrongs of the past are so easy to identify that it can be hard to appreciate the pieces that feel right. What feels right about the story isn't the style of the houses or the size of their respective yards, but that it defines affluence in terms of breadth. It's a picture that can't be reproduced today, when the California housing story is about a growing market for homes that cost $30 million and up, Silicon Valley software engineers who consider a $400,000 annual salary middle-class, and teachers who get up at 4:00 a.m. to drive to work and along the way pass tent cities under freeways.

This book is about that new, less flattering version of California. Most of it takes place in the San Francisco Bay Area, the nation's foremost center of technology and a place where housing costs are routinely described as "a crisis." The region's cost problems are so longstanding and extreme that it provides a bright and fully formed picture of how housing goes wrong and the mix of solutions that can help fix it. But San Francisco is just an exaggerated example of the geographic inequalities that are rising in tandem with global income and wealth gaps, and a cautionary tale of what happens when you combine a highperforming economy with decades of antigrowth sentiment. You can find the same basic story, in different shades and tones, in Seattle, Minneapolis, and Nashville, or Vancouver, London, and Berlin—cities that are economically leaving their peers and where a steep rise in housing costs has made it harder for lower-income people to benefit from the fruits of growth.

City planners started documenting the urban housing shortage in the 1970s, and in the decades since economists have shown that many of the country's highest-income regions have become so expensive that they have all but gated out middle-class jobs and people. According to some studies, the exorbitant cost of living in such places is distorting state-to-state migration and reducing the entire nation's economic growth. The ability to move to a high-opportunity city is a huge and vastly underrated piece of how societies get richer. Growing cities tend to have the highest economic mobility, and there's plenty of data and common sense to support the idea that people's lives can be vastly improved by going from a place that doesn't have much work to a place that has a lot of it.

And yet, at a time when America is facing big questions about how to make the economy better and more just, the idea that we should be making it easier for people to live in high-mobility places gets little attention outside academic circles. This is not to suggest that politicians should start telling the residents of depressed places to abandon their homes for cities that are better off, but they could at least try to make it easier for those who would like to. When the country's highest-growth regions become so expensive that it is considered an extravagant luxury for people to live near jobs and industries that everyone in America has played at least some role in building, that qualifies as a major national issue.

Golden Gates is the story of how we got here and some of the early efforts to solve what is fast becoming a national housing crisis. It's a story about one group of people searching for new homes while another group of people clings to the ones they have. The struggle at the center is the struggle to make space and coexist. This is fundamentally a struggle of politics, but those politics do not conform to a red/blue map. Cities are ultimately about people, so this book is too.

There is an upstart activist who helps create a national movement that says yes to new development, a fifteen-year-old girl who leads her apartment complex in a fight against eviction, a suburban city manager who goes rogue in a crisis of conscience, a developer who spends his golden years trying to build housing on an assembly line, a South LA anti-gentrification activist who builds alliances with politicians in Beverly Hills, and a nun who becomes a property mogul in an effort to outmaneuver gouging landlords. Sometimes together and frequently in opposition, these people meet in the halls of democracy to chart a new course for urban America while reconciling with capitalism, each other, and the nation's oldest sins. If they succeed, they will have undone some of the deepest tribal patterns and answered the endless question of civilization, which is where we're all going to live. They won't succeed, by the end of this book or in their lifetimes. But together they could make things better, or at least we should all hope.

CHAPTER 1

MEMBERS OF THE PUBLIC

THE POLITICAL REVOLUTION known as BARF began during a seven-hour-and-fifty-two-minute planning meeting inside San Francisco City Hall. It was half a century in the making and in the space of two years would upend California politics and help to spawn a national uprising of angry, millennial-aged renters. But there on that first day you almost had to squint to see it. The meeting was in the judicial-looking chambers of the San Francisco Planning Commission, and it had been going for about three and a half hours when the commissioners turned their attention to a proposal for a new building that would have eighty-three subsidized apartments reserved for low-income households in the impoverished Tenderloin neighborhood. When it was time for public comment, a nervous young woman in a striped sweater and shorts walked from her seat to the audience microphone and addressed the semicircle of commissioners sitting on the platform in front of her.

"Hi, my name is Sonja Trauss," she said. "I'm just a member of the public, and I'm here because there is a housing shortage in San

Francisco. And, um, I look forward to as much new housing being brought to market at all levels, uhh, as possible. I mean, quickly as possible. Thanks."

Whoever this Sonja was, she was obviously not alone. Over the next hour, she and a bearded friend kept using the public comment time to say they were in favor of every project in the pipeline, as well as more housing generally. It began with the 83 subsidized apartments in the Tenderloin, then continued with the 111 units at 650 Indiana Street and the 259 units at 1201 Tennessee. Through hastily prepared comments that she strung together with a surplus of "ums" and "sos," Sonja proceeded to lay out a platform that would make her a housing celebrity and inspire a run for city office: how expensive new housing today would become affordable old housing tomorrow, how San Francisco was blowing its chance to harness the energy of an economic boom to mass-build housing that generations of residents could use. She wasn't there to complain about shadows over her yard or a lack of parking on her street. She didn't care if a proposal was for apartments or condominiums or how much money its future residents had. It was a universal platform of more. Sonja was for anything and everything, so long as it was built tall and fast and had people living in it.

"I decided to come speak in support of large housing projects when I realized that the entitlement process is biased against beneficiaries of new building," she told the commission when the Indiana Street project was up. "So neighbors around the projects, with valuable opinions, um, you know, get notified, but the potential probably two hundred new residents have no way of giving input into whether, like, this project or any similar project gets to be built. . . . Sooooo, I'm part of the general community of renters in the Bay Area, so I'm affected by the lack of housing through high rent and lack of options, so I'm here on behalf of myself as, like, a general part of the public. So yeah, so, in general, I'm here to remind the planning commission to consider all the people that will benefit from this once it's built. Because they don't exist yet as, you know, as renters."

The rhetoric wasn't new. The term "NIMBY," developer shorthand for "not in my backyard," had been around for at least four decades at that point, and there were numerous books, countless news articles, and an entire sub-specialty of economics to show that the Bay Area was the national capital of NIMBYism. Had she been a man with white hair or identified herself as the employee of a real estate developer, chances are nobody would have noticed. But for a young adult with no obvious signs of intoxication to show up at a midday city meeting to say she was just generally in favor of housing because San Francisco didn't have enough of it? That made no sense.

Nobody attended eight-hour city meetings if they didn't have to, and while the planning commission was a place of arguments and strange behavior, it was also a place where people at least knew where each other's lanes were. The people who showed up to speak in favor of new projects were the developers who'd proposed them, the trade organizations they paid to shill for them, the unions who worked for them, and the community organizations whose wheels they had successfully greased. The people who showed up to oppose new projects consisted of environmentalists, angry neighbors, and community organizations that felt their wheels hadn't been greased enough. Sonja claimed to be none of these—"just a member of the public."

After the meeting, people walked up to her in the marble hallway to try to figure out if someone had sent her. *What's your name?* Sonja. *What do you do?* I'm a high school math teacher. *What brought you here today?* I'm just a member of the public. The sorts of people who were usually against things asked Sonja questions that were designed to figure out which developer she secretly worked for. The developers she secretly didn't work for tried to figure out if the opposition had recruited her as a reverse-psychology trick. Whichever side they were on, bystanders wanted to know where she had come from and if she had a hidden angle.

Sonja was a grad school dropout who had moved to the Bay Area because she was too embarrassed to move home. She was originally from Philadelphia and ended up in California after bailing out of the economics PhD program at Washington University in St. Louis. Technically speaking, she'd left with a master's, but school had not gone well, and because she was too proud to go back to Philadelphia after telling all her friends that she was off to become Dr. Sonja Trauss, she continued west to El Cerrito, a few miles north of Berkeley, to help her dad's cousin Myrna while she went through chemotherapy. It seemed like a good thing to do for family while she figured out what to do with herself, although that figuring was a lot easier when you had someone you could stay with.

After Myrna's treatment, when Sonja went looking for work and an apartment, she joined the long line of people who'd discovered that the Bay Area was an easy place to get a job and an impossible place to afford rent. She and two friends got a West Oakland apartment that cost $3,000 a month, and Sonja started teaching math at a pair of across-the-bay community colleges for $20 an hour, before quitting to make $10.50 an hour at a nearby bakery that didn't involve commuting. It made sense: once she subtracted the cost of all the buses, trains, and ferries that sat between her place and the two teaching jobs, the bakery's take-home pay was the same. It was also depressing: working the night shift twisting pretzel dough was not what she'd expected to be doing at thirty.

She'd never really had it together in the career department. Sonja graduated from Temple with a philosophy degree, then went to law school and dropped out. Later came the economist phase that sent her to the Midwest before she left. She'd been a bike messenger, a window washer, and a legal aide. She worked at a neighborhood association and answered the phones at a mortgage hotline in the throes of the financial crisis. Sonja liked reading and school, and her mom was a nurse and her dad was a lawyer, so the professional expectation was there. She just could never throw herself into the pursuit of a real job or credential the way she could so totally throw herself into the new hobbies and activist side projects she picked up whenever some problem or perceived injustice appeared along the way.

This had started early. In seventh grade Sonja got sent to detention after she and a friend persuaded their science class to be dead silent for an entire class period to punish the teacher for telling the class to shut up. No questions, no greetings, nothing but eerie preteen stares for forty-five straight minutes. She'd been arrested for protesting a city plan to renovate a popular park so that it wouldn't be so attractive to skateboarders, and later spent a year organizing friends and sewing spandex costumes as part of the founding of a thirty-person comedy troupe, the Vaudevillains, that marched in the New Year's Mummers Parade. When the owner of a printing press across the street from her house in Philly started operating at all hours, Sonja turned it into a months-long war that began with a noise complaint to the city, escalated to more complaints about the city's lack of responsiveness, and ended after she started calling the owner of the printing press's cell phone and leaving messages that consisted of nothing but the sound of his press in the background while she held the phone out of her bedroom window, then kept calling, over and over, until the voice mail ran out of space and the owner asked a judge for a restraining order.

In Philly, you could afford to be a marginally employed rabble-rouser because everything was cheap. Sonja had a cheap four-bedroom house that had open walls with exposed wiring, and she packed it with cheap artist and musician roommates who turned the place into a subcultural melting pot of punks, rappers, artists, zinesters, graffiti writers, Hollertronix DJs, and grad students. Years later, the people who lived and hung out there would describe it with strange vignettes, like how Spank Rock and Santigold once filmed a music video in the living room, or how there was this one period when Sonja got really into weight lifting and another when she was all about role-playing games, and how on occasion these interests would overlap and one day you'd come home and find her in a circle with a bunch of buff dudes drinking protein shakes while playing *Call of Cthulhu*. Bargain rent was the backdrop, the freedom that brought these scenes into existence. And it was 180 the experience of the Bay Area, where art seemed to be defined by political activism and the struggle of just being there.

This was never more true than it was during one of the region's periodic tech booms. During the late 1990s dot-com boom, a group called the Mission Yuppie Eradication Project started encouraging residents of San Francisco's Mission District to vandalize parked SUVs on the logic that this would prompt young professionals to move to neighborhoods where their cars were safer (and the restaurants who catered to them to go out of business). Two decades later, when Sonja arrived at the beginning of a new boom tied to smartphones and social media, the yuppies had traded their SUVs for Ubers, so activists had instead taken to spray-painting the sidewalks with phrases like "Tech Scum" in nicely stenciled lettering. Things started escalating in 2013, when a group calling itself Heart of the City descended on the annual Pride Parade with a white bus emblazoned with a banner that read "Gentrification & Eviction Technologies OUT" (GET OUT) in Google font and coloring. Later that year, on December 9, 2013, the same group created a human blockade that prevented one of Google's employees-only shuttle buses from leaving a stop in the Mission en route to the company's headquarters, which sat thirty-five traffic-choked miles away in the Silicon Valley city of Mountain View.

Anyone in search of a meme-ready example of the "barbell economy"— bulges of rich and poor separated by a rail of middle class—would have a hard time doing better than the Bay Area tech buses. They were hulking double-deckers with velvety seats and fast Wi-Fi and tinted windows to hide the private lives of software geeks. It wasn't just that tech jobs paid well and came with a ride to work. They had good health care and free lunch and gyms and laundry, and the people who got them were "talent." The spectacle of a bus full of talent being protested by several dozen people holding signs that said things like "Stop Evictions Now" and "Warning: Two Tier System" seemed to encapsulate America's vastly more unequal direction, and within a few hours the story, which had been heavily chronicled on Twitter, was splashed on newspaper home pages around the world.

Sonja was plenty bothered by rising rents but had a different view on what the problem was. Having spent most of her life in Philadelphia, a city with blocks of empty property that had lost about half a million people from its 1950 peak, she knew what a troubled city looked like and was not going to blame anyone for moving to a region that to an outsider felt like an economic wonderland. It had been only a few years since the Great Recession. Most of America was still grappling with what the pundits called "a jobless recovery" (whatever that meant), while the Bay Area lived in a bubble of exuberance and self-satisfaction. Google had just revealed its self-driving car project, Facebook was gearing up to go public, and the venture capitalist Marc Andreessen was coining the phrase "software is eating the world." Sonja thought it was exciting to live in a place with so much optimism and easy employment, and when she heard people complain about how San Francisco was being murdered by runaway growth, she regarded them as ingrates who didn't know or didn't care what places like Philly and St. Louis looked like.

So, no, the problem was not too many jobs, which is fundamentally what the tech protests were about. The problem, as Sonja saw it, was too little housing. She was two years removed from economics school. The law of supply and demand was still fresh in her mind. She'd also found it shocking just how flat Bay Area cities seemed to be given how much it cost to live there. There were some skyscrapers and a few Parisian-height neighborhoods around the core of San Francisco and Oakland, but most of the rest was single-family houses, and the region's two major commuter rail lines, Bay Area Rapid Transit (BART) and Caltrain, were surrounded by empty fields and sprawl of the sort Northern Californians supposedly scoffed at LA and Orange County for. The mythical Silicon Valley, charter of America's future, was a land of unremarkable cul-de-sacs with unremarkable $2 million houses, surrounded by a bunch of office parks and strip malls that could be mistaken for the suburbs of Phoenix. And yet seemingly anytime someone talked about building a duplex or triplex, let alone a five- or six-story building, it was tarred for having too many shadows or being "out of character."

Out of character was a concept Sonja had failed to absorb. She grew up in a three-story house in Germantown with enough rooms to test your vocabulary (study, cloakroom) along with a suburban-scale yard with a swing set surrounded by thick greenery. The building next door, which filled the view from her childhood window, was a four-story apartment complex. It sat across the street from an even taller public housing project, near a single-family house that had been turned into a halfway home. The walk from Sonja's house to a nearby strip of beauty shops and discount stores had houses next to schools next to offices next to a convalescent home, which was near a park next to a coffee shop that sat across the street from the historic Germantown White House, which is a little gray building that according to an outdoor plaque is where George Washington lived for a few weeks during the yellow fever epidemic of 1793, back when Germantown was a rural village. This was Sonja's version of normal, and it made her psychologically out of place with most Americans' notion of what an orderly neighborhood should look like.

Patterned on the American mind, in ways we rarely stop to notice, are layers of zoning and land-use rules that say what can be built where. They are so central to how American cities look and operate that they have become a kind of geographic DNA that forms our opinion of what seems proper and right. The idea is to divide cities up based on what should go near what, which clearly has some logic to it. The classic defense of zoning is that you wouldn't want to make it legal for someone to build a chemical factory next to a school, and you can find at least some kind of building regulation, at least by custom or culture, in essentially every city on earth going back to ancient Babylon. Napoleon appears to have pioneered the idea of separating housing from polluting industries by royal decree in 1810. Germany invented municipal zoning a few decades later, and it spread around the Continent before jumping to America, where it became something else entirely.

Unlike Europe, where zoning started as a centralized endeavor that consisted of a few relatively simple rules for how a city should be laid out, American zoning was local and community-centric, which is another way of saying haphazard and idiosyncratic. Part of Germany's logic for zoning was to make private land less expensive by regulating how it could be used. In America, zoning was often used to raise or at least protect property values, and over time this caused people to see office and residential neighborhoods as rigidly distinct and to treat single-family houses and apartment buildings as alien forms of living.

Cities started dividing up housing types around the turn of the twentieth century, and it was Berkeley, in 1916, that wrote what was probably the nation's first ordinance creating neighborhoods with single-family houses only. Rules are full of paradox, and so it is with land use and zoning. One person's protection is another person's exclusion, which is why just about every city hall zoning fight can be summarized as one side talking about its freedoms and another side answering, "Free for whom?" Does zoning protect property rights or restrict them? Does it promote economic freedom or hamper it? Is it capitalist or socialist? There is no single answer, which is why zoning says a lot about who we are and who we are becoming. At least at the local level, zoning is democracy, and democracy is zoning.

Philadelphia is as regulated as any other place is, and Sonja's neighborhood wasn't exactly unplanned. Still, she only knew what she'd grown up with, which was a block whose mash-up of history stretched from the colonial period and Revolutionary War through industrial growth, industrial decline, urban blight, and urban revival. It was a mix of squat and tall, commercial and residential, historic and new, and it gave her a centuries-long sense of just how much the inner lives of buildings changed with the passage of time.

Take, for instance, the Fairfax, which was the name of the apartment building that filled the view from her bedroom window. The Fairfax was a stately brick building with portico balconies and an arched entryway that according to a 1914 advertisement was intended for "a most discriminating class of prospective occupants." Back then, the rent included bellboy service and maids by the hour, and the ad described Germantown as "fashionable" and boasted about the three-minute walk to the Chelten Avenue train station. Those attributes fell out of favor as America built the freeways and Philly saw a good chunk of its population bolt to surrounding suburbs. By the mid-1980s, the Fairfax was in the hands of a pair of debt-burdened investors who presided over an ignominious period of burned-out lightbulbs and unanswered tenant complaints.

It was right around the moment when the dumpsters started overflowing that Sonja's dad, Irwin Trauss, surmised that the owners had probably abandoned the building. It was also around that time that the building's front-door call system stopped working, and Sonja got used to a nighttime routine in which she would lie on her bed looking at the fluorescent stars on her ceiling while listening to Fairfax visitors announce their arrival by yelling to a friend's window and asking him or her to drop the keys. Then someone shattered the glass front door, and yelling was no longer necessary. The Fairfax's abandonment was great for the building's superintendent, who converted his sudden unemployment into a lucrative business pocketing rents before disappearing with a cash nest egg. The remaining tenants picked up the enterprise by renting kicked-in apartments to random people off the street, and from there the building was overrun with squatters and a crack dealer who often had dozens of antsy customers waiting in the marble hallways during his peak Friday night hours.

It's one thing to have your city decline in the pages of a local newspaper. It's another to see it fester next to the home where you're raising your children. The only perimeter between the Fairfax and Sonja's house was an old cedar fence that was leaning and full of holes, and the family lost a number of TVs and VCRs to burglars. This was reality for some people, but families with options had to ask hard questions about just how long they were willing to hold on. For Irwin and Sonja's mom, Georgette, the answers for how to deal with the problem were diametrically opposite. Georgette started looking at potential new houses in the suburbs, while Irwin started looking for investors and worked out a plan to buy the Fairfax so that he could clean it up on his own.

Irwin's parents were Polish Jews and Holocaust survivors who had moved to Philadelphia after the war. Sonja's grandmother, Blanka Trauss, was in the Warsaw ghetto during the uprising and made it through Majdanek, Auschwitz, Bergen-Belsen, Aschersleben, and Theresienstadt before the Russians freed her and two remaining sisters (Blanka was one of eight girls and each of her other five sisters were murdered by the Nazis). After liberation Blanka sailed to America with Sonja's grandfather Kazimir, and along with her siblings produced a brood of social justice–minded shrinks, teachers, and civil rights lawyers. Irwin, the youngest, was a nonprofit housing lawyer who defended homeowners from foreclosing banks. After a career of fighting bad actors, he was intrigued by the challenge of trying to rescue the Fairfax from negligence and return it to stability. Neighbors thought he was delusional, and the week before the purchase was finalized, a police raid left one of the apartments with splintered furniture, broken windows, and a thoroughly demolished bathroom. Many people would see an omen. Irwin reasoned the wrecked unit had probably held the most criminally inclined tenants, and if their apartment was now uninhabitable, the building could only get better from there. And after years of night and weekend renovations, it did.

Sonja would later recall all sorts of little lessons from this experience. How an excess of property leads to lower rents. How once high-end buildings filtered down the income ladder. Also, her father's gumption. Before the Fairfax, all she knew of her dad and work was that he was a lawyer who took an elevator up an office building and sometimes went to court. Buying and running an apartment complex seemed like some special skill that certified apartment people were supposed to handle. And yet, when her mom was out engaging in the sensible business of shopping for a new house, Irwin was calling investors and talking to banks and dealing with tenants and haggling with contractors and doing repairs. The impression it made on Sonja was that it was possible for a regular person to insert himself into a big and complicated problem that he seemingly had no business getting involved in.

When the tech bus protests broke out in San Francisco, Sonja was dating a software engineer named Micah Catlin, and one of their frequent outings was to go to a bar called the Trappist and loudly agree that the Bay Area didn't have enough housing. The bus protesters were right to be angry about rent but were focusing on the wrong things. The data was on Sonja's side here. In the time she had lived in California, the Bay Area region had created about eight new jobs for every new housing unit, way beyond the figure of one and a half jobs per housing unit that planners considered healthy. In essence, the policy was to enthusiastically encourage people to move there for work while equally enthusiastically discouraging developers from building places for those people to live, stoking a generational battle in which the rising cost of housing enriched people who already owned it and discouraged anyone who wasn't well-paid or well-off from showing up.

Even if local politicians never set out to create the perfect conditions for punitive housing costs and a frenzied market beset by dangerous overcrowding and speculators that displaced poor renters who were already barely holding on, this was nevertheless what they had done. It was easy and satisfying to characterize this as Google buses versus everyone else, but when you got behind the numbers and discovered that behind each job was someone like Sonja, a local teacher, or Micah, an engineer from Salina, Kansas (population: 47,716), the caricature was harder to hold. Even the anti-gentrification activists were frequently from somewhere else, making them agents of the forces they were protesting, whether they admitted it or not.

By now Sonja had left the bakery and become a high school math teacher. The practical thing to do, at thirty-two, was to focus on stability and make the job stick. But she could never ignore a cause, so she started writing letters. In February 2014, two months after the first bus protest, she sat down in her Oakland apartment and wrote to the San Francisco Planning Commission in support of an upcoming proposal for a new apartment building. She signed it "Sonja Trauss, President, SF Bay Area Association of Renters." To keep track of new projects, she signed up for a city service that sent paper mailers to anyone who wanted to be alerted to new permit applications. There ensued a torrent of envelopes addressed to Sonja Trauss of SF BAAR.

After seeing enough of this mail, her roommate Max suggested she change the group's name to SF BARF. This on the logic that nobody was going to care what a nonexistent organization called SF BAAR thought of the local housing situation. Nobody was likely to care what SF BARF thought either, but they would at least notice it. The acronym could stand for SF Bay Area Renters' . . . and the *F* would be "Federation," like the United Federation of Planets in *Star Trek*. Sonja thought it was funny and went online to see if the sfbarf.org domain name was available, and sure enough it was, and she bought it. Not long after, she and Micah took a day off work to go to San Francisco City Hall and speak in favor of some projects and prove SF BARF was for real.

CHAPTER 2

ORGANIZING THE UNORGANIZABLE

IF THE PEOPLE OF San Francisco were surprised by Sonja Trauss, they shouldn't have been. The emergence of her or someone like her had been forecast by decades of books, newspaper articles, and academic studies that had made all the same observations about a housing shortage years before she was born. The question wasn't whether she had a point about the Bay Area underbuilding housing, but whether she or someone like her could create a political movement to challenge the entrenched constituency of homeowners that had a strong financial incentive to see housing affordability get worse. That was another subject people had started contemplating even before Sonja was born, and the consensus they had come to, in a pre-social-media world, was that it would be all but impossible to organize a group like SF BARF. How do you stoke the outrage of people who don't live somewhere *yet*? And even if you do stoke their outrage, how do you change policy when most of those people can't vote in the place that is refusing to build housing for them?

The first time someone asked those questions, at least the first time housing economists remember someone asking those questions, was in a 1979 book called *The Environmental Protection Hustle.* The author was an MIT urban planning professor named Bernard Frieden who had done his research during a one-year residency at UC Berkeley. Frieden wrote in the preface that he had gone west with the intention of writing a book about things the federal government could do to improve housing affordability for young families, and upon arriving in California and encountering the Bay Area's rampant and toxic NIMBYism, had decided to change course and write about local housing policy instead. California was far from the only place where antigrowth politics were conspiring to raise prices for entry-level buyers, but it was way ahead of the rest of the country, in regulation and housing costs too.

The book was unforgiving, and its tone veered from incredulous to disgusted. Frieden used phrases like "arrogant," "self-serving," and "moral righteousness" to characterize the Bay Area's land policies, and used example after example to call into question the region's already-well-established reputation for progressive social policy. He wrote about how the region funded its BART commuter rail system with a series of regressive taxes that fell harder on poor people, then used strict anti-growth policies that had the effect of preventing those people from living near it. How the Sierra Club would oppose exurban housing for creating more commuters, suburban housing for not being closer to central cities, and urban housing for using up city space. Frieden spent an entire chapter bashing Marin County, a woodsy enclave that sits across the Golden Gate Bridge from San Francisco, employing a series of devastating anecdotes like hikers who protested measures to make nature more accessible to disabled people and homeowners who used environmental logic to fight a subsidized housing development for the elderly.

Frieden was no zealot, and *The Environmental Protection Hustle* was not the Fox News screed that the unfortunate title conjures. The book had all sorts of caveats about how the Bay Area was an especially scenic place, and it acknowledged the region had done plenty of good by protecting natural treasures like Napa Valley and Muir Woods from the eyesore of overdevelopment. His contention was that festering antigrowth politics, which began as a very reasonable backlash to sprawl, had swung way in the other direction and were now using the front of environmentalism to prevent people from moving to denser corridors where housing was actually supposed to go.

Frieden didn't believe nature had much to do with this—such policies were actually anti-environment, because they only promoted sprawled growth elsewhere—and he seemed baffled that the press wasn't calling it out. In the years Frieden was writing his book, newspapers were running headlines like "The American Dream Becomes an American Nightmare," and *Time* magazine had a cover story titled "Sky-High Housing" that included a picture of a couple and their dog looking upward at a house floating above their heads and out of reach. "Although local hostility to growth has attracted some national attention, very few reporters or researchers have connected it to the rising cost of new homes," he wrote. "These have been separate stories: headlines such as 'Nation's Cities Fighting to Stem Growth' simply had nothing to do with the other headlines about the end of the American Dream."

As for how to fix it, Frieden seemed pessimistic that a political solution could be found. The people who got hurt didn't know whom they were supposed to be angry at and had no way to conceptualize the nonbuilding of homes they might have lived in if only they'd been built. Such people, Frieden wrote, "are unorganized, and probably unorganizable."

And for decades it was true: unorganized and unorganizable. Frieden's book caused a minor stir among land-use scholars who had never seen the growing environmental movement called out so forcefully, and while the book did not bring the Bay Area or the nation any closer to solving the NIMBY problem, it staked out a new policy issue and inspired generations of economists to take his ideas and build on them. The first person in this chain was one of Frieden's former students, an economist named Ken Rosen, who became a professor at Berkeley shortly after Frieden returned to Massachusetts. Rosen would go on to produce a number of influential studies that essentially put numbers on the arguments in *The Environmental Protection Hustle*. The studies wouldn't do much to change policy, but they helped bring attention to the housing shortage—"Changing San Francisco Is Foreseen as a Haven for Wealthy and Childless," blared a *New York Times* headline in 1981— and would in turn inspire more economists to do more studies as the problem continued to metastasize.

Three days after the *Times*'s "Wealthy and Childless" headline, one of Rosen's students, an undergraduate named Larry Katz, graduated as Berkeley's top economics student and gave an entire commencement speech about the Bay Area not having enough housing:

> I would like to begin my discussion with the following observation. This observation is that although it is fairly well-known that California in general and the San Francisco Bay Area in particular hold the dubious distinction of having the highest housing prices in the country, exceeding the national median by well over 50 percent, I believe it is not nearly as well-known that this is a very recent phenomenon and that as little as 10 years ago California house prices were not much greater than the national median.
>
> As my fellow graduates surely must be thinking, a primary economic issue here is the identity of those supply and demand factors which can account for this sharp relative price acceleration. The standard explanation has relied solely on demand factors such as the recent upsurge in California household formation and California's vibrant economy. Yet, the empirical evidence suggests that the strong demand for housing can only partially explain this rapid house price inflation. The fact that California experienced even greater demand pressure in the late 1950s and early 1960s without a similar relative price explosion supports the view that the demand size does not provide a full explanation. Thus, there is a missing ingredient, and I contend that this missing ingredient is some sort of supply constraint.

Katz's speech ended on the same political conundrum Frieden had identified, which was that high-voting homeowners had every reason to see the status quo persist. "I believe, regrettably, that this will require some sort of state or federal action," Katz said. He left Berkeley for MIT a few months later and went on to become a Harvard professor and one of the world's foremost labor economists.

It was hard to see this so clearly back then, but America was in the middle of a vast realignment that was fundamentally altering where we live, how we work, and the structure of our families. The early markers were all there. After decades of depopulation and white flight, cities were slowly coming back to life and attracting young professionals. Inequality was rising, homelessness appearing on city streets, and Silicon Valley establishing itself as the nation's foremost center of technology and a really good place to get rich. Zoning rules and NIMBYism had nothing to do with these underlying trends. They would nevertheless run into them. The collisions grew in intensity and raised the cost of living a little more each decade, until you had a thirty-year trend that, upon being amplified by the Great Recession, threw the housing market so out of whack that it started distorting the entire national economy and became impossible to ignore.

In those early moments, however, housing still seemed like a local enough problem that it was hard for anyone with a national viewpoint to get too worked up about it. Poverty. Rising health-care costs. The continued loss of factory jobs. America had plenty of other, more pressing issues, and higher-level policy makers were necessarily more concerned with guiding the country through each particular boom and rough patch than taking a time-out to reconcile with just how radically the world was shifting.

There is an arc to technological progress, and the arc goes something like this. A group of people start playing around with a new invention that has the potential to make them and society richer by solving a big problem that currently requires a lot of work. Investors rush in, companies compete like mad, a handful of those companies win, the big companies eat the little ones, and jobs that once required a large labor force are either automated by machinery or moved to cheaper places. In the early twentieth century, when automobiles were a hot new thing, Detroit was a hive of speculative investment and audacious start-up founders like Henry Ford, Ransom Olds, the Dodge brothers, and David Dunbar Buick. As car companies and other manufacturers got their technologies pretty well figured out, they shifted from inventing new things to making those things widely available and cheap by distributing their production away from headquarters cities to plants around the country. It was an egalitarian moment, filling small towns and suburbs with millions of new factory jobs that paid a solid wage yet were simple enough to perform that broad swaths of the population could get them without having to go to college. It was also a perilous moment for cities, which began to shed their base of jobs making cars, garments, appliances, and every other factory-built product (which eventually became so easy to produce that jobs that had left cities for cheaper places in America would be sent overseas).

By the early 1980s, America was solidly at the end of the mid-century manufacturing boom that gave us cheap consumer goods and a broad middle class built around suburbs. Cities like Detroit were spinning into decay, but other cities were reinventing themselves. Places like New York, San Francisco, and Seattle all got rocked by all the same forces that rocked the industrial Midwest. The difference was a hard-to-replicate mix of an educated populace and the presence of one or several good research universities, which helped them bounce back from industrial rot and become the beneficiaries of a new inventive arc that was tied to computers and resulted in the various digital devices that we now watch and date movies with.

Big metro areas are where companies want to be at the beginning of a technological leap, because leaps are the product of collaboration. Whenever the economy hits a particularly innovative period and cities fill up with new kinds of jobs and industries that gather in some district so that they can steal designs and each other's employees, what's happening is less like a competition and more like an informal, society-wide meeting where a bunch of different actors are all feverishly trying to figure out what to do with whatever new tool we've just invented. Dense spaces are a good place to have this meeting because whenever people are struggling to figure something out, they seem to want to be around a bunch of similarly occupied people whom they can watch and borrow ideas from and/or ask for help. This is why the people who predicted that the internet would lead to the death of centrally located offices were wrong. Try to put your most complex thought into an email and then go meet someone and try to explain it in person, and think about the banter and the smiles, and gauge the effectiveness of seeing someone be excited when you're onto something, and the polite head shakes when you're not, and then ask yourself which of those two methods is a better way to communicate a half-formed idea. Density gave us cars in turn-of-the-century Detroit and would give us computers in the information age.

Urban cores started recovering in the 1980s and 1990s, and by the early 2000s, cities—in particular, cities with big tech and finance industries—were back in roaring form. Companies were moving downtown, *Sex and the City* was in its heyday, and yuppies were engaging in strange new trends like going to goofily hidden cocktail bars and the next day soothing their hangovers with $4 pour-over coffee that takes about thirty-five minutes to produce. It was not unlike the early twentieth-century boom, when America grew into a consumer society and New York—which was already a well-developed place at that point—added three and a half million people between 1900 and 1930.

Except this time, after decades of suburban and exurban housing growth, and the creation of so many new zoning and land-use regulations, cities and their surrounding suburbs were politically ill-equipped to add people, and they were especially ill-equipped to add them in city neighborhoods and closer-in suburbs that were home to reactive homeowners of the sort Bernard Frieden wrote his book about. So instead of becoming vastly bigger as cities did in earlier eras, the brain centers that were becoming America's new industrial powerhouses started to become vastly more expensive, stoking waves of gentrification and displacement and limiting the new golden age to a relative and privileged few.

Layered on top of this were a bunch of related trends that only made housing demand stronger and housing prices more expensive. Young people started delaying marriage and having fewer or no children, which had the effect of increasing the number of households within a set population; even in the late 1970s, when San Francisco was still losing people, it was already starting to add households. Add in income inequality, which exploded as good-paying factory jobs went away and were replaced with low-end service and retail positions, while engineering and other high-skill professions pulled away from the rest. All of this met in the dense confines of cities, where tech and finance workers sought the face-to-face contact that fuels creativity, and lower-paying service professions sought the higher-paid employees who could afford massages, gym classes, and frequent restaurant meals.

Unless you were a planner or economist who thought about far-out projections, it was hard to see how these trends related to housing policy, because there was always some cyclical up and down to obscure the long trend of declining affordability. A month after Larry Katz delivered his Berkeley speech warning about California's housing troubles to come, the United States entered a recession, and in the following years mortgage rates plunged. In the mid-2000s, banks made it temporarily easier to buy homes by giving out the easy-money loans that would stoke the housing bubble and bust. Then the financial crisis hit, and the news was full of stories about empty subdivisions and underwater mortgages.

Finally, during the long recovery from the Great Recession, every single thing about housing became horrible at once. Tech took over the economy and fomented an explosion in software jobs that would create America's first trillion-dollar companies. The boom was exacerbated by a population bulge of millennials—on their way to becoming the largest generation in U.S. history—who started leaving college and their parents' homes in search of apartments in city neighborhoods, only to discover that older millennials and Gen Xers weren't starting families or leaving for the suburbs so readily as previous generations had. Cities weren't ready for it, and even if they had been, the building industry was still hobbled after the wave of bankruptcies that had accompanied the Great Recession and had caused millions of tradesmen to flee the industry. The builders who did survive tended to be more conservative, and across the industry developers focused on higher-end projects whose rent and sale prices could overcome steadily rising labor costs and the various fees and layers of process that were now baked into how cities did things.

Just as all this was happening, a revival of the exclusionary zoning research of the sort first kicked up by Bernard Frieden started seeping into urban politics, led by a Harvard economist named Edward Glaeser. Glaeser was an urban romantic who grew up in Manhattan riding graffiti-covered subways in the late 1970s. Now he studied cities in an imperial, six-columned building on the edge of Harvard Yard. His office was comically messy, full of disjointed stacks of books and paper and a collection of stained teacups with dried-out bags still inside them, and this seemed reflective of his academic specialty, which was to plumb the hidden economic order that lies below the chaos of urbanity. Most of Glaeser's work centered on why some places prosper while others fall into decline, and in the late 1990s he branched into housing research after selling a Boston-area house for a 33 percent profit after living in it for all of two years.

He picked up more or less where Ken Rosen and Larry Katz left off, partnering with a Wharton School professor named Joseph Gyourko to author a series of studies that used construction industry data to create a national figure for how much it cost to build a house or apartment, and from that showing that the harsh zoning and land-use restrictions that had raised prices in Northern California were now conspiring to make housing scarce and expensive in big metro areas around the country. This wasn't about explaining why it cost $2 million to live in a small condo in a popular neighborhood of San Francisco. It was asking how it was possible that in a place like San Leandro, an industrial city that sits across the bay next to Oakland, a cracked stucco house with a dirt lawn and boards on the windows sells for something like $500,000. Glaeser's studies broadened the housing debate, but his contribution was political as well as academic. He started blogging about housing costs and writing op-eds about housing costs and becoming the subject of various newspaper profiles where he called the advent of strict zoning the most important shift in the U.S. housing market since the adoption of the automobile. More than anyone else, it was Glaeser who pulled NIMBYism out of planning and economics journals and into the mainstream policy conversation, where it would eventually get picked up by Sonja.

By the end of the 2000s, the idea that a surfeit of land-use rules was making housing needlessly expensive was getting regular treatment in the press, often with a quotation from Glaeser. Soon influential policy writers like Ryan Avent, a reporter at the *Economist*, and Matthew Yglesias, then a Washington-based columnist for *Slate*, were advancing the idea that urban liberals needed to put aside their reflexive suspicion of developers and embrace an agenda of more housing. The intellectual fuel for some sort of anti-zoning political movement was now sprayed across the ground, and the invention of Twitter, then just a few years old, had created a new and potent accelerant by allowing pissed-off millennials to find each other. Three decades after *The Environmental Protection Hustle*, the ability to organize the unorganizable was suddenly right there, looking for a spark.

AFTER THAT FIRST San Francisco bus protest in late 2013, similar blockades continued off and on through the next year, spreading to Oakland and Seattle and escalating from stopped buses to broken windows and slashed tires and an April 2014 incident in which a group of protesters stopped a purple Yahoo bus and climbed atop the roof. One of them vomited down the bus's windshield, and for a day or two afterward news sites carried a much-retweeted/republished picture of a trail of yellow puke chunks smeared across tinted glass. Two weeks later, a writer named Kim-Mai Cutler published an article on a site called

TechCrunch that carried the headline "How Burrowing Owls Lead to Vomiting Anarchists." Cutler grew up in Apple's hometown of Cupertino and had a decades-long sense of just how radically the region had been transformed by tech, but was also sympathetic to incoming tech employees, who were genuinely baffled as to why they were being protested. "Burrowing Owls" was an attempt to capture this nuance with a dense, fourteen-thousand-word explainer on the history and thorny politics behind the Bay Area's long-standing housing shortage. It began with a promise: "This is a complex problem, and I'm not going to distill it into young, rich tech douchebags versus helpless old ladies facing eviction."

This was no bluff. The story had a dozen numbers in the first few paragraphs and continued with a flowchart of San Francisco's planning process, a spreadsheet of business taxes, a summary of Ed Glaeser's housing research, and a history of the 1970s that included diversions into the Jonestown massacre and the assassination of Mayor George Moscone and Supervisor Harvey Milk. To make the reading more manageable, Cutler broke the post into twenty-one parts that carried subheadings like "Fuck, this is complicated" and "So complicated!" and "We're fucked." There was a subtext to all this complexity, and that subtext was a message to TechCrunch readers that said, *This is not your fault.* As patient readers would learn, the title was inspired by a controversy that had erupted in Mountain View over a proposal to develop housing on a piece of marshy, bay front property that sat near Google's expanding headquarters but was also the site of a local burrowing owl population. The idea was rejected and no alternative proposed. Cutler's logic was this: Mountain View doesn't build housing → more Google employees move to San Francisco → Google sends buses to get them → someone pukes down a bus window during a protest. Burrowing owls lead to vomiting anarchists.

TechCrunch was not unfairly maligned as a repository of short news stories and barely rewritten press releases about start-ups receiving new rounds of venture capital, so Jeremy Stoppelman, the chief executive of Yelp, spoke for everyone when he opened the article on his phone and after a few minutes of reading and scrolling found his initial reaction to be, how is this on TechCrunch? He did keep scrolling, however, well past the introductory lines. Stoppelman read "Burrowing Owls" just as he was struggling with that most tech CEO of problems. Yelp had gone public two years earlier, and he was now worth a few hundred million dollars. He'd written checks to various causes but wanted to be more directly involved in some sort of policy goal, and housing costs interested him.

This was not altogether altruistic: to keep up with high housing costs, Yelp's salaries were rising faster than he liked, and the company was about to start shipping lower-paying sales jobs to cheaper cities like Phoenix. Stoppelman had more than enough money to become a player in local politics if he wanted, but he didn't believe traditional politicians would engage the kinds of radical solutions he was interested in unless someone reframed the conversation. After reading "Burrowing Owls," he asked Cutler for a meeting to see if she would consider starting some sort of group to realign local politics around the housing shortage she'd laid out in the piece, but she turned him down. Then, two weeks after the piece ran, Sonja and Micah showed up at San Francisco City Hall for SF BARF's first public unveiling.

By the standards of her future reputation, Sonja's first performance at a public microphone had been mild, even agreeable. She was generally positive and paid deference to dissenting neighbors with "valuable opinions." Had she continued on that trajectory, it seems unlikely that she would have become one of the more divisive personalities in San Francisco or, for that matter, a personality in San Francisco at all. Years later, when she was trying to tidy her public image during a suicide run for a seat on the San Francisco Board of Supervisors, Sonja would say that she never regretted a decision that seemed like the right decision in the moment. And what she needed in that moment was attention.

A month after that first San Francisco Planning Commission meeting, when the Oakland City Council met to discuss a big redevelopment project that would add housing across her own neighborhood in West Oakland, "valuable opinions" Sonja was gone and abrasive Sonja showed up. This was in the spring of 2014, or right about the time that the Bay Area started accepting that the current crop of techies was not going to be as fleeting as the ones from the late 1990s, which had been hobbled, if not exactly eradicated, by the dot-com bust. Before the meeting, protesters marched a mile from a park to city hall, and two people were handcuffed when they tried to block others from entering the building. Inside the chambers, when a city planner introduced the proposal, the crowd screamed, "Satan!" During the public comment period, when her name was called to speak, Sonja walked to a lectern in white cowboy boots, a black tank top, and leggings with fluorescent sawtooth patterning.

"So, when two things happen at the same time, sometimes it's confusing which is the cause of the other," she began. "I see umbrellas and rain at the same time. Do umbrellas cause the rain? Or did the rain cause the umbrellas? You can do an experiment."

"What's your point?" someone said from the crowd in the rows of chairs behind her.

Sonja turned around and snapped, "You'll see."

"You can open an umbrella. Does it cause rain?" she said.

"No. It does not," she answered herself.

She continued, "Rents rise and new homes are built at the same time. Which causes the other? Do new houses cause rents to rise?"

"Yes!" several people yelled out from behind her.

"Nooooo. Rising rents cause capitalists to build houses," she said.

"Take those culturally appropriated leggings and go somewhere," someone yelled out later.

"These leggings are sweet!" Sonja said back.

People loved her. People hated her. They could not and would not ignore her. Sonja drove a glittery orange Crown Victoria, tweeted as @SFYIMBY (*Yes* in My Backyard), and would say things like NIMBYism is so entrenched and rooted in nostalgia that you could propose new apartments on an abandoned lot and still have someone protest the building on the grounds that the abandoned lot "was the first place I got fingerbanged." Sometimes she sounded like a starry-eyed optimist, asking people to consider how much better the world would be if, rather than working so tirelessly to stop growth for fear of traffic, people put their energy toward improving local transit options. Other times, most of the time, she resorted to performative provocation. Like sitting down next to anti-development gadflies at public meetings and telling them that San Francisco's housing problems were their fault. Or proclaiming that people who were put off by the name SF BARF were acting as instructed. Then there was the inadvisable tweetstorm where Sonja tried to argue that one benefit of gentrification is that it justly rewards longtime homeowners for having invested on blocks that are well-located and beautiful but whose value banks and white homeowners had long refused to recognize. It was a subtle point whose subtlety she pulverized by beginning her tweetstorm with the statement: "Gentrification is what we call the revaluation of black land to its correct price."

The details were always more thoughtful than her loudest moments. When someone on Reddit asked Sonja to square her pro-development aims with anti-displacement measures like rent control, she responded that she was all in favor of rent control and did not see tenant protections as being incompatible with new building, arguing that it was possible to create one set of policies that made it punitively expensive and time consuming for investors to buy buildings and jack up the rent while simultaneously creating a second set of policies that made it financially attractive and bureaucratically easy to build on empty lots and parking garages. She was also equally clear that her aims were more revolutionary than political, telling people that her ultimate goal wasn't to pass some big new housing policy but to alter the social mores so that neighbors who fought new development ceased being regarded as anti-capitalist heroes and instead came to be viewed as selfish opponents of housing.

"When people have some idea about what they want their neighbor-hood to look like, when they are like 'We think we should be able to tell some other landowner how to build,' that's a feeling people have, and it's not a *logical* thing, but it's a feeling everybody reinforces," she explained in BARF's early days. "People also have feelings like 'I don't feel like going to work' or 'I want to cheat on my spouse.' And those are feelings that we as a society are like 'We know you feel that way, but if you act on that we're going to think you are an asshole.'"

Even by local activist standards, BARF was an amateur operation, but amateur was the point. Sonja built a 90s-inspired website with blinking text, comic sans font, and sentences that used "u" instead of "you." She recruited members on Twitter and by messaging people who espoused pro-development views in the comments sections of local news stories about new buildings. The SF BARF mailing list grew to a few hundred in a few months, attracting political novices who saw video of Sonja at public microphones and thought, "I guess you can do that?" Soon enough, a half dozen or more young professionals were showing up at afternoon planning meetings when everyone was supposed to be at work, and several times that at the biggest and most controversial or nighttime meetings, which were often followed by a trip to the bar. Sonja called it "socialization with a purpose."

Local media attention was immediate, and national attention followed. One of those early stories made its way to a retired English teacher in Virginia who happened to be Jeremy Stoppelman's mother, and she proceeded to forward it to her son. After reading the story, Stoppelman had one of his policy people contact Sonja for a meeting.

Jeremy Stoppelman was in his mid-thirties, still young enough to relate to the annoyance of high rent, and he was reared in a Silicon Valley culture that believes if you give the right people money to start something new, chances are they will figure it out along the way. Yelp began when an investor gave Stoppelman and a co-founder $1 million to pursue a concept they had for a website that would review local businesses. The investor had no idea what sort of business they would come up with, just that they would probably come up with something, and if they didn't, well, hey, it was worth a shot. Stoppelman applied this same line of thinking when Sonja showed up at Yelp's San Francisco headquarters and laid out her plans to build a movement for more housing.

After wrestling with the thought for a few weeks, he sent Sonja $10,000 via PayPal to keep doing what she was doing.

Sonja had arrived in California professionally lost, and the cost of rent had seemingly made the Bay Area a poor place to find direction. It turned out to be the best place for her. Every city had patrons looking to give money to people who wanted to change the law, but San Francisco had to be one of the few places in America where the multimillionaire CEO of a publicly traded company would make his first foray into local politics by organizing a meeting with the founder of a group called SF BARF. Had it been a different time in a different city, Sonja would probably have been dismissed as nothing more significant than a younger and more excitable version of the same old gadfly eccentric who commandeers the open microphone at city meetings across America. In the smartphone-boom-era Bay Area, however, she finally found an issue that could turn a life of diversionary passion projects into something like a career, and by the end of 2014 she'd quit her teaching job to make a run at becoming a full-time activist.

It helped that economists were still producing studies and that those studies were becoming ever more severe in their conclusions and commanding ever higher levels of attention. Two of Ed Glaeser's former students published a paper that argued antigrowth land-use policies had raised housing costs to the point that zoning rules were now stunting American migration and raising inequality by making it prohibitively expensive for people who didn't have a high-paying job or family money to move to cities where the best-paying jobs were growing fastest. A second pair of economists put the cost of this problem, tallied across all the lost jobs and missed opportunities that people who would have moved but didn't missed out on, at about 10 percent of U.S. gross domestic product, or $1.7 trillion a year. These studies all came with caveats and were thoroughly critiqued, but the critiques, at least the serious ones, tended to be studies that concluded thriving cities were indeed short on housing but that the focus on zoning discounted the broader role of income inequality in economic segregation. What this amounted to was an argument between one set of studies that said zoning was a hugely important thing making America less equal, along with a bunch of caveats about how income inequality was also important, and a batch of separate studies that said the bifurcation of the economy was making America less equal, along with a bunch of caveats about how the lack of housing was also important.

Either way, as housing became an ever-hotter topic, seemingly each new speech and study was amplified by Twitter, newspapers, and the extended urban planning blogosphere, before migrating to more official channels. In late 2015, Jason Furman, chairman of President Barack Obama's Council of Economic Advisers, gave a speech titled "Barriers to Shared Growth" and cited exclusionary zoning as a growing cause of inequality. The following year President Obama himself called out land use and zoning in a speech to the U.S. Conference of Mayors: "We can work together to break down rules that stand in the way of building new housing and that keep families from moving to growing, dynamic cities."

Back in the Bay Area, Sonja was making friends in city hall and amassed a growing list of members whose telltale characteristics were millennial, professional, and new to the Bay Area. They descended on Twitter and government meetings like a roving political gang. These appearances were never very well received, but the disagreements changed depending on what sort of city they were in. The first fight was in the lower-density enclaves of Silicon Valley or across the Bay Bridge in the East Bay suburbs, where owners of single-family houses rejected the more housing message with the familiar argument that more development would increase traffic and reduce property values. In San Francisco, SF BARF experienced much of the same in the lower-density neighborhoods on the city's west side, but also found deep ideological resistance from leftist groups like the San Francisco Tenants Union.

While it wasn't uncommon to hear someone in a low-density suburb say they didn't want more housing, period, that was a rare line of attack in San Francisco where it was usually a version of *more housing is great so long as it is affordable housing.* Affordable housing sounds like an apartment that has low rent for some obvious reason—maybe because it's small and in an old building that sits next to a truck depot. Actually, it refers to subsidized buildings that are built with help from the federal government and have apartments that are restricted to people who make below their area's median income. You can't find these places on Craigslist. People find them by demonstrating they have a middle to low annual income and then apply for one of a relative handful of subsidized apartments, at which point they get their name on a years-long list or a chance to enter a housing lottery that they have almost no chance of winning. Policy wonks referred to it as capital *A* Affordable Housing to make it clear that these units are part of a government program and not the naturally cheap apartments that most people imagine them to be.

Sonja's position on affordable housing was that affordable housing was great and that cities should build as much of it as possible and also raise taxes so that they could build even more. The first project she ever spoke in favor of, during SF BARF's first public appearance, was an affordable housing complex. But since there would never be enough affordable housing for everyone—publicly-subsidized apartments were only a tiny fraction of the market and most people would by definition never qualify for them—she was also for for-profit builders erecting as many duplexes, condo towers, and backyard cottages as they could build. She rationalized this by parroting economists' arguments that more housing, even more market-rate housing, would help prices for everyone by taking pressure off lower-cost housing stock whose rents were rising because higher-income tenants had few other choices. And it was her "build everything" position, and SF BARF's comfort with for-profit development generally, that put Sonja and her group in conflict with the city's nonprofit establishment, which tended to look skeptically on any building that wasn't 100 percent subsidized and tarred privately built apartments as "market-rate luxury housing."

There was some truth to this. In San Francisco, where a market-rate one-bedroom rented for somewhere between $3,000 and $4,000, nonsubsidized prices were high enough that essentially everything could be classified as luxury housing. But that was the point. New housing has always been expensive—hence why poor people almost always live in older homes and apartments—and it was precisely because there was a lack of it that old housing was becoming expensive too. It would, of course, take decades for new housing to become naturally affordable, so the Bay Area would also have to build a ton of subsidized housing and extend some sort of added protection for tenants to have any kind of chance at keeping the region from being economically cleansed.

These were facts that many SF BARF critics brought up, as well as facts that almost nobody—Sonja included—disagreed with. The difficulty was that among the hard left, the idea that building more market-rate housing could be part of a balanced solution was dismissed out of hand and tarred as the "supply-side theory" and "trickle-down housing." Many people went so far as to argue that the Bay Area was a kind of economic inversion zone in which new housing led to greater demand and higher prices, all but ignoring the role of job growth in drawing people there. This ran counter to progressive national politics, yet was an oft-repeated talking point in local circles that got presented at public hearings and distributed on pamphlets that dismissed decades of economic studies as "the filtering fallacy."

On the surface, these fights took on the familiar frame of socialism versus capitalism. SF BARF was the "pro-capitalist" organization that wanted "Hong Kong by the Bay," while tenant groups were arguing for "a seat at the table" and "the right kind of housing." One side would talk about the supply crunch, and the other side would ask whom that building should be for. The Tenants Union would talk about "luxury apartments," and SF BARF members would answer back with a screed against "luxury single-family homes." Under the surface, however, the fights really seemed to be about people who'd lived in San Francisco a while, or had moved there thinking it was something else, having to accept the reality that they had no control over the city's destiny.

The Bay Area, once considered a good place to chill out and drop out, was now the burning-hot nucleus of some of the most epochal forces in human history. The ability to have all the information in the world in a search engine, the smartphone that allowed you to carry that information in your pocket, the apps that let you broadcast your life to the world, the multiplying microphones and cameras, the cars that drove themselves, and the trillions of dollars that came with it—it was here and more was coming, and nothing that happened in local government could do much to change it. San Francisco was far from the hollowed-out manufacturing towns where factories rotted while jobs went overseas. It did not have those problems. But it was no less immune to global forces, and in an economy this lopsided even a winning city has its losers.

The SF BARF message was that there was no way to stop what was happening, only a choice in how to embrace it. It was true. It also hurt and came off as entitled arrogance, especially when the message got weaponized on social media. SF BARF members made boogeymen of their opponents, starting useless Twitter wars and posting the home values of antidevelopment crusaders in the nonprofit and local media worlds to accuse them of using the veneer of social justice to protect their investments through "planned shortages." The median SF BARF member was a classic center-left Democrat who supported affordable housing and rent control, and aside from the cat GIFs and the occasional image of a NIMBY with a Hitler mustache, the conversation in SF BARF's Google Group was for the most part dedicated to economics papers, news stories, recaps of city meetings, and discussions of how to become better friends with anti-gentrification groups. But when that energy got filtered through the rage spiral of social media, the politics of ideas devolved into the politics of personal attack.

That was the danger of building attention through bombast and noise. Anyone who read a series of tweets from Sonja and other BARFers—from the many thousands to choose from—would walk away having learned little about the housing shortage and a lot about the general tone of nastiness and disrespect that is the coin of Twitter's realm. Attention was attention, however, and Sonja was featured in ever more news stories and started getting invited to give talks around the country. Along the way she discovered that there were various other groups around the country and world who were also organizing around building housing and, like her (and in several cases in response to her), had started calling themselves YIMBYs*. In the summer of 2016, a Colorado group called Better Boulder organized a nationwide YIMBY conference. It was funded by the Open Philanthropy Project, the foundation of the Facebook billionaire Dustin Moskovitz, and was attended by 150 or so pro-housing activists who flew in from tech-heavy cities like San Francisco, Seattle, Portland, Boston, and Austin.

The first-ever YIMBYtown conference was held in a Boulder Hyatt and, aside from the swag bags with trucker hats, had all the superficial markings of a hotel conference (name tags on lanyards, coffee and pastry buffets) attended by associations of office brokers and insurance underwriters. Sonja was the conference's first keynote speaker, and when she was introduced that morning in the ballroom, she hobbled from her table to a lectern wearing an orthopedic boot. A few weeks earlier she'd been the subject of a big story in the *San Francisco Chronicle* and was so excited about the coverage that she jumped up in elation and broke her foot on landing. Sonja often told the press that she'd gotten into activism after seeing housing opponents with signs and thought "I can make a sign too," and her comments in Boulder were in line with the sentiment.

"The biggest danger to the health of your young organization is that you will lose interest in it," she said. "So make decisions about your organization. Whether it's the name or the place and time that you meet, the priorities, the activities that keep you interested. Don't worry about what seems legitimate or formal unless that keeps you interested. Your idiosyncratic club will attract people that are amused by the same things that you're amused by, which makes the club more fun for you, and

---

* The first pro-development group to use the term "YIMBY" appears to be YIMBY Stockholm, which was founded way back in 2007.

generally a more rewarding social experience for everybody. 'Cause that is what we're doing, is building a social world."

The conference's days were professional, full of meeting room break-out sessions with titles like "Building a Progressive Urbanist Coalition," "Data-Driven YIMBYism," and "Reforming the Sacredness of Single-Family Zoning." The nights were twee, full of beer and the excitement of several dozen people who thought they were the only person in the world thinking something and were now at a national conference of People Like Them. One evening, during a post-conference gathering at a dusty beer garden, attendees were invited to walk up to a microphone and answer the question "Why am I a YIMBY?" in three minutes or less. The first person sang a song. There was a haiku shortly after. *Urbanism. Climate. Bike lanes.* One guy got up to say that one time he overheard someone in a supermarket asking what "YIMBY" meant, and so he took it upon himself to explain the acronym and its greater meaning ("It's our collective backyard"), and at the end of the explanation the supermarket stranger hugged him, and so, yeah, that's why he was a YIMBY. Someone else said they were a YIMBY because parking is important. Just that.

As the conference continued through the weekend, it started to head toward a delicate discussion of how they might establish some sort of common standards and principles. Most of the attendees identified as liberal, but the YIMBY movement had also started to attract a contingent of anti-regulation conservatives. During a breakout session one troubled lefty said he didn't want to be associated with a movement that accepted "libertarian fuckboys." And what to do about developers? The overall goal of the YIMBY movement was to increase the amount of housing and pace of construction, which almost inevitably meant making life easier for builders. How to do that without having that movement devolve into a bunch of shills.

There was also a lot of talk about talk. How to talk on Twitter, how to talk to the media, how to talk to NIMBY parents, how to talk to preservationists, how to talk to spouses who are annoyed that housing politics are all you talk about. Sightline Institute, an urban think tank in Seattle, would end up running a focus group on YIMBY messaging that showed "homes" tested better than "development" and "density" should be eschewed for "walkable and convenient." Nobody ran this test, but it seemed likely that such phrasing would do even better with opponents when the messenger didn't sound like a patronizing asshole. That sentiment was telegraphed by the conference's second keynote speaker, a Seattle planner named Sara Maxana, who began her speech by calling a volunteer to the stage and playacting an argument about supply and demand that ended with her calling the volunteer morally inferior and an idiot. "We know a couple things that aren't working," she said to the crowd after the performance. "We know that spouting off evidence and data, that's not working. Inducing shame is not working."

Probably the biggest question of the conference was why most of the people there, and the YIMBY movement generally, were white. Different backgrounds, different incomes, different genders, identities and sexual orientations: the pronouns and points of view were diverse and represented, but most of those points of view came from people who were well educated and white. It was the self-conscious brand of white. The kind of white that acknowledged privilege and said "kale tacos are so white" while eating kale tacos. The kind of white that did not want to be called a gentrifier or to be at a mostly white conference. Not that YIMBYtown was *all* white, but when you're at an urban-minded conference where you have to say, "Well, it wasn't *all* white," there you go. During a breakout session called "Why Is the YIMBY Movement So White?," a small subset of people had a tortured discussion about how they could forge alliances with tenant organizations who didn't like them very much and fought new housing on the grounds that it would foment gentrification and displace low-income people.

The room had the tension of people who wanted to live in a pleasant urban neighborhood while knowing that in the current state of things that desire often meant someone else, usually poorer and not white, had to leave. Below the pleasures of urbanism and highbrow concepts like design was the realization that you couldn't touch the housing issue without also touching America's deepest and most radioactive questions. The nature of capitalism. The legacies of slavery and segregation. The cudgels of institutional power. Immigration, inequity, community, agency, and whether it's better to work in an imperfect system or tear that system down. History was defined by episodes in which the powerful removed the less so from land, and cities were now at the center of the same ageless battle.

One guy said that before the conference he posted a rather innocuous Facebook post about flying to Boulder to attend, leading a self-described radical to comment that YIMBYs were a neoliberal movement that was erasing the voices of displaced communities. He had no idea how to respond to that and wished he did. A nearby woman said they were running into decades of racist housing decisions and somehow had to rebuild trust, but how is that even possible after so many bad policies had gone wrong? Another person said their group was making rent control front and center in their platform. There was also a broad acknowledgment that YIMBY groups were universally enthusiastic about making it easier to build affordable housing. Couldn't that be something that they and other groups could work on together? Finally, a woman told the room that everyone should go to places where lower-income community groups meet and hang out there regularly for six months, but never actually say anything. Don't talk to anyone who doesn't talk to you. Don't say anything about your little housing group. Just show up, shut up, and sit there for half a year, listening.

CHAPTER 3

NO HAY PEOR LUCHA QUE LA QUE NO SE HACE

THE HOUSE IN East Palo Alto had ten people and two families. Ismael Pineda slept in a room with his two brothers. Their mother and father were nearby. The landlord slept on the other side of the house with his wife and daughter. The landlord's teenage son enjoyed the relative privacy of the living room couch. People left early, quietly. They came home late, quietly. Everyone was courteous to each other, and the landlord told the tenant Pinedas that they should feel welcome in the living room and watch TV on the couch normally as if it were their own place. It was a nice gesture, but the Pinedas never really took him up on it. They'd moved to East Palo Alto from a house in Redwood City after their old landlord told them he was going to renovate and they had to leave. The crowded new house was the best place they could find on short notice. They were confident it would be temporary and didn't want to be there for much more than sleeping.

So instead of coming home to face the weirdness of trying to feel normal on another person's couch, Ismael and his brothers, Cesar and

Jesus, who lived together and worked together and hit salsa clubs together, improvised by going to the gym. Long days of construction were followed by long nights at 24 Hour Fitness, where the brothers pumped iron and took showers. It went chest day, leg day, tris and bis, shoulders and back. Repeat. It was a heavy pace that, like the house, would be a short-term affair. The Pineda family was not going to be paying $2,400 for two bedrooms in an overstuffed house in East Palo Alto forever any more than the brothers were going to keep up a perfect workout routine forever. It was all just a non-ideal waypoint until they found a new place with their own living room and did not have a live-in landlord to think about.

Ismael and his family were part of a frenzied and ongoing migration of janitors, nannies, maids, landscapers, and construction workers who ricocheted around Silicon Valley's dwindling supply of cheaper housing and crowded into tighter quarters with each move. They traveled along a jagged line that hugged the eastern part of San Mateo County, moving from Redwood City into an unincorporated area called North Fair Oaks and down to East Palo Alto. They were industrial neighborhoods cut up by freeways and train tracks and historically were composed of poorer white families and the community of African Americans that on account of redlining guidelines—mortgage rules that made it nearly impossible to get a home loan outside white-only neighborhoods dominated by single-family houses—had been relegated to East Palo Alto.

In the 1940s, that gradually started to change as several less desirable areas transformed into barrios to house and feed and entertain the growing numbers of Mexican workers. San Jose and the surrounding agro-industrial towns had long had sizable Mexican American populations to work the orchards and railroads in present-day Silicon Valley, but it was during World War II that Mexican labor officially became an extension of the U.S. economy. In 1942, the United States and Mexico brokered the bracero temporary work program (named for the Spanish word *brazo*, or "arm") to backfill agricultural jobs during the war. Jobs in *el norte* were advertised in poor, agrarian Mexican states like Michoacán, Zacatecas, and Jalisco, which had been decimated by industrialization after the 1910 revolution and became known as "sending states." Some early braceros started permanent communities in California and Texas and Arizona, but most went back to Mexico for the winter. After the war, U.S. farmers, now addicted to cheap labor, successfully lobbied to extend the bracero program.

In North Fair Oaks, a piece of unincorporated county land that sits next to Redwood City and is impossible to distinguish without a map, the barrio began with a group of farmworkers from Aguililla, Michoacán. The Aguilillans had been working as braceros an hour south in Salinas, and eventually they moved north to work in local grocery stores during the winter. It was a small group of mostly male laborers, and they lived in and around a green apartment complex. The bracero program ended in 1964 after a backlash from domestic workers, but by then it had become easier for businesses to sponsor migrants for citizenship or pay them under the table. As Silicon Valley's Latino population surged, bringing more women, and then children, the North Fair Oaks retail strip sprouted taquerias and *quinceañera* shops, and the area earned the nicknames Little Aguililla and Little Michoacán.

By the 1970s, when companies like Atari and Apple and Oracle took root in Silicon Valley, many of the earliest migrant families were on their way to the middle class, buying homes, owning businesses, and sending their kids to college. They were followed by subsequent waves of migrants who worked in the expanding service sector tied to tech money, but as housing prices shot up and the economy became more stratified, the immigrant trajectory started to change. Where in the 1950s and 1960s it wasn't out of the ordinary for migrant workers to make enough to buy a house in North Fair Oaks or East Palo Alto or East San Jose, that dream shifted out of reach in the 1970s and 1980s as worker wages stagnated and housing grew more expensive. Some Mexican homeowners cashed out and used their proceeds to buy bigger places in the Central Valley or Arizona or Texas, in the process sacrificing the good schools and higher pay in Silicon Valley that promised mobility for future generations. Those who stayed faced immigration crackdowns after a surge in illegal border crossings during Mexico's financial meltdown in the 1980s, which made undocumented workers easier to exploit. And rents kept going up.

North Fair Oaks and East Palo Alto were put in the perverse position of being poor areas whose role was to effectively subsidize richer neighbors. They took in the linchpin service workers that places like Palo Alto drew on as a cheap pool of labor, but because they were technically separate governments, better-off cities didn't have to fund their schools or social services. The divisions of wealth were startling. Driving south from the Middlefield Road retail strip that makes up the heart of Little Michoacán, you pass a block with the Chavez *supermercado*, Recuerdos Mex, and Piñata Surprises. Just down the street sits a sign that says "Town of Atherton City Limits." As you pass it, the sidewalk ends, block-long fences rise, and over the tops you can see the batting cages and public-park-sized playgrounds that are required backyard amenities in a city that is home to several billionaires and where the median house value is nearing $7 million.

So that was North Fair Oaks' status: a place that was ignored but also mostly undisturbed, a hamlet of the working poor that was surrounded by Silicon Valley excess and sat just a few miles from the expanding headquarters of Google and Facebook. It was a place nobody wanted, until of course they did.

SISTER CHRISTINA GOT the Buckingham call in July 2016. Sister Christina Heltsley was a nun who ran a Catholic nonprofit called the St. Francis Center, which sat in the heart of North Fair Oaks, a block away from the train tracks on a street where houses have large dogs and boarded windows and backyards consumed by faded cars in a state of dismantling. She was sitting at her desk, next to a bookcase decorated with pictures of smiling children and a woodcut that read "Peace," when the phone rang. The call was from a man who worked for a Los Angeles private equity firm called Trion Properties. He said his company had just bought the building across the street from her—a forty-eight-unit apartment complex called the Buckingham Apartments. It was one of the largest buildings in the vicinity and home to dozens of low-income Latino families who depended on St. Francis's food pantry, clothing donations, and immigration counseling, and sent their kids to an adjoining school. The man said he'd heard Sister Christina was a force in the neighborhood, and so he just wanted to call and tell her that his company had bought the building and wanted to be a good neighbor.

Sister Christina felt her insides drop. She knew where this was going and that the families who lived across the street were as good as gone. Nevertheless, she asked the man what "good neighbor" meant. The man responded in generalities. They just wanted to be good neighbors. Sister Christina's interpretation of good neighbor was that the people from Trion were hoping that by calling her to say they'd bought the building, that by telling her themselves instead of waiting for her to find out from angry tenants after they got their inevitable rent increases and move-out notices, that this was paying some kind of fealty that would persuade her to bless or at least forgive what both of them knew was coming next. There would eventually be a moment of gallows humor when Sister Christina discovered that Trion's managing partner was named Max Sharkansky, but aside from a few shark jokes the experience was mostly awful.

She spent the next few months hustling for extra donations and trying to find homes for displaced tenants and having cartoon steam come out of her ears whenever she heard the phrase "underperforming asset." Still, she never accused Trion of lying. After all, aside from the good neighbor bit, the company had been straightforward about its plans. Shortly after buying Buckingham, Trion created an online presentation that boasted about its purchase of "48 non-rent controlled units in gentrifying market of Redwood City." The presentation laid out the renovation and rebranding plans and talked about the 40 percent upside that could be gained from increased rents. There were pages of large-font numbers next to multiplying *X*s and double-digit percentages along with summaries of various office expansions by tech companies including Facebook, whose headquarters sat just a few miles away from the St. Francis Center. "Facebook has offered its employees $10,000 to individuals and $15,000 to families that live within 10 miles of the campus," it said.

Housing troubles were, of course, nothing new. Sister Christina worked with poor people. Poor people have money troubles. She was also plenty familiar with the buy-and-displace business plan, and she knew, long before Trion showed up, that the phenomenon was creeping further into the neighborhood. Still, the indignity of losing a building that was directly across the street and filled her office window, of having a group of investors from LA straight-up declare their intention to rid North Fair Oaks of the people she'd dedicated her life to helping—that was too much to take. That October, Sister Christina and the Buckingham tenants and four hundred angry neighbors marched in front of the building and down El Camino Real holding signs that read "Stop Displacement Now" and "Trion Please Don't Evict My Family" and chanting, *"Esta es nuestra casa. ¿A dónde vamos a ir?"* (This is our home. Where are we going to go?) They made a lot of noise and got a lot of press, but it was clear what the odds were. The real question was how to prepare for the more Trions that were coming, and how to find a way to get in front of it. In the months after the building was purchased, Rafael Avendaño started assembling an army that would try.

Rafael Avendaño was the enthusiastic and whistle-wearing director of a gym called the Siena Youth Center, which was part of the St. Francis Center and sat a block away from the Buckingham Apartments and Sister Christina's office. It was a multipurpose community building that with the aid of some folding chairs and a few chirps from the whistle could be arranged and rearranged to accommodate indoor soccer games, neighborhood meetings, youth groups, fandangos, and homework sessions. Avendaño immigrated to San Francisco from El Salvador as a child before moving south down the peninsula for high school. Now he was a teacher/mentor/guardian whom adults called Rafa and kids called Coach Rafael.

After the Buckingham disaster, Coach Rafael had an idea. Local immigration organizers had started training people on how to use smartphones to quickly amass crowds of neighbors to film and otherwise intervene if ICE was harassing somebody, and he thought something similar might work for housing. He envisioned a minutemen squad of teenagers to organize tenants and flash protests. That way, instead of being behind as they were with Trion, instead of organizing one-off protests after tenants were already being displaced, they would have a team ready to confront every price-gouging landlord almost as soon as he raised the rent. Coach Rafael couldn't really stop investors from coming, but if they made enough noise and got enough attention, they could at least drag rent increases out and raise the cost of displacement by escalating political pressure and making gentrification plays like Trion's considerably more uncomfortable.

He had to do something, anyway, because his kids were getting picked off and leaving the neighborhood for cheaper homes seventy miles away in Tracy, or welling up with stress knowing that it could happen at any moment. Coach Rafael convened a meeting with Siena Center parents to ask if he could have permission to start training their kids in activism (yes), then started working with a nonprofit called Community Legal Services in East Palo Alto (CLSEPA), so that this rapid-response team of anti-eviction teenagers could have their own legal advocate more or less on retainer. They called the group Rents Too High, and one of the leaders was a fifteen-year-old named Stephanie Gutierrez who went to nearby Sequoia High School and walked to the Siena Center down a mile-long strip of El Camino that had thrift shops, liquor stores, and a Ferrari dealer. The way it worked was that once a week on Tuesdays, Stephanie and the rest of the group leaders would gather to write letters to landlords and assemble protest signs—"Stop Displacement Now," "Hear Our Cry, Rents Too High"—from wood, paper, markers, and a stapler. Coach Rafael stockpiled the signs toward the front of a supply closet that sat just off the gym floor. The closet also had a bullhorn, inflatables, board games, and a shelf of sleeping bags for camping trips. As far as the actual protests, Stephanie would help younger kids write speeches and try to psych them up for being in front of a crowd and news cameras, and over time the mass actions took on the motions of a field trip: permission slips beforehand, pizza parties after.

The Tuesday night meetings also doubled as an emotional release in which kids would talk about the helpless feeling of seeing so many friends leave and lose their homes while Coach Rafael sat admiring and quiet watching teenagers be consumed by empathy. Displacement was a virus, and as it spread, they all knew they could be next. Sometimes the meetings had guests, who did things like explain how the local legislature worked. Other times, the kids did circular icebreakers with adults from the area so that they would have lots of allies to talk to and work with. If there was one thing Coach Rafael wanted kids like Stephanie to absorb, one all-important lesson that was the foundation of everything they were trying to accomplish with Rents Too High, it was this: tell someone. If you hear about evictions: tell someone. If your own parents get a big rent increase: tell someone. Once the kids told someone, Coach Rafael would be ready to pull out the signs and the bullhorn and a nonprofit lawyer would be there to write letters and raise the specter of future court, but they had to do it fast. The point of rapid response was to avoid another Trion where the protests didn't get started until the saga was already over. Rapid-response protest meant rapid response. So Stephanie knew exactly what to do that day when she came home after school and discovered that her building's new owner had taped a packet to her front door.

Stephanie lived in a two-bedroom apartment with her divorced parents and little brother. Her dad worked early to late doing construction. Her mom, Sandy Hernandez, made about $14 an hour cleaning houses and taking care of elderly people. Sandy's schedule went something like this: leave at 6:30 a.m. to take care of an old lady for the morning, drive half an hour to clean a house in Millbrae, drive half an hour back to take care of an elderly couple in the afternoon, drive back to take care of the old lady from the morning for the evening, go home to see the kids and make dinner, after dinner drive to an office building where she cleaned after the workers cleared out, then drive home again, walk in around midnight, and catch a bit of sleep before leaving at 6:30 again the next morning.

After Stephanie walked into the apartment that afternoon, she called her mom at work to tell her something had arrived. Sandy said to open it. Maybe the landlord needed to fix something.

Thank you for your continued residency at 1207 Hopkins Ave.—Unit 5. Please be advised that due to current market events and conditions, the decision has been made to raise the effective rent for your unit. We have reviewed the local rents for comparable units in this area and find an increase to be both reasonable and justified.

You are hereby notified that effective 2/01/2018 your monthly rent, which is payable on or before the first day of each month, will be $2,750.00 instead of $1,898.00, the current monthly rent.

Except as herein provided, all other terms of your tenancy shall remain in full force and effect.

Regards,
CREI LLC

Stephanie called Sandy back. The rent was about to go up $852 a month. This was an impossible number. At $14 an hour, $852 was sixty more hours that time did not have. Their faded green apartment complex had worn carpets and bleeding hinges and amenities like an unkempt yard with a dismembered bike locked to a pole. It was an old building on the cheap side of Redwood City, right next to North Fair Oaks. The rent wasn't exactly affordable: Sandy and her ex-husband spent more than half their wages to cover it. But if the rent was now going higher than *that*, where else could they go? Stephanie hung up and cried. The virus she'd been protesting on behalf of friends was now coming for her. It was a private cry, and she never told her mom about the tears. Instead, she told her not to worry and started texting grownups from the Siena Center. A 45 percent rent increase was a brutal thing for a teenager to be trained for, but she at least knew what to do.

STEPHANIE STARTED SPENDING her after-school hours knocking on her neighbors' doors and asking them if they wanted to organize and challenge the landlord. Neighbors who didn't answer got letters in Spanish and English. Some of them were gone in days. They saw the new rent and just left. But a small handful said they wanted to hear her out, and in the course of all the door knocking Stephanie discovered that a nearby building had been purchased by the same owner and the tenants there had also gotten notices of a rent increase. Some of them wanted to challenge it too, and after a brief meeting in Sandy and Stephanie's living room, a group of a dozen or so tenants from the two buildings decided they would follow Stephanie's lead and start organizing. *"No hay peor lucha que la que no se hace,"* someone said. There is no worse fight than the one that isn't fought.

The group officially formed a tenants' union a few weeks before Christmas during an evening meeting at the Siena Center. Adult tenants like Sandy went upstairs to consult with Daniel Saver, a lawyer who worked for CLSEPA. Saver was a Harvard Law graduate who had a long history of war protesting and human rights activism, and after law school and a prestigious clerkship took a $46,000-a-year job at a legal nonprofit whose offices sat next to a junkyard. He'd never studied or even been particularly interested in housing before joining CLSEPA, but he'd told people he wanted to be a nonprofit lawyer who did whatever a community needed him to do, so now here he was, dealing with the rent.

While Daniel was upstairs going over the legal stuff, Coach Rafael and his wife, Ana, were downstairs on the gym floor talking about human rights with a dozen or so kids. Stephanie kicked off the conversation by reading a poem about displacement, and Coach Rafael explained to the group that this was rapid response in action.

"How does it make you feel?" he asked.

"I feel sad because the owners are kicking them out," a girl said.

Another girl replied, in English and again in Spanish, that her family had to leave their apartment after the rent was raised from $2,250 to $3,000. Even the kids had the rent memorized.

Ana Avendaño queued up a short video about the North Fair Oaks neighborhood: how it came to be called Little Michoacán, how evictions were spreading, pictures of the protests that Coach Rafael had guided Stephanie and others in staging. When the video was over and the gym lights were back on, Ana passed out a stack of blue pocket-sized pamphlets that read "Universal Declaration of Human Rights." She asked a volunteer to read article 25 on page 16. A young girl raised her hand and began reading.

"Everyone has the right to a . . . standard of living adequate for the health and well-being of himself and of his family, including food, clothing, housing and medical care and necessary social . . . services . . . and the right to security in the event of unem unem . . . ployment?"

"Mm hmm."

". . . sickness, disa . . bility?"

"Mmm hmm."

"Wid. Widowhood?"

"Mmm hmm."

"Old age or . . . other lack of live li hood . . . in . . . Cir . . ."

"Circumstances."

"Circumstances . . . Beyond. His. Control," the girl finished.

"That was a lot of words," Ana said.

She continued, "What are some of the things you took away from that?"

A girl said, "Things needed for health?"

"Oh yeah, things needed for health," Ana said. "What else?"

"Everyone has a right," another girl said.

"Everyone has a right, yeah."

The group took a moment to translate into Spanish.

"Everyone has a right to housing," Ana continued later. "What we're doing, what you guys are doing, what you're fighting for is a human rights issue."

Ana found another volunteer to read article 27 on page 17.

"Everyone has the right freely to participate in the cultural life of the community, to enjoy the arts and to share in scientific . . . advancement. And its benefits," another girl read.

"Mmm hmm. What do you guys hear when you read that one?"

"Everyone, like, has the right to, like, participate," one girl answered.

"When you think about North Fair Oaks or Little Michoacán or Little Aguililla, however you want to call it, what kind of cultural life is there? What's happening that you can take part of? Are there any events that you know of?" Ana asked.

Kids talked about friends' birthdays and the previous week's Our Lady of Guadalupe celebration.

"If I wasn't living here and I had to live in Tracy because I couldn't afford to live here anymore, then I wouldn't have access," Ana said. "That's why I felt that article 27 was also important for us to learn because that's also what we're fighting for. We're fighting for housing, and we're fighting for people to stay here and be a part of this community."

When Sandy and the rest of the tenants came down after their meeting, Daniel explained that the group had decided to have him write their landlord a letter. This was about the only recourse the tenants had. The area didn't have rent control or any significant tenant protections. It would just be a simple and nice letter, co-signed by a lawyer, that said the rent increase was unfair and that these were good and loyal tenants who wanted to stay in their homes but had no ability to absorb an $852 rent increase, and so they were writing to him through their lawyer to see if they could work something lower out. Left unsaid in the letter was that if the landlord didn't work with them, they were standing ten feet away from a closetful of protest signs and a bullhorn. Still, there was no reason to escalate now, everyone had agreed. You never knew until you asked. Maybe the landlord would respond quickly and with a great deal. Maybe.

Stephanie arrived at the protest in a white hoodie. As the cool evening became a cold night, she pulled the hood over her head and snug around her face. It had been six weeks since her family had received the letter from CREI LLC. Two weeks more until the rent went up and her family either moved out or got pushed out. At Siena, she became an organizational busybody, making signs and hounding kids for permission slips and calling nearby youth groups in an effort to bulk up their protest numbers. At home, she worked the phones until late. Sandy was a combination of proud and worried. Here was her teenage daughter juggling all these adult tasks and leading a group of adult tenants against a landlord with all the power. All these people were looking up to her and saying, "Ah, mi hija, muchas gracias." But also here was her teenage daughter absorbing adult levels of stress and spending the bulk of her after-school time trying to prevent her family from becoming homeless.

Stephanie barely slept the night before the protest. Before bed, she thought about what she might say to the hopefully large crowd in the inevitable moment when Coach Rafael handed her the bullhorn. It wasn't really the butterflies of public speaking that kept her up so long. It was the feeling that all this work had somehow turned into a promise to her neighbors, to her family, to herself, that somehow she could work this out. And what if she couldn't? Silicon Valley was full of homeless camps and recreational vehicles parked on side streets and in big-box parking lots. Clearly the worst happened.

The crowd, at least, did not disappoint. About a hundred people showed up at the protest, and as they packed tightly onto the small sidewalk in front of the landlord's office, the mass swayed with the group energy of a concert. Passing cars honked and the crowd returned it with woo-hoos, and neighbors from other apartments came over to observe and chant with them. In the weeks since the tenants had received their notice of a rent hike, someone had figured out that one of the people behind CREI LLC was a landlord named Jesshill Love, and the discovery had manifested in a bunch of protest sign Love puns ("No 'Love' Here" and so on). Not everyone had made time for original work. That was okay because Coach Rafael had vanned over a boxful of his "Stop Displacement Now" signs. All the noise woke up a homeless couple who emerged from a camper across the street and checked out the protest before wandering into the night to panhandle by a freeway entrance.

The media didn't disappoint either. Lots of note-taking newspaper reporters and TV crews with shoulder cams that blasted the crowd in white light. Some politicians showed up too, and while their words weren't exactly encouraging, they did at least show up. Ian Bain, Redwood City's mayor, told the crowd he would call and write the landlord and that city hall was looking into new renter protection measures. When someone grilled him on rent control, he said he wasn't getting into a debate on rent control. "Our children, your children, should not have to be doing this," said a city councilwoman named Janet Borgens. "I don't know how to fix it . . . I can't make promises I can't keep. I won't do that to you. I will not stand before you and lie to you. But I will tell you my heart breaks for all of you."

When Janet Borgens was finished, Stephanie finally got her chance at the bullhorn. Coach Rafael described her as a leader he was blessed to know and whom he expected great things from in the future.

"It's very hard," Stephanie began.

"Louder!" the crowd yelled.

Stephanie pressed the bullhorn into her face.

"It's, like, stressful for all of us," she continued. "Um, because. I do think about where we're going to be. What is the future for both of us, not just for myself, but for my little brother. Um. Going through this, I have learned a lot of things. We should appreciate what we have and not be greedy about how things just come and go. And I thank you all for coming here because it does mean a lot. We are all here for each other at the end of the day."

Neither Jesshill Love nor any of the building's other owners were there to hear Stephanie talk about the stress of them pushing out her family. They had all long since gone home. There had been some earlier discussions about possibly having the protest in the middle of the day so that the landlords would be there and feel maximum discomfort, but the real goal was max turnout, and you weren't going to get a max turnout of working people if you asked them to forfeit their already-too-low wages to protest the cost of rent at 12:30 p.m. on a Tuesday. Nevertheless, they'd made a lot of noise and gotten a lot of coverage. Jesshill Love would know what had happened on his sidewalk (if he didn't know already). Just to be sure, a woman called out the management company's office number to the crowd, twice. Before leaving, a group of kids pasted the window with hand-scrawled notes, including one that read "Jesshill Love Have a Heart."

JESS LOVE HAD been renting apartments in the Bay Area since 1989, when, at nineteen, he used the savings from years of summer jobs to make a down payment on an $89,000 condo in Palo Alto. He rented to a group of tenants while he was off at college in Connecticut and used the next spate of summer jobs to refill his mortgage and repairs account. Love graduated and went to law school and spent two decades as a lawyer, but all along the way he kept building a real estate side hustle— trading up his properties, using his nights to do repairs, putting cash flow into new buildings. Finally, he was in his fifties and quit the law firm to become a full-time investor.

Love liked real estate because he was good at it. He could do basic things like lay tile and sweat copper and install water heaters and repair cabinets. He could do sly things like find off-market deals through estate sales. He could do smart things like look at a spreadsheet detailing a barely profitable rental building and see the bottom line growing with new water meters and power-saving lightbulbs and more expensive laundry machines. The real estate business was full of stupid and inexperienced people who paid too much for buildings and couldn't change a toilet flusher and gave it all over to a property manager who ripped them off. Love operated with the comfort of knowing that he absolutely wasn't one of them.

He wasn't naive about how hard rising rents could be on a family, but he took the market as a fact and had a lawyer's way of intellectualizing what is and is not legal. Rents were rising: fact. Being a landlord was legal: fact. Anyone who doesn't accept those facts is living outside reality, and they know, or should know, that the market will come for them soon enough. When Jess Love thought about who was to blame for the protest that had come to his office doorstep, the person he blamed was the old landlord for neglecting to raise the rents to market.

But Love had also never been protested before, and he didn't like how it felt when he walked into work the day after the demonstration and found a pile of the kids' signs sitting on a table in his office. One of them said "Jesshill Love Have a Heart." He placed it on his couch and looked at it throughout the day and thought about what it said about him. That night at eight o'clock he called Daniel Saver to offer the tenants a deal. Saver wasn't there so Love left a long and rambling voicemail about how he'd spent the day with the "have a heart" note, and he was thinking of writing his deal proposal on the card and taking a picture of it and texting it back to Daniel, and so, whoever the kid was, Daniel could tell them that she'd changed his mind. Love's change of heart didn't make the tenants feel much better, however, because the deal he followed up with was a deal that would allow them to stay in their apartments slightly longer and for slightly less rent.

THE TENANTS' NEXT meeting was held in an upstairs room of the Siena Center and overlooked a Zumba class that had taken over the basketball court. It began with a generous spread of food. The food had been delivered by a nonprofit organization that distributes Silicon Valley's vast supply of uneaten office buffets to other nonprofits and community organizations. Thus, as the group came into the room to talk about how they were about to be displaced by a landlord who would use proximity to the tech industry as part of his rationale for raising the rent, they were greeted by a mustardy potato dish and a salad of cherry tomatoes and quinoa that were the leftovers of some venture capitalist or software engineer.

Stephanie had arrived early to set up the meeting and stood on a chair taping butcher paper to the wall for group thoughts and notes about next steps. The mood was glum and tired as it started to set in that even if they could delay it a bit, the rent would be going up, soon, and a lot of them would be moving out. The group sat in a rough circle fuming and commiserating in Spanish. Two decades earlier, when the Siena Center opened, the neighborhood's main problem was being the site of a turf war between the Norteños and the Sureños. The center had combated the influence of gangs by becoming a well-lit place where kids whose parents worked two or three jobs could play and do their homework surrounded by watchful adults and an uplifting soccer mural. Gang members had initially protested by showing up at the grand opening and stabbing a man with a screwdriver on a sidewalk just outside the window, but the violence had since faded, and Siena was now a community bedrock, and the sidewalk outside the window was safe (or safer). It seemed unfair, after all that, that some landlord should now force them to leave.

"Do you feel this protest achieved what you guys wanted?" Sandy asked in Spanish.

"I don't know if we've achieved what we wanted, but I saw that at least the mayor and a city council member were there, so something is happening," Coach Rafael said.

"The mayor wrote me that same night," Daniel said. "When I got to my house very late, he had written to me, saying that, you know, I'm the mayor, I'm going to try to put something on the agenda, we're looking into it, asking me things about rent control, because he doesn't think it works."

"*¿Dónde vive?*" (Where does he live?), another tenant said, to laughter.

"And tomorrow fourteen of our youth will write the mayor an email," Coach Rafael said.

"I already have two jobs, what do they want, for me to have another job and not sleep anymore?" Sandy asked. "My Brian sometimes cries, 'Mommy, don't go to work.' Now he wants me to have three jobs? And then how will we sleep? He wants us to have three jobs, and not sleep, or what do they want?"

"And there are bigger impacts to the community," another tenant said. "It's hard for kids when their friends have to leave because they're losing their friends, their best friends from school. The community is going to change with these practices."

Still, Jess Love had offered a deal, and it was probably the best deal they could get. Pride wasn't going to prevent them from taking it, even if they didn't think it was fair.

A week or so later the tenants gathered in Sandy's apartment to sign Love's offer. Happy or unhappy, a gathering is a gathering, so Sandy had laid out a spread of taco shells next to bowls of chips, shredded lettuce, salsa, and cotija cheese. The living room walls were still hung with decorative plates. Stephanie's room still had a collection of teddy bears on her turquoise bed, which sat next to her turquoise desk and under a picture of her smiling in her turquoise *quinceañera* dress. The move had already started, though, and would soon get going in earnest. Stephanie had packed some of her clothes and Sandy had a stack of yet-to-be-unfolded boxes that she'd gotten from a recently departed neighbor who hadn't bothered to join the fight. Her son's room was still in order and covered in Raiders posters. Too young to fully understand what was going on, he stayed in there to focus on *Grand Theft Auto* while the group talked about the contract they were about to enter.

Sandy's bed was in the living room—she took the living room so her kids could have their own rooms—and Daniel Saver sat on the edge of it and went through legalese. The agreement was four pages, and the guts of it were that the rent would still go up $852 but now the price increase would happen in May instead of February, as had originally been planned. If the tenants left right away, they would get $1,500 in moving expenses, and if they left before the end of April, they'd get $1,000. The group laughed with derision when Daniel explained that Love thought the higher rents were fair and that he was actually being a nice guy because he could have raised them higher. Economically speaking, however, this was more or less true. Stephanie periodically distracted herself from the meeting to scroll through apartment listings on her phone, and the other two-bedrooms she'd found in the area were going for somewhere between $2,500 and $2,700.

After Daniel fulfilled his lawyerly obligation to go through every single line of the agreement in an uninterrupted hour of Spanish that ended with an exhausted "whoo," he continued with a pep talk.

"*¿Primero ustedes la otra vez escucharon este mensaje de Jess, cierto?*" (First of all, you heard the other day that message from Jess, right?), he began. "You heard how he reacted, exactly, and how he reacted to the protest. In a way, you . . . it's not like you touched his heart, but you affected him. What you did, the protest, I'm not going to say he was very genuine with us, but he had to change what he wanted to do, because you created power and pushed your voices forward, and forced him to change. When we started with this, he had all the power, right? Do you remember how you felt when you got that notice? How that impacted you?"

"Surprised, like we weren't expecting it," Sandy said.

"Exactly, and almost like desperate," Daniel said. "And starting at that point, him with all the power and you without any, and that increase, we reached a point at which you affected him, you made a change in your own situation. That's a win. Second, well, the protest was very impactful. The mayor of Redwood City was there. You called the attention of the public to this problem, not just for your own benefit, but for that of all of the area."

"Now we see that if tomorrow, or in the future, we can stage a protest, we can organize ourselves more, because Rafael has so many people," another tenant said.

"You have already started the process to make those who have the power accountable, both the owner and the members of government," Daniel said. "One has to stay vigilant, because as soon as they find out that no one is looking at them, they'll keep doing the same thing."

He added, "*Es una lucha larga, pero la peor lucha es la que no se hace.*" It's a long fight, but the worst fight is the one that you don't start.

THE PINEDAS GAVE up on finding a single-family house like the one they had before their old landlord booted them to do renovations, but they didn't give up on their plan to leave the overstuffed place in East Palo Alto. Rents being what they were, the only way to make it work was to either move two hours east and commit to a life of zombie super commuting, or downsize to an apartment. So when they heard there were vacancies in a little green building in Redwood City that had just been purchased by new owners and was renting two-bedroom apartments for $2,750 a month, they reached out to apply, and got one. The rent was $350 more than they were paying, and the brothers would still have to triple up a bedroom. It was still their own space. The higher rent was worth it to regain the privacy of a one-family household.

Five weeks after Daniel Saver sat on the edge of Sandy's bed in the living room and explained Jesshill Love's buyout offer, the Pinedas were moving in to the newly vacated unit. The living room was freshly painted. There was a flat-screen mounted on the wall and beyond it stand-up speakers and shelves of AV equipment. Sandy's wedding picture had been replaced with an Our Lady of Guadalupe print. The room where Sandy's son used to play *Grand Theft Auto* was darkened by a stack of bunk beds pressed against the window, so close to a king mattress that the only way around the room was a tiny lane of floor. The Raiders posters were gone and a cross was in their place. A dream catcher dangled above the top bunk from the ceiling.

Economists were almost universally in agreement that the Bay Area had a housing shortage, and they were right. But when tenants showed up at meetings to say fancy new buildings did nothing for them and someone had to pay attention to the even bigger shortage in affordable housing—the regular, nonsubsidized kind—they were right too. Over three decades of steadily declining affordability, the housing markets of both the Bay Area and the nation could be reduced to a pair of diverging lines in which the supply of people paying more than half their income on rent grew while the supply of affordable apartments went further and further down.

Some units were literally lost, to age or demolition. Many others were figuratively lost, to rising rents. Put these forces together and America's largest metro areas now had about thirty-seven affordable homes and apartments for every hundred very-low-income renter households. Sometimes that led to the classic version of displacement with the yuppies and the coffee shops. Just as often it led to something that was less like gentrification and more like a state of churn where crowded apartments were the norm and working-class tenants bulked up to outcompete one another.

A few months before Jesshill Love bought Sandy's apartment, researchers at UC Berkeley published a study of a hundred low-income tenants who had been displaced from houses and apartments in San Mateo County. The study found that about 40 percent of the displaced tenants stayed within five miles of their old place, and two-thirds stayed in the county limits. Tenants in the study had an average of three people per bedroom when they stayed within a mile of the place they'd been pushed out of. Given the choice between leaving the state, moving to Tracy, or piling together, most people chose to pile in.

Half a mile away from her old apartment building, Sandy and her kids were stuffing themselves into a new one-bedroom in downtown Redwood City. Sandy still slept in the living room a few feet from the kitchen, but because their new living room was smaller, she had replaced their larger couch with a love seat that pressed against the foot of her bed. Her ex-husband claimed an air mattress that he inflated each night and laid on a strip of wood between Sandy's bed and the wall. As always, the kids got priority and the bedroom, which had a neatly gendered split: The left side, Stephanie's side, had a pink canvas that read "Be Happy, Be Bright." The right side had one Raiders poster.

The hard part for Stephanie was that somewhere along the way she had allowed herself to hope. For weeks, she was always busy, making signs, calling allies, preparing for the protest. There was a rush of responsibility and obligation and the comfort of being smothered in Coach Rafael's encouragement and so many friends and strangers' support. It wasn't as if she thought their rent would stay the same, but there was so much energy at the protest—Redwood City's mayor came!— that she started to believe her family and their neighbors would at least get a deal that would allow all or most of them to stay. Then it was over and almost everyone left.

Just before they moved out, Stephanie began to unravel. She started having panic attacks and wanted to be alone in her room, but the room made her heart race and breath short, so she spent a week at her older brother's house in San Jose to get away from everything for a while. She was barely talking to anyone when she went back to the apartment one last time to lug out what was left in Target bags and cardboard boxes. Sandy had to work during the move, so it was Stephanie who precariously pulled most of the family's furniture up to a second-floor balcony from the bed of a pickup truck. After their stuff had been moved and the new one-bedroom apartment was full of boxes of clothing and shopping bags stuffed with knickknacks, she accepted having fought and lost. Stephanie barely ate and missed a month of school. She decided to take some time off from the Siena Center to stay home, where she mostly just slept. Another teenager in another building would have to organize the next protest.

It almost broke Sandy to see her daughter crumble. She also knew they were lucky. Only a few families from the complex had stayed in Redwood City near the kids' schools. It seemed like divine intervention that they qualified for a subsidized apartment that was connected to the St. Francis Center and cost $1,425 a month, less than she was paying before. It was too small for four people, but the apartment had a nice kitchen and was close to the big house in the hills that Sandy cleaned. Stephanie didn't complain. She'd become an adult in all this, and now she knew they were lucky too. When Stephanie's little brother asked why they had to live in such a small space, Sandy put things in perspective: "We're rich because we have somewhere to be."

CHAPTER 4

PLANS OF OPPRESSION

BEFORE YOU CAN UNDERSTAND how housing went from the symbol of middle-class affluence to an engine of inequality, or why the 1950s compact of having cheap suburban housing in segregated neighborhoods built on federal subsidies and endless freeways contained the seeds of its self-destruction, or how a well-intended redevelopment agenda got turned into a racist program to clear out black neighborhoods, or why the 1970s growth backlash that set California on a path to becoming the nation's most expensive state was less a calculated conspiracy than it was best-laid plans, before all that, first you have to go back to September 2, 1945, the day World War II ended, when fifteen years of depression, war, and rationing had left America with a housing shortage that was even more dramatic than today's.

Home builders had essentially stopped building during the Great Depression, and during the war their main growth area was temporary housing in defense centers like California. Families doubled up with other families. People lived in greenhouses and chicken coops. Old trolley cars were sold as homes. A person in Omaha placed an ad for a large icebox and suggested someone could sleep in it; a pair of New York newlyweds spent two days living in a department store window to publicize their apartment search. Dorms, shift sleep, converted garages, streets of campers, live-in cars: all the totems of a housing shortage were there, and the surge of welcome-back peace babies, which followed the surge in goodbye war babies, would only make things worse.

In 1947, two years after the war ended, San Francisco's district attorney, Edmund G. Brown, whom everyone called Pat, commissioned a report on the city's living conditions. The report cited rats in South of Market rooming houses and the sight of Chinatown families huddled into "dark cubicles." Nearby in North Beach, a sick-looking family of seven occupied a damp and crowded apartment whose rigged-up wiring seemed destined to be the origin of a future and tragic fire. Housing problems were not the sort of thing the district attorney usually worked on, but Pat Brown was outraged that San Franciscans were living in such conditions and that slumlords were profiting so handsomely from it. He'd marshaled a staff to investigate on the logic that poor housing equaled high crime.

Brown had grown up a Republican back when San Francisco was a Republican town. He switched parties during the Depression after becoming exhausted with the Right's devotion to free-market principles in the face of so much suffering. Brown believed government had a duty to try to help people when the private market couldn't, and shortly after producing his San Francisco housing study, he trekked to the state capitol in Sacramento to urge the legislature to vote for a new public housing bill to supplement the federal public housing program, which was out of funds and had already been waiting for two years for reauthorization.

California's Republican legislature voted against it, and during the hearing lawmakers were vocally disdainful of the idea of using public money to solve San Francisco's housing problems. Brown blamed the defeat on politically connected landlords and the next day wrote an angry letter to the chairman of the legislative committee he'd testified in front of, calling the hearing "disgraceful" and suggesting that rural state senators might feel differently about fiscal austerity if their own districts faced the kind of crowding that San Francisco did. Then he continued to loudly advocate for the state and federal governments to finance new building to help alleviate the shortage, and expanded housing subsidies for those who couldn't afford it. "We do not permit bad and defective meat to be sold because we know that it is dangerous to the community," Brown wrote in a letter to the editor of the *San Francisco Call Bulletin*. "The same is true of housing. Slums are injurious to the health of the community and must be eliminated. The only possible way that this can be done is with government aid and assistance."

Another tool was redevelopment, or "slum clearance." Around the country, the deteriorating conditions of urban housing had prompted a number of states to create new redevelopment agencies that could use the power of eminent domain to demolish and rebuild old neighborhoods in partnership with private developers. California followed New York in creating its state redevelopment program in 1945, and four years later Congress passed the Housing Act of 1949, providing federal funds to seed new renewal programs and accelerate, and subsidize, the ones already in place.

In San Francisco, the redevelopment effort was pushed by a number of progressive-minded planners and architects who were alarmed by the crowded and unsafe housing Pat Brown documented in his report. They saw a new building program as a way to use the power of government to get rid of negligent slumlords and the antiquated system of small urban lots that they thought contributed to overcrowding. Many had dreams of rebuilding the urban core with high-quality new housing that would come at a variety of income levels and also be racially integrated.

In the meantime, however, America started building the postwar suburbs. After the war, as GIs returned home and baby making accelerated, the cause of American government and industry shifted from defeating foreign adversaries to building a vast middle class that would be defined by single-family-house living. The federal government called on private builders to construct five million new homes, and there were new billions for freeways, infrastructure and home loans for veterans.

There's a good deal of mythos around the idea that America is an "ownership society," and an important part of maintaining that mythos is a politics that regards Pat Brown's request to build public housing to alleviate crowding as a communist plot yet considers the federal government greasing the sale of single-family houses as free-market forces at work. Federal programs also supported construction of apartments, but the dream of owning a house was ingrained in the American conscience. Renters were regarded as people who had failed, and buyers' preference for detached houses with a small yard were rooted in pastoral notions older than the country. Compact buildings like row houses and cooperatives (a precursor to condominiums) were doomed to be a sliver of the market.

It was a good time to be a home builder. Beyond the explosion in demand, the federal government had bought into the real estate industry's contention that the loan insurance programs developed by the Federal Housing Administration (FHA) during the Depression should continue to provide a generous backstop to the private housing market, allowing far more people to qualify for mortgages and creating an even more vast market for single-family houses. Builders started construction on 114,000 homes in 1944. They started 1.7 million in 1950. The surge of new building transformed America's real estate industry from a collection of small one-at-a-time or a-few-at-a-time home builders to a business that was dominated by a handful of large regional builders that squeezed and streamlined until the haphazard world of outdoor construction was a tight industrial process on par with a General Motors assembly line.

The template was Levitt & Sons, a New York–based home builder run by William Levitt, along with his brother Alfred. The Levitts were early adopters of the prefabricated walls and roofs that would come to define the tract home, and over time the brothers reduced house building to a twenty-seven-step process in which single-task, unskilled and un-unionized workers only painted or only tiled or only hammered. They also vertically integrated their company to take control of their own concrete and timber production. Despite what the cultural snobs would say about cookie-cutter communities, the techniques pioneered by Levitt and other home builders constituted a lightbulb moment of genuine innovation that made housing profoundly cheaper and Americans better off. Levitt produced dozens of new houses a day and sold them for a monthly payment comparable to rent. The 17,400 houses in the first Levittown development, about thirty miles outside New York City, were modest by today's standards—a two-bedroom Cape Cod had white metal kitchen cabinets, an unfinished attic, and just 800 square feet—but went for about $8,000, or roughly $90,000 in 2019 dollars.

As low-density suburbs arose on the edge of every city, low-cost houses with abundant space and creature comforts became a singular symbol of progress and proof that the American way was winning. Compared to the rest of the world, American houses were large and full of modern furnishings, the latest appliances, and a range of packaged foods and consumer products like Frosted Flakes, Oreo cookies, Hawaiian Punch, Tupperware, Minute Rice, TV dinners, Play-Doh, Frisbees, and Barbie dolls. In 1959, during a walk through an American exhibition in Moscow, Richard Nixon, then the vice president, highlighted a six-room model ranch house to the Soviet leader, Nikita Khrushchev. "Soviet propaganda had been telling Russians in advance that the ranch house they would see at the U.S. exhibition was no more typical of workers' homes in the U.S. than the Taj Mahal was typical in India or Buckingham Palace in Britain," according to a *Time* magazine story. "Nixon made a point of telling Khrushchev that the house was well within the means of U.S. working-class families."

Assuming those families were white. There was an invisible wall around subdivisions, erected in the form of dehumanizing racial covenants in which the prohibition of nonwhite owners was just an ordinary rule listed alongside the typical homeowners' association requirements like keeping up your yard's appearances and not putting billboards on the roof. On top of that were the redlining guidelines that prohibited even well-off families from getting loans to buy homes in black or integrated neighborhoods. Postwar suburbs didn't create segregation, but they expanded it, industrialized it, and turned subdivisions like Levittown into a government-sanctioned apartheid: the mortgage guarantees that the federal government made to banks and mortgage brokers were premised on white-only neighborhoods; you could not get an FHA-backed loan in mixed-race neighborhoods. "If we sell one house to a Negro family, then 90 to 95 percent of our white customers will not buy into the community," William Levitt said in a 1954 interview with *The Saturday Evening Post*. "That is their attitude, not ours. We did not create it, and we cannot cure it. As a company, our position is simply this: We can solve a housing problem or we can try to solve a racial problem, but we cannot combine the two."

It was clear where the suburbs were headed, but America was on an unbendable building program, and California was the national exaggeration. The state's post–World War II growth was a bigger and grander extension of this new mass migration to what by the early 1950s some were beginning to call sprawl. Recruiting newcomers had long been a commercial way of life for the Golden State economy. By 1945, the state had been at it for more than a century, and whether it was through pamphlets or radio or pop music or the movies, it was almost always the same general sales pitch of nice weather and an affordable house with a yard full of bright vegetation.

The war years had created an industrial base that would help seed the conditions for a future economy based on technology, and as the pent-up demand for postwar housing started being satisfied, the state's population surged, growing from 6.9 million in 1940 to 10.6 million in 1950 and 15.7 million in 1960. "The houses in this suburb were built the same way," wrote D. J. Waldie in *Holy Land*, a memoir of growing up in Lakewood, in southern L.A. county. "As many as a hundred a day were begun between 1950 and 1952, more than five hundred a week. No two floor plans were built next to each other; no neighbor had to stare into his reflection across the street."

Pat Brown went back to Sacramento. He'd gone from San Francisco district attorney to California attorney general and in 1958 was elected California's thirty-second governor after campaigning on a program of growth, growth, growth. Brown was a consummate booster who had gotten the nickname Pat after a seventh-grade performance in which he had so enthusiastically executed the teacher's assignment to sell Liberty Bonds with the slogan "Give me liberty or give me death!" that his classmates dubbed him Patrick Henry Brown and the joke stuck for life. Now he was selling California as the nation's foremost attractor of new people.

Growth had never been a concept Californians universally signed on to—you can find examples of antigrowth sentiment going clear back to the gold rush—and when Pat Brown ran for governor in 1958, there were already plenty of people who thought newcomers were ruining the life of abundance that the state had long been in the position of trying to simultaneously protect and sell. Too much traffic. Not enough infrastructure. Elimination of precious open space. Brown's counter was to frame population growth as a catalyst for equal opportunity prosperity. He relabeled "problems" as "challenges" and ran ads saying the state's "abundance is here for all to share." It was an appeal to state pride and the idea that California, with its growing economy and multiplying electoral votes, was becoming a national leader. And you can't be a leader of much of anything without catering to new followers.

When Brown was elected by a margin of a million votes, he took it as a mandate to spend. And so he spent, pushing plans to expand public universities, increase the breadth of social programs, and build lots of freeways. His biggest achievement, one that had eluded various other governors, was to ensure a new Southern California water supply by persuading voters to approve $1.75 billion in new bonds (a little over $15 billion today) to begin construction on the California State Water Project, a vast system of dams—at the time the largest state public works project ever—that redirected river water from the rainy upper part of California through a 400-mile aqueduct that flowed through the arid Central Valley, over the Tehachapi Mountains, and into Los Angeles, where population was growing fastest.

That was what it meant to be a Democrat back then. California voters approved the water project's funding in November 1960, and less than a year later Brown was wearing a hard hat in front of news cameras, ceremoniously setting off three hundred pounds of dynamite to get it all started. Because dynamite for infrastructure was liberal. Damming rivers was liberal. Building a four-hundred-mile aqueduct through nature and building power plants to propel it to factory farms and over the mountains into a parched south land, and doing all this for the purpose of continuing the mass building of new subdivisions, that was liberal too. It wasn't an environmental pillage; it was an act of progressive governance that would create a better life for the little guy. Also, people wanted to move to California, and Brown seemed to find it all but inconceivable that the state would *not* spend several billion dollars in public money to invite them. "What are we to do?" Brown wrote to a newspaper publisher in 1960. "Build barriers around California and say nobody else can come in because we don't have enough water to go around?"

Brown's enthusiasm for newcomers was such that at the beginning of 1962, a few months before he defeated Richard Nixon for a second term, his office declared that on December 21 California would pass New York as the nation's most populous state and that at the end of the year there would be a four-day party to commemorate the historic realignment. The milestone was coming eventually; that was a certainty. But the idea that anyone in the governor's office could determine the state's population trajectory with the precision of a day was bananas. News stories pointed this out, and in private letters Brown wrote that nobody had any idea when the exact date would be. Whatever. On December 28, he held a capitol ceremony in which a bunch of men on horseback wearing Davy Crockett hats presented him with a leather scroll proclaiming California No. 1 and fired off their muskets. For the next week, city leaders and chamber of commerce types wore celebratory buttons and organized moments of synchronized horn honking and in one case trekked out to the Nevada border to flag down incoming families to welcome them to California.

"California is proudly flexing its sun-tanned muscles these days over the fact that, sometime in the last few months, it surpassed New York as the most populous state in the Union," wrote Eugene Burdick, a Berkeley political scientist and co-author of the novel *The Ugly American*, in an April 1963 column for *The New York Times*. "The individual statistic who tipped the historic balance past the 17,300,000 mark may have been a newborn baby, or a young physicist from M.I.T. winging his way across Lake Tahoe. More likely, it was someone in a station wagon crowded with children and weary parents."

Rick Holliday was one of those kids. A few months after Burdick's column, his family crossed the Nevada border and over the Donner pass after the cross-country drive from Pittsburgh. There were seven people in the car—two parents, five kids—and it happened to be Rick's tenth birthday. Aside from that detail, the main thing he remembered was sitting in a rear-facing seat tripping out on the bigness of the trees and mountains. Ten was old enough to grasp the life-altering bigness of his family moving to the West Coast, yet young enough for him to be excited about it instead of forlorn like his older brother who had left a teenage life behind. A few hours later, when the family stopped at the Nut Tree restaurant in Vacaville and bolted across the parking lot to food, Rick lingered behind on the station wagon's gate and thought about the significance of these being his first steps in California. The moment was interrupted by the sound of his dad yelling to get the hell out of the car.

Rick's dad, Malcolm Holliday, was a well-known pediatrician doing pioneering work in the field of infant kidney transplants, and his decision to bring the family west was bound up in Pat Brown's growth policies. Malcolm Holliday had been poached from the University of Pittsburgh to set up a research partnership with the expanding University of California, from which he planned to give and receive: five was a lot of kids to put through college, and his plan for not going broke was to send all of them to affordable UC schools. After eating at the Nut Tree, the family drove to the San Francisco suburb of Orinda, where they lived in a ranch-style house with an avocado-green refrigerator and started engaging in strange local customs like cooking on an outdoor barbecue. Rick felt like he'd been living in black and white and had now discovered color. A few months after arrival, he foreshadowed his future career by stealing a bunch of wood from a construction site and building a tree house above a nearby creek bed.

BY THE 1960S, the grand redevelopment plans that had been hatched to modernize cities and alleviate postwar crowding were finally underway. In New York City, Robert Moses, the infamous "Master Builder" who was never elected to public office but led various government agencies (including several at once), was pushing through slum clearance projects like Lincoln Center and executing his vision for a more car-centric metropolis built around elevated freeways. Bay Area leaders were way behind Moses, having spent a good deal of the 1950s going block by block designating certain areas as blighted, and accomplishing little else. When they were finally ready to build, it was clear that a flight to the suburbs was well underway, and the more equal-minded redevelopment ideas, like using federal money to erect mixed-income neighborhoods (ideas that were put forth when the faces of housing troubles were mainly white), lost their political salience.

There were some scattered examples of the utopian dreams that the more forward-thinking planners had in mind, like the 299-unit St. Francis Square housing cooperative in San Francisco, a racially integrated complex for working-class people developed by the International Longshore and Warehouse Union and the Pacific Maritime Association pension fund. More often redevelopment became an excuse to demolish homes in black neighborhoods like West Oakland and San Francisco's

Fillmore District, thinning out the population and adding civic projects that businesses like department store owners had pushed for in hopes of luring the middle-class from the suburbs back downtown.

As cities tore down ageing tenements and converted Victorians and evicted tens of thousands of black tenants, planners engaged in the old fallacy of thinking of cities in primarily physical terms and believing that if old structures were cut away and replaced with new ones, and old pockets of poverty could be blasted out, this would somehow solve America's oldest racial and economic inequities. The author James Baldwin called it "Negro removal." Some of the displaced residents were homeowners who got paid for their property, but most of them were renters who got either nothing or meager relocation assistance and a vague promise that they might get rehoused later, a promise that was rarely if ever fulfilled. In the Bay Area and around the country, tens of thousands of black residents who had been legally banned from the suburbs fled their bulldozed homes and crowded into nearby neighborhoods, where landlords promptly started subdividing their units and people began huddling into unsafe quarters of the sort Pat Brown had originally written his 1947 report about, and that the redevelopment agencies who were creating this mess had originally been created to solve.

Implicit in William Levitt's statement that his company could solve a housing problem or a race problem was an admission that the decision by home builders and the federal government to bar black families from all but a few designated new subdivisions amounted to a vast moral debt whose societal costs were being passed on to future generations. It was fitting that the repayment would begin in California. The early 1960s roughly marked the moment when social critics started framing the state as an early look at the nation's cultural and political future. It was a construct, but it worked: from the massive scale of its subdivisions to Hollywood and fashion trends and the nascent microelectronics industry that was just getting going in what would become Silicon Valley, California was becoming a national bellwether. And in 1963, when Pat Brown began his second term looking to pass a piece of nation-leading civil rights legislation, it was an early indication of how ugly the fight for fair housing would be.

William Byron Rumford had been a state assemblyman for fourteen years at that point. Rumford was a pharmacist from Berkeley who was the first black person elected to state political office from Northern California. He'd become an effective legislator almost immediately, allying with Governor Earl Warren, the future chief justice of the United States, to pass various civil rights bills that grew steadily more ambitious. There was a law to integrate the California National Guard. Bills to curb prejudice in teaching and school administration jobs, and a law that made it illegal for insurance companies to refuse to cover black drivers. Rumford frequently teamed up with Augustus Hawkins, a black assemblyman from Los Angeles, and the two spent more than a decade trying to pass a bill to outlaw employment discrimination. The California Fair Employment Practices Act was finally passed in 1959, and Pat Brown signed it during his first year in office.

Four years later, Rumford was walking the halls of the capitol looking for co-sponsors on a bill, to become known as the Rumford Act, that would outlaw racial discrimination in the sale and rental of housing. This would be a major leap—for Rumford and California. The 1968 Civil Rights Act, which banned housing discrimination nationally, was still five years away. And while white Californians liked to think of themselves as more liberal and enlightened than other Americans, the state's cities were still thoroughly segregated. Lest anyone have any doubts about this, Brown began his push for a fair housing law with a report from a special state commission that showed the vast majority of California's black population was concentrated in a handful of neighborhoods. Of the 350,000 homes that were built over the period of one study, a little fewer than a hundred had been sold to nonwhite households. Much more than Rumford's car insurance bill, or even the Fair Employment Practices Act, a ban on housing discrimination was a huge political risk because it had the potential to significantly change how the real estate industry operated and what white homeowners were now accustomed to.

Brown was nevertheless an enthusiastic backer. The bill passed the state assembly but ran into predictable trouble in the more conservative state senate, where it was held in a crucial committee whose chairman kept scheduling the Rumford Act for a hearing and then canceling it. The bill had a shot at passing the broader senate if it could get out of committee for a vote, but with just a few weeks to go before the end of the legislative session, it remained stuck. At that point, members of a group called the Congress of Racial Equality (CORE) began a sit-in that would ultimately end with them sleeping on air mattresses in the capitol rotunda for a month. They got a visit from the actors Paul Newman and Marlon Brando, and Governor Brown was generally approving of the protest. After more legislative stall tactics, CORE members lay down in front of the doors leading to the senate to block senators from walking in.

Finally, on the last day of the legislative session, the bill got a hearing and made it out of committee with a few amendments. At that point, Hugh Burns, the senate president pro tem and a conservative Democrat from Fresno, attempted to run out the clock by declaring that no bill would be taken up out of order, a move that would put hundreds of bills in front of the Rumford Act, with just a few hours to go. Over in the other chamber, the state assembly Speaker, Jesse Unruh, tried to pressure the senate by deciding, around 10:00 p.m., that the assembly would refuse to take any more senate bills unless the higher chamber dealt with pending assembly bills (of which the Rumford Act was one).

When that failed, a pair of Democratic senators executed a legislative technicality that allowed them to pull the bill to the front of the line by scheduling debate on a specific bill at a specific time—a move that, according to senate rules, did not allow the bill in question to be debated; that is, conservative senators could no longer continue to run out the clock. When Burns rose to say the senate had to take bills in order, a senator named Joseph Rattigan jumped up to say that his motion couldn't be debated. After a roll call, the Rumford Act was scheduled for an 11:00 p.m. debate, and senate Democrats spent the next twenty minutes whipping up votes. The Rumford Act passed the senate and was hurried to the assembly, where it passed again, sending the bill to Brown's desk, for a guaranteed signature, a few minutes before midnight. Joseph Rattigan cried. The CORE demonstrators sang. The victory was sweet, but the victory was short.

In 1911, looking to curb the influence of monopolistic corporations and politically powerful railroads, progressive reformers led by Governor Hiram Johnson, a liberal Republican, instituted a citizens' initiative system that allowed California voters to make and repeal laws—and rewrite the state's constitution—by putting their own legislative proposals on the ballot. Anyone who could get signatures equal to 5 percent of the votes cast for governor in the previous election could put his or her own law on the ballot. Anyone who could get signatures equal to 8 percent could put forth a proposal to amend the state's constitution. Pretty much the second the Rumford Act passed, the California Real Estate Association, the trade group for real estate agents, started gathering signatures for a scorched-earth initiative that would not only repeal the fair housing law but amend the state's constitution so that the right to *not* sell or rent homes to people based on race could be enshrined.

As goes California, so goes the nation: it was a construct, but it worked. A long-held theme of civil rights is big victories followed by crushing losses. The measure to repeal the Rumford Act, called Proposition 14, was part of an emerging white backlash that gave an early look at the race-neutral language with which the fight against future civil rights measures would be waged. Instead of the full-throttle hate and violence that marked the civil rights battles that were simultaneously going on in the Deep South (this was only a year after Alabama's governor, George Wallace, gave his infamous "segregation now, segregation tomorrow, and segregation forever" speech), the California Real Estate Association framed Proposition 14 as a battle over property rights. This gave white voters the comfort of voting for what was effectively a statewide segregation bill without having to feel as if it were about race. One Republican state senator said that the Rumford Act was a step toward "dictatorship."

Governor Brown blasted Proposition 14 as a vicious and bigoted idea that would be a "blow to decency," and he furiously campaigned against it. When voters overwhelmingly passed it that fall, it was an ominous sign for Brown's future, because the measure was supported by many of the blue-collar white union voters who had put him in office. Proposition 14 passed in the same election in which California voters also overwhelmingly supported Lyndon Johnson for president, who nationally represented the kind of liberalism Pat Brown had perfected in California. But this wasn't so much inconsistency as an example of how voters were theoretically for civil rights at a vague national level yet would immediately draw the line when they were asked to desegregate their own city or neighborhood. Despite the property rights sales pitch, the Prop 14 voting results skewed heavily along racial lines. Some of the most lopsided precincts were around Oakland. In San Leandro, voters in majority-white areas were 80 percent in favor of Proposition 14. Majority-black districts across the city line in Oakland voted against it by more than 90 percent. "You could draw but one conclusion from the vote on 14 and that is that the white is just afraid of the Negro," Brown wrote in a letter to his daughter.

Proposition 14 was eventually nullified by the California Supreme Court, which reawakened fair housing as a campaign issue in 1966, when Brown ran for a third term against an actor and political novice named Ronald Reagan. Reagan would end up defeating Brown by carrying many of the same white Democratic voters who had passed Proposition 14, and during the campaign he said the right to rent or sell property to *anyone* was one of Americans' "most basic and cherished rights."

It would be way beyond a stretch to say that Reagan won by opposing fair housing. Pat Brown had been governor for eight years, and he'd been damaged by his handling of the 1964 Berkeley protest in which thousands of students took over Sproul Hall as part of a free speech sit-in that resulted in eight hundred arrests and a flood of negative news coverage. A year later the Watts riots, often called the Watts Rebellion, led to six days of smoldering buildings, two dozen deaths, a thousand injuries, and the National Guard going to Los Angeles. But Reagan's campaign, coming after the Rumford Act, the Free Speech Movement, and Watts, was an unmistakable appeal to white swing voters that *those people* were dragging the state down. He railed against a bloated government, portrayed Berkeley students as spoiled eggheads, and talked about the "jungle paths" of California streets, pioneering what would become a popular national electoral strategy of combining the fear of black people (Watts) with the resentment of white liberals (Berkeley) and antipathy to taxes (Orange County).

CALIFORNIA VOTERS HAD accepted Pat Brown's growth plans, but after two decades of excess, two decades in which each new freeway and sports team and subdivision had been hailed as a sign of progress, people were getting tired. One of the earliest signs of fatigue had actually come a bit earlier, in the mid-1950s, when San Franciscans started fighting against a proposal for a new double-decker freeway that was intended to travel along the Embarcadero to the Golden Gate Bridge.

This was a good fight. The Embarcadero Freeway would seal off miles of bay front and run directly in front of the city's Ferry Building. And this was just the beginning of a vast state freeway plan that intended to blanket a relatively small city—San Francisco is just forty-seven square miles—with seven crosstown freeways, including several through Golden Gate Park. It said most of what you needed to know about what sort of future state highway engineers saw for the Bay Area that one of the Embarcadero Freeway's proponents had argued it would increase access to scenery by allowing people to glimpse the bay and Alcatraz from cars traveling on the top deck. The project was so vehemently challenged by citizens groups that the San Francisco Board of Supervisors refused to let the state finish it, "and today the blunt stub of it still stands nearby the waterfront, a monument to the public's determination," wrote the *Los Angeles Times* a decade later.

In defiance of state planning, over the next few years San Francisco built a grand total of 4.4 miles of freeway. When the federal government warned the city that if it didn't start building more it would lose $235 million in matching funds, a crowd of four hundred mostly anti-freeway protesters packed the chambers of the San Francisco Board of Supervisors, where they booed, hissed, and popped balloons anytime someone spoke in favor of taking Washington's money. What became known as the Great Freeway Revolts spread to Marin County, Los Angeles, and northward to Seattle. In San Fransisco, the protests fomented a shift in local political power, away from the collection of growth-oriented business, civic, and labor groups that were collectively known as "downtown" and toward smaller, neighborhood-centric groups that upon being activated by freeway fights became highly skilled at organizing.

By the mid-1960s, the idea that California had too much unrestrained growth had become a mainstay of local politics and created a subgenre of books (*California Going, Going . . .*), songs ("Little Boxes"), and magazine articles ("California: Too Much, Too Soon?"). And much like the original freeway revolts, these critiques were generally sound. San Francisco tore out Victorians, developers plowed over farms, and highway engineers built multilevel stacked interchanges. The logical extension of California-style growth seemed to be that cities would be nothing but offices and freeways, hills would be nothing but tract houses, and bays would be nothing but concrete. But for a group called Save the Bay, planners would probably have executed a plan to turn a majority of the San Francisco Bay into landfill.

"Everyone who has lived in California more than a few months remembers a pleasant orchard that has been uprooted for a factory or shopping center, a favorite picnic spot that has been graded for tract houses, an unspoiled beach that has been paved for parking, a living stream that has been entombed in a culvert, a rustic country lane that has been converted into a roaring highway," wrote Harold Gilliam, the *San Francisco Chronicle*'s environmental writer.

In 1965, when Macmillan published a book called *The Destruction of*

California by a conservationist named Raymond Dasmann, it was interpreted as a sign that a major New York publishing house now saw California's soothsayer status as a cautionary tale for the nation. Dasmann opened his book with a memory of driving across the Bay Bridge to San Francisco in early 1963. Looking to dramatize the population race with New York, the state division of highways had installed, with Pat Brown's encouragement, a New York versus California population counter that showed California was adding dozens of people an hour while New York barely grew. Dasmann thought new people were nothing to celebrate, and his book went on to argue that the state should try to arrest growth by simply not planning for it.

"This means not encouraging new industries to move into an area," he wrote. "It means not developing our water resources to a maximum, and thus not providing the water that would make possible additional urban or industrial growth, or bring into production new farming areas. It means not building those new power stations or those new freeways. No real-estate development will be built in an area where electricity and water will not be provided. No industry will come where it will not receive space, power, or water. People will not come where there are no new jobs or new housing, or if they do come they will not stay. Immigration is not excluded, but the immigrants will be a minority willing to compete for existing jobs and housing space."

The Destruction of California was just one among a collection of books, published between 1962 and 1968, that collectively assailed the sprawl-centric growth model and called on planners, activists, and politicians to initiate a program of corrective action. Exactly how this might happen was not so clear. In the mid-1960s, the broad ideology that we now call environmentalism was still in its infancy and had a lot more in common with age-old conservationism than what we think of as environmentalism today. The Sierra Club was a small regional organization, and environmental activists, such as they were, were predominantly focused on things like protecting waterways from corporate agriculture and preserving distant nature and wildlife by fighting extractive industries.

It was inside the new suburbs, the suburbs whose creation had fomented so much antigrowth rage, where environmentalism broadened into a mass movement. The U.S. homeownership rate jumped from around 44 percent in 1940 to 63 percent in 1970, and in 1966 the number of people living in suburbs eclipsed the number of people living in central cities for the first time in U.S. history. Suddenly there was a large group of Americans, from a range of income levels (though still overwhelmingly white), living with more yard space, increased contact with animals and vegetation, and the fear that it would be destroyed by further sprawl. It wasn't nature so much as an approximation of it; the suburbs made lawns a point of pride and caused the number of U.S. dogs to quadruple. Still, you had a large cross section of Americans developing a greater appreciation of outdoor life and an interest in maintaining spaces that were at least semi-wild, and this appreciation was broadening the definition of "the environment" to include city margins as well as distant lakes and forests.

As the Sierra Club started dabbling in urban politics and tackling issues like protecting parks, its suburban membership expanded and environmentalism grew into a potent political tool that, unlike old-line conservationism, could move majorities at the neighborhood level. A large-lot home ordinance was more environmental because it left more grass. Open space was a place to walk your dog. Toxins were the smog you breathed in the air and the poisons people used on neighborhood plants. During the first Earth Day in 1970, some of the highest rates of participation were at high schools in low-density suburbs with high home values, and one of the more common environmental activities was group trash pickups. Think globally, act locally.

The good intention of stopping sprawl soon became cover for stopping everything. In 1970, Ronald Reagan signed the California Environmental Quality Act (CEQA), a landmark law that paralleled the 1969

National Environmental Policy Act and subsequent creation of the Environmental Protection Agency. CEQA ("see-qua") required cities to analyze and adopt measures to mitigate all environmental impacts identified in their reviews of local land-use decisions. The state saw an immediate explosion in environmental impact lawsuits around new housing developments—lawsuits that, in contrast to the aims of true environmentalists, would grow to be more numerous around dense "infill" developments in established neighborhoods than they were around the edge-city sprawl that the masses were (rightly) so concerned about.

The Greater Bay Area typically built around forty-five thousand housing units a year in the early 1970s. Between 1972 and 1975, environmental lawsuits challenged developments that accounted for twenty-nine thousand, and by 1976 California was producing four times as many environmental impact reports as the federal government. In 1972, the San Francisco chapter of the Sierra Club opposed a bond measure to bring more water to the job-rich suburbs around Silicon Valley on the grounds that this would increase sprawled growth at a time when San Francisco was losing population. A few months later, the same group supported a proposal to discourage high-density construction by limiting building heights around the city. In a somewhat famous case from 1973, a sixteen-year-old Boy Scout in San Francisco was able to use CEQA to halt the construction of a two-hundred-unit condo project for a year and a half.

The embodiment of the new and more environmentally conscious California was Pat Brown's son, Jerry, who was elected governor in 1974, at thirty-six, just as Reagan was leaving office to build a presidential platform out of the antitax/antigovernment reputation he'd cultivated in California. Jerry Brown was a Yale Law graduate who had spent three years training to be a Jesuit priest before leaving for college at Berkeley, and while he became famous for his philosophical ramblings and earned the nickname Governor Moonbeam, his governance seemed to be grounded in Catholic asceticism and the near-constant belief that something very bad, be it a recession or nuclear apocalypse, was right around the corner. In his first State of the State speech in 1976, he declared it "an era of limits":

> We face a new challenge. It is not the one faced by those who preceded us. For them, the task was how to cope with tremendous growth. But for us, it is a far more subtle and difficult undertaking. Throughout much of our recent past, the economy and the environment generated a surplus out of which new social programs could be financed . . . The country is rich, but not as rich as we have been led to believe. The choice to do one thing may preclude another. In short, we are entering an era of limits.

Brown grew up in San Francisco and had memories of playing touch football games in front of his house that were only rarely interrupted by cars. He'd watched the southern part of the peninsula go from a rural expanse of farms to a mass of offices and new subdivisions. He was the person whom writers like Harold Gilliam were talking about when they talked about the people who knew the open fields and hillsides that were now being consumed by growth. Young governor Brown became known for his hatred of freeways, for refusing contact with the wealthy developers who bankrolled his father's campaigns, and for handing out copies of *Small Is Beautiful*, a book by the economist E. F. Schumacher that argued for a less consumptive form of living that Schumacher called "Buddhist economics."

Jerry Brown lived as he preached, flying commercial and eschewing the governor's mansion for a matress on the floor of a Sacramento apartment. And while he pursued an inclusive-sounding agenda, like diversifying state hiring, proposing an anti-redlining law, and talking incessantly about the environment, Democrats were endlessly frustrated with his stingy budgets and doubts about the efficacy of social programs. He became, to some, the symbol of a state where seemingly liberal people had become uninterested in tackling the big social issues that required money and action, and were instead focused on easy and symbolic stuff like an Earth Day full of trash clean ups.

"Like most Westerners, Californians are foursquare for clean air, open space, equality, and decent housing, and against smog, dirty streams, inflation, and big oil spills in Santa Barbara," wrote Arthur Blaustein in a 1977 essay in *Harper's Magazine*. "But beyond that the commitment fades. Behind the façade of cultural hype, the new Western politics is, in essence, the old selfish privatism. Instead of efforts to redress social, economic, and political inequalities, the voters are offered only vague upward psychic mobility wrapped in the mantle of rugged individualism or deep asceticism. The 'new activism' is one that is actively committed to passivity, a state of mind which refuses to undertake the slightest personal inconvenience to intercede on behalf of those in our society who are suffering most."

More than anything else, the thing that characterized Jerry Brown's first governorship—the thing that would forever change America, the housing market, and become the most disrupting force in California history—was inflation. In the early 1970s, after the Organization of the Petroleum Exporting Countries cut oil production and declared an embargo on the United States for supporting Israel in the Yom Kippur War, U.S. consumer prices shot up and continued rising throughout the decade, sometimes more than 10 percent a year. It was a developing world episode of the sort that Americans, accustomed to stability, were wholly unprepared for. One day they'd go to the grocery store and find out that they couldn't afford the staples they'd bought a week earlier. Another they'd find out their electric bill was up 20 percent. People ended each year with the anxiety that their raise would not cover the rise in living expenses—which it often didn't—and long-term saving plans like how much to put away for your kid's college became complete question marks. For a decade, every president talked about it. For a decade, none of them could solve it.

When historians look back on "the Great Inflation," they mark it as a moment when Americans started losing faith in their leaders—Vietnam and Watergate didn't help—and when the economy started becoming more vicious and unequal. It was when union membership was heading into free fall. It was when middle-class factory jobs started being erased and CEO pay began its rise to today's obscene levels. The 1970s were notable for another, related reason: they were also the moment when residential real estate became a good financial investment. Until about 1970, home prices never rose fast enough to outpace the stock market, and Americans still regarded houses as first and foremost a place to live. They certainly didn't expect to *lose* money on a home, but to the extent they thought about the money they would get when they sold it, they saw it as money stored instead of money multiplied.

That started to change in the early 1970s, when the cost of homes, like the cost of everything else, spiked upward. It was devastating for young couples looking to save what was left of their inflation-eroded paychecks for a down payment on their first house. For anyone who already owned a home, however, the declining buying power of their own salary was offset by the fact that they now owned an asset that was performing like a hot stock. This added a powerful financial motivation to the multiplying list of reasons to oppose nearby development. Homeownership not only was suddenly very profitable but acted as a financial hedge against rising prices elsewhere, because most homeowners have fixed-rate mortgages whose monthly payments never change. Also, unlike renters, they can deduct their mortgage interest and property taxes from their federal tax bill.

By the end of the decade, as real estate grew to encompass a much larger share of American household wealth, suburban cities became increasingly bold in passing growth moratoriums to slow the pace of new development and large-lot zoning ordinances to guarantee that whoever bought the small amount of housing that was being built would come with money. In a 1977 paper on growth controls, Robert Ellickson, then a law professor at the University of Southern California, described suburban homeowners as "a profit-making cartel." He further warned that suburbs, with their small and homogeneous populations of land-owning households, were just the sort of tiny undemocratic government that James Madison had warned about all the way back in the Federalist Papers: "The smaller the society, the fewer probably will be the distinct parties and interests composing it; the fewer the distinct parties and interests, the more frequently will a majority be found of the same party; and the smaller the number of individuals composing a majority, and the smaller the compass within which they are placed, the more easily will they concert and execute their plans of oppression."

William Fischel called them "homevoters." Fischel was an economist who spent the 1970s and 1980s developing a theory of suburban behavior that he eventually called "the homevoter hypothesis." The theory went like this: Homes are an all-eggs-in-one-basket kind of investment. You can't diversify them like a stock, and you can't buy insurance on falling values. People can get their money back in the event their home is actually destroyed: you can buy fire insurance and flood insurance and earthquake insurance. But the one thing you *can't* buy insurance on is the thing homeowners fear most, which is the fear that their neighborhood will go to hell and they'll be stuck in a house nobody wants to buy.

And so began a vicious cycle in which the more home prices went up, the further people had to stretch to buy a home, the more motivated new homeowners became to protect their investment, the more home prices went up, the more people had to stretch, and so on. According to a Google analysis of old books, in the 1970s "housing prices" went from being a phrase that was only rarely used to a phrase that was so common it was used several times more frequently than "stock prices." The phrases "exclusionary zoning" and "growth management" went from rare to common usage over the decade. Soon after they were joined by "NIMBY."

IT WAS AN ODD TIME to be a twentysomething embarking on a career as a city planner, which was what Rick Holliday was now doing. Rick had rewarded his father's decision to move the family to a state with an inexpensive university system by graduating from Berkeley, and he had absorbed the 1970s ethos that the best kind of housing was affordable housing built densely, preferably at state expense and in an environmentally conscious manner. Later, when Rick started doing internships to learn the practicalities of his career choice, the on-the-job lesson he walked away with was that the things they told you in planning school were not the things they told you in real life. He got a vivid illustration of this during an internship in Moraga, a suburb next to where he grew up in Orinda. One of Rick's jobs was to take a sleeve of markers and fill an orthogonal city zoning map with different shades based on what kind of housing was allowed on each parcel. Single-family housing was yellow. It was the only marker he used.

Not long after, he decided Moraga wasn't for him and instead went to graduate school, again for planning, though mainly he was trying to stave off adulthood. Rick took uninspiring classes on things like zoning and municipal finance. One day, on the advice of a friend, he skipped whatever lecture he was supposed to be in and sat in on a class taught by a professor named Don Terner. Don Terner was housing famous. He'd helped start a nonprofit that was a precursor to Habitat for Humanity and organized Bronx residents into cooperatives that used public money to rehabilitate decrepit apartment buildings where they could then live affordably. Terner regaled the class with stories like how the co-op members insisted he work with them and would always give him the worst job (like shoveling squatter shit out of a basement). Then there was the time his work site was thrown into chaos by the arrival of overhead helicopters and a pack of black limousines, one of which turned out to contain President Jimmy Carter.

Rick went home and told his wife, Nancy, he wanted to be the West Coast Don Terner, and dedicated the rest of his time in graduate school to writing a thesis for a program that would try to replicate the Bronx co-op project in Oakland. Terner helped Rick turn the thesis into a proposal for a new law that would set aside a few hundred thousand in grants to help low-income residents rehabilitate local buildings. A year later, Rick and Terner traveled to the state capitol to try to turn Rick's graduate thesis into some kind of state grant for rehabilitation money. They got a bill passed, and shortly after Jerry Brown appointed Terner head of the state's Department of Housing and Community Development.

Rick stayed in the Bay Area and took a job helping the City of Hayward design a program to have private developers give the city land (which they could deduct from their taxes). Then the city would build low-income housing on it. There was just one problem. Way back in 1950, the same real estate agent groups that would try to undo the Rumford Act had passed another constitutional amendment, called Article 34. That one said cities couldn't build public housing without having voters approve it, and had all but ended public housing construction, even in big cities like Los Angeles. The chances of public housing being approved in Hayward were about zero, but Rick decided to go for it and ran the yes campaign while working for the city, which was probably illegal. The measure lost, of course, and Rick told Nancy he was going to quit his job. Instead he tried one more idea.

The idea was to find a developer to build subsidized housing with city money, which would end-run Article 34 by taking government out of the building role. The city agreed to the plan, which meant all Rick had to do was find a developer. He went to a volunteer group called Eden Housing, which was founded to enforce fair housing laws after the federal Civil Rights Act passed and was now helping low-income families build homes. Rick told them that the City of Hayward was looking to give a bunch of cash to an affordable housing developer, which meant Eden could apply for the cash and use it to hire staff and build subsidized housing, and, oh, by the way, he wanted to run the organization if they got it.

In other words, Rick was trying to get Hayward to take some of the money it was supposed to spend on public housing and use it to make him the head of a nonprofit developer. When he got the job, he asked the state for a grant under SB 910, that is, the program he had created with Don Terner as part of his master's thesis. The program that Terner was now up in Sacramento running! An enterprising newspaper reporter could have made quite a mess of things if he or she had decided to follow the paper trail and ask how it was that a twenty-five-year-old whose only known project was a tree fort behind his parents' house had all of a sudden become a government-contracted developer. But those were the kinds of shenanigans you had to pull if you were going to get subsidized houses past a wary public, and anyway he made $14,000 a year.

PRETTY MUCH BY DEFINITION, the basic concept of government is to spread the costs of an organized community across the entire populace. You can't have a fire department for one house, and unless the block is very wealthy, you can't have a fire department for ten houses or fifteen houses either. Nor could you have cops, a sewer system, parks, libraries, power, water, and the rest. This mathematical fact tends to put a limit on just how far a city will go in resisting new growth. It's something of a natural law, tied up in the cycle of life, that the costs of living in society are shouldered by different people at different times, which is why a broad and growing tax base is central to a healthy government. Put in more practical terms: cities that oppose growth forever will either start to fall apart or find their homeowners stuck with cripplingly high property taxes.

In the late 1970s, the latter started to happen. Homeowners' apparent windfall from rising home prices was offset by tax officials, who steadily raised property taxes as local values inflated. Stories of 50 percent tax increases became common, and as city coffers swelled, neighbors descended on assessors' offices to argue their bills could tax them out of their homes. This created a lightning in a bottle moment for a gadfly named Howard Jarvis. Jarvis was a wealthy entrepreneur from Utah who in the 1930s had moved to Los Angeles, where he owned various manufacturing businesses before retiring in 1962 to spend his golden years railing against the cost of government. He'd since become a well-known crank whose presence at city councils, school boards, and county boards of supervisors was so predictable that it often prompted government officials to use his few minutes of allotted testimony time as an opportunity to leave for a break or phone call. From 1968 to 1977, Jarvis made three attempts to gather enough signatures for a proposed statewide initiative to freeze property taxes. He ran a stunt campaign for mayor of Los Angeles to generate publicity for his third attempt, and as he wrote in his autobiography, *I'm Mad as Hell,* later that spring, when the state informed him that his petition didn't have enough valid signatures to qualify for the ballot, he started collecting signatures for a new petition the next day.

Part of the logic behind California's initiative system is to make elected officials more responsive to the people they are supposed to represent. It's a ruthless political temperature taker, one that is much more severe than a standard election, because unlike a standard election, revolts of initiative make law. And those laws can't be changed by the legislature: laws made by initiative can only be changed by another vote of the people. Therein lies one of the system's main detracting points, which is that it leads to extreme political decisions—decisions that are difficult to change—and in doing so makes long-term law from short-term chaos. Jarvis argued that the intention of his property tax initiative was to make taxes more equal, which was diametrically the opposite of what he would eventually accomplish.

Two decades earlier, when Pat Brown sold his growth plan to Californians, he did it by imposing new taxes broadly. Now there was an emerging mind-set that new people—be they actual newcomers or California natives who wanted to buy a home—should pay more of the state's financial burden. Hence a bunch of new developer fees, which were immediately passed on to new home buyers and shifted a larger share of the cost of things like new parks and infrastructure onto incoming residents. Jarvis's 1978 initiative, later called Proposition 13, would exaggerate this disparity even further. Proposition 13 asked voters to pass a constitutional amendment in which property taxes would be immediately rolled back to 1976 values and from then on would never rise more than 2 percent a year, regardless of a home's value. Properties could be reassessed only after they were sold. This meant that assuming California homes continued to appreciate in value, which they did, anyone who had recently bought a home would have to pay far higher property taxes than their neighbor across the street, even if that neighbor was in an identical tract house.

With antitax fervor brewing across the state, Jarvis's group collected twice as many signatures as needed, and in 1978 Proposition 13 passed with just under two-thirds of the vote. Over the next few decades, Proposition 13 would make the California housing crunch considerably worse, by making NIMBYism a far more profitable activity than it was with rising property taxes, and by discouraging cities from adding housing that strained local finances; absent rising property taxes, new housing could cost cities more than it brought in through taxes. Before the election, Pat Brown had said, "If I were a Communist and wanted to destroy this country, I would support the Jarvis amendment." Jerry Brown said it would be a "monster."

Once the results were in, however, Jerry Brown called it "the strongest expression of the democratic process in a decade" and set about reforming the state's finances. Jerry Brown's administration had long pushed a more contained and city-centric model of growth, and a handful of his staff would later become recognized as early leaders of the environmentally friendly, mass-transit-oriented design movement that became known as new urbanism. The administration tried to ratchet that philosophy further up after Proposition 13, and Brown argued that the sprawl of his father's California, which the state could no longer pay for, was over. "We will have to focus development in the cities and in the older suburbs, and as we do, inevitably we will have to increase the density," Brown said in his 1979 State of the State speech.

This was exactly what the activists who had so vehemently opposed suburban growth had long been theoretically arguing, emphasis on theoretically. Antipathy to development was often just as strong in cities as it was in suburbs, and sprawl was an easy way to build housing because sprawl displaced farms and cattle, neither of which complained about the hordes of new people, and because edge land was also much cheaper to build on than the tight spaces within cities. Infill might be smarter, greener, and cheaper to service, but sprawl means building houses where people aren't, and infill means building houses where people are. As Rick Holliday had learned in his yellow-square-coloring internship, the things students learned in planning school and the things environmental design wonks told governors in their office were not the same things homevoters actually wanted. Sprawl was a political contradiction, containing both the logic of its failure and the voting conditions that make its growth model almost impossible to stop.

By 1980, with housing costs untenable and rent control legislation popping up around the state, Jerry Brown issued an executive order for a Task Force on Affordable Housing to tackle the crisis of having average home values exceed $100,000. Two months later, a week after the task force's first meeting, Rick was one of fifty developers invited to a private breakfast in Los Angeles where Brown promised "fundamental changes" in state housing policy. Later that year, he signed a package of housing bills and an executive order that were supposed to speed up housing construction and force cities to think regionally and allow housing at all income levels.

Two years later, just before he left office, Brown signed another bill, called the Housing Accountability Act. It allowed people to sue cities that actively tried to block higher-density developments. There is hardly any record of its passage, and nothing resembling a fuss. For years it just sat there, barely noticed, rarely used, until one day several decades later Sonja Trauss came across an article about it in the newspaper and thought, "Huh."

CHAPTER 5

SUE THE SUBURBS

TONY LAGISS WAS a feisty old real estate agent who lived alone in a rickety two-bedroom bungalow on Deer Hill Road that sat next to a guest house and a small office building from which he ran his business. His structures were worth nothing. The land around them could be worth many millions—twenty-two acres of hillside that bordered the 24 Freeway and was a short drive from a BART station and the strip of storefronts, Starbucks, and supermarkets that make up downtown Lafayette, California. Near the freeway and town was a profitable space for Lagiss. He'd owned land in the Bay Area since the 1940s, when he returned home from the merchant marine, and over the next few decades he watched the value of his investment appreciate as bulldozers turned the East Bay into San Francisco's bedroom district. Lagiss spent a good portion of the '50s and '60s in court battling the state over its decision to condemn his property to build the 24, and eventually got a settlement that included undisclosed cash and an agreement that he could keep the portion of his parcel that the freeway didn't consume. Around Lafayette he was known for the typewritten antitax screeds he mailed to city hall and local newspapers, and for the yellow Oldsmobile he drove around town, which had "LAGISS" on the plates.

Not many people knew this, but buried under Lagiss's land was one of Lafayette's oldest secrets. The secret was that many decades earlier, when California was in its go-go growth phase and the area was evolving from a bunch of farms around a mill wheel to a wealthy commuter suburb that sits a tunnel away from Oakland and a thirty-one-minute BART ride from San Francisco, the county zoned his land for high-density apartments. And in the 1950s, that seemed to be the trajectory Lafayette was on. The population jumped from five thousand in 1950 to nineteen thousand in 1965, before halting in 1968, when Lafayette incorporated into a city so that it could wrest land-use power from the county and put a stop to growth. The incorporation play worked. Decades later, the Bay Area had doubled in population while Lafayette kept a steady twenty-five thousand residents who used phrases like "small town" and "semirural" to describe the local character. A number of the neighbors seemed to think Lagiss's twenty-two-acre parcel was protected open space closed off to future development.

It was anything but. Unbeknownst to a good amount of the city and the various executives and sports stars who had moved into the multimillion-dollar homes that dot the hillside above Deer Hill Road, Lagiss's property had always remained zoned for the high-growth vision of the 1950s. In theory, a developer could build something like eight hundred apartments there if it wanted to, and someone would definitely want to. The parcel was so prime for real estate, so perfectly situated around the freeway, downtown, and BART, that way back in 2002, when Lagiss was in his eighties, the city tried to proactively scare off developers by using a planning document to declare its intention to rezone his property for low-density single-family houses to match the rich homes up in the hills. Later that year, Steve Falk, Lafayette's longtime city manager, asked the city council to officially downzone the land and requested $150,000 to cover the various administrative and legal costs it would take to get the process started. The council thought $150,000 was too much, so the property remained zoned as it was, empty and awaiting a proposal.

THE APPLICATION LANDED in March 2011. If it wasn't so thick and thorough, Steve might have assumed it was a joke. According to documents filed with the city's planning department, Tony Lagiss's daughter, Anna Maria Dettmer, had teamed up with a developer named Dennis O'Brien to propose a complex of fourteen buildings and 315 apartments to be spread across the Deer Hill lot. The application called it the Terraces of Lafayette. Steve's back-of-the-envelope mental calculation was that the Terraces would be the largest development in Lafayette history and also never happening. He figured the size was a negotiating tactic. Developer proposes 315 apartments, neighbors freak out, developer shrinks it down, everyone gets a victory.

On the other hand, there was no way that's how this would go, and the developer should have known that just as surely as Steve did. It had been only a few years since the neighbors went nuclear over a city council debate to put a mere fourteen houses on the same lot. There was no world in which those people would be okay with someone scattering 315 apartments along the hill, no world in which they would be okay with the 315 apartments being whittled down to 215 or 115, and probably no world in which they would be okay with anything having anything to do with apartments whatsoever. This left two possibilities. Either Lagiss's daughter had teamed up with an idiotic developer who had no idea how Lafayette operated, or the developer knew something Steve didn't. And the developer wasn't an idiot. Dennis O'Brien had been building houses in the Bay Area since the 1960s and was on the board of directors of BRIDGE Housing, a national affordable housing developer that Rick Holliday and Don Terner founded in 1983. Whatever game Dennis O'Brien was playing was a game Steve Falk wasn't familiar with.

O'Brien revealed his strategy in a letter that arrived at city hall a few months later after the city council predictably started scrambling to re-zone the property so that it would be illegal to build more than four houses on the site. The letter said O'Brien's company intended to have the Terraces carry below-market rents, and in accordance with section 65589.5 of the California government code it would sue the city if it went through with its intended downzoning of the land. Steve was not familiar with section 65589.5. What he and the rest of the Lafayette government learned in the subsequent weeks of legal opinion getting was that section 65589.5 was a law known as the Housing Accountability Act (HAA). It said cities couldn't rezone their land just because a developer proposed something they didn't like on it, or exactly what Lafayette was planning to do.

Even though the Housing Accountability Act had been on the books for decades, developers rarely used it. That was why nobody in Lafayette could see O'Brien's angle in advance. In public, developers would tell you they didn't use the HAA because they would never dream of suing a responsive local community and the esteemed city councils that they had a great working relationship with. In private, they'd say it wasn't worth getting into a pissing match with a bunch of NIMBYs because that would only antagonize local politicians and inspire future city councils to make their lives a living hell the next time they proposed something. O'Brien was an exception. Rival developers told him Lafayette would fight him no matter what he proposed, so he should come in with a credible threat, and he found one. It took only a few weeks before Steve Falk and the rest of the Lafayette government realized O'Brien had them legally boxed in, but neighbors didn't get it and were incensed that the city couldn't just dismiss his apartment proposal out of hand.

"Traffic," "too aggressive," "not respectful," "overburdening," "an embarrassment," "outraged," "audacity," "very urban," and "will allow more crime to be committed" were some of the things people said in an early public meeting about the project. "Deeply upset," "unsightly," "monstrosity," "inconceivable," "simply outrageous," "vehemently opposed," "sheer scope," "too much," "semi-rural," "very wrong," "blocking views," "inconsistent," "does not conform," "not distinctive," and "property values will be destroyed" were some of the things they wrote in letters. "The project would strain our already crowded and underfunded schools." "I do not understand why Lafayette would approve additional housing when there is already plenty of housing available within commuting distance of San Francisco." "Don't expect my vote in the future if this passes." "I have a huge concern with locating a multi-unit apartment complex in such close proximity to the High School," one woman wrote. "Exposing them to a complex that will house 315 different types of families/tenants increases their exposure to many of the elements we strive to keep away from our youth."

The Lafayette City Council met on the second and fourth Monday of each month in an auditorium next to the library, and they sat on a foot-high stage behind nameplates and skinny microphones. The audience sat in rows of chairs in front of them and off to the side was a communal table where the city attorney and other staff sat in a line waiting for questions. Steve Falk was usually a few feet behind the staff, alone in a chair by the fire exit so that he could observe the dynamics of each meeting from the widest possible vantage point. Steve did abstract paintings on the weekends, and after a career of watching development fights, the subject of zoning had so deeply penetrated his psyche that his house was decorated with canvases of colorful boxes on wobbly grids. Being the city manager was kind of like being the city CEO, especially in a small community like Lafayette, where the council was a part-time operation. But it was still a democracy of the people, and Steve, who had a master's from Harvard's Kennedy School of Government, thought it was deferential to that idea for him to be off to the side and out of view while the council was in session. For the same reason, he almost never spoke during council meetings, except when he was delivering reports.

It wasn't that he considered it wrong or off limits to advise the council on their decisions. He just preferred to do it in private so that whenever a big and controversial vote came down, the faces of that vote would be people in elected office. Such was the case with the Terraces of

Lafayette. A few meetings in, Steve could already see how the project was going to go. First there would be two years of design reviews and historical assessments and environmental reports and planning hearings. Then the development would go to the city council for approval, and voters would show up in droves to protest. The council would deny the project, Dennis O'Brien would sue, and the city would spend several months (or longer) mired in an expensive lawsuit that it would very likely lose. Steve's feeling was that anything he could do to prevent that fate would be serving the public interest, so one day in 2013, after a crowd of about fifty people showed up at the city council meeting to lose their minds about the Terraces, he approached the council during a closed session to ask if he could call Dennis O'Brien to request a private meeting. Maybe they could work out a deal. The council doubted this could be done. They'd already accepted a destiny in which they would deny the project, get sued, and let a judge figure it out. Still, the worst that could happen was that the deal would fall apart and they'd get sued like they already planned to. If Steve wanted to get in the middle of that, he was free to go ahead and try.

Steve had taken a negotiation class in graduate school, and one of the lessons he always remembered was that people were supposed to be more reasonable when they bargained over food. To prepare for his meeting with Dennis O'Brien, he walked from his office to a deli and bought fresh baguettes, a wheel of brie, and bunches of red grapes. He laid the spread on a conference room table and cut the bread into slices and put down little cheese spreaders and surrounded it with the red grapes. Dennis O'Brien was roughly the color of those grapes when he walked into city hall for the meeting, and Steve accepted that for the next few hours he would be the recipient of two years' worth of O'Brien's frustrations. But before it got to that he wanted everyone to eat. That's what Steve told the room as they sat down at the table. The room was silent. Steve explained the whole deal about how he once took a negotiation class and people were nicer around food. The room remained silent. Steve looked at Dennis O'Brien and said, *Dennis, look, I don't even know you, but you have to eat something, even if it's one grape, before I'll talk to you.* That at least got people laughing. Steve stayed serious and said he meant it. He wouldn't start the meeting until everyone in the room ate something from the table. For anyone who wasn't Steve, the meeting seemed to be turning into a conference room version of one of those dinner parties where the host tries to executive produce all seating and conversation, but much like one of those parties once you're stuck you're stuck, so everyone grabbed some bread and cheese and grapes.

In addition to all the food, the room had a whiteboard where Steve drew a Venn diagram with three circles. Residents. Developer. City. The resident circle wanted less traffic and no more than four houses. The developer circle wanted profit, which would involve a lot more than four houses. The city circle wanted to placate the neighbors. Where between the numbers 315 and 4 could they find a place to meet? The initial conversation went well enough that after several hours of talking and white boarding and grape eating, the room agreed to have another meeting. The second meeting turned into a dozen meetings and several conference calls, and after many more hours of talking and white boarding and eating, Dennis O'Brien decided to submit a new plan for forty-four single-family houses. In addition to downsizing the project, O'Brien agreed to reorient the development so that traffic was aimed away from an already-choked intersection, and to build the city a sports field and dog park.

This is what developers mean when they talk about being extorted by a city for a building permit. It was also how business got done, because now, in theory anyway, each circle on the whiteboard had been filled with something it wanted. The angry neighbors got an almost tenfold reduction in density, no nearby apartments, and a traffic circle that aimed cars away from their intersection. Dennis O'Brien got to build and sell forty-four houses and an implicit promise from the city that his path to construction would be easier. The city got a bunch of recreational goodies that it could present to residents as a concession and build a small constituency around.

Steve was a frequent user of the analogy about sausage making, and this was definitely some sausage, but he walked out of his talks with Dennis O'Brien feeling like an A-plus public servant who might have a second career in conflict resolution. A month later, he presented the new plan to a relieved and happy council. "Given that the developer has indicated that if the project is denied it will file a lawsuit against the city, and given the risks to the city presented by that potential lawsuit, and particularly those associated with California's Housing Accountability Act . . . ," Steve told the council during his windup to the new project presentation, in hopes of making it clear that this was the last and final choice.

Then: two more years of waiting. Two more years of applications and studies and environmental impact reports. Two more years of Steve receiving angry letters and watching neighbors complain about the proposal. Finally the council was set to vote on the new project on August 10, 2015. Forty-four houses was still more than many of the neighbors wanted, but the apartment complex was now gone, and a number of residents had been swayed by Steve's efforts to get them a new field and dog park. All of that was enough to persuade the council to vote the project through and officially end what had now been a four-year process. About a week before the meeting, Steve was sitting at his desk when he got a call from a woman he'd never heard of. Her name was Sonja Trauss.

STEVE FALK HAD BEEN GOING to zoning and land-use meetings for twenty-five years. Until the day Sonja called him, not once, not ever, had he heard someone complain that a project was too small. Sonja being Sonja, she volunteered to Steve that she was looking for some advice on a potential lawsuit against the city. That was another first, and Steve naturally tried to dissuade her from filing it. *You'll be suing the wrong city*, he said. Whatever a small suburb like Lafayette was supposed to be doing to encourage housing and density, Steve believed it was doing it. There were new apartments going up all around the BART station, and over the previous decade the city had approved all but one of the multi-family projects that had been submitted to the planning department, and built eight new multifamily units for every one new single-family house. The exception was O'Brien's proposal, but Steve told Sonja that if she drove out to Lafayette she'd see for herself that the project was far from the urbanist dream. The site was a mile from downtown, toward the bottom of a high-speed hill with no sidewalks. Nobody who lived there would walk anywhere. An hour or so later, Steve hung up feeling as if he'd persuaded Sonja to drop her plans. Of course, he never had a chance.

Four days before the August meeting where the Lafayette City Council was set to approve Dennis O'Brien's new single-family-house project, Sonja sent Steve a letter from SF BARF formally threatening to sue. The following Monday before the council meeting, Steve was sitting in his usual spot on the side of the room, watching people filter into the library auditorium, when he noticed a gaggle of young adults throbbing with the conspiratorial energy of teenagers before a prank. The comment microphone was already going to be crowded. In the years since Dennis O'Brien had first made his proposal, neighbors who lived up the hill from Tony Lagiss's land had formed a nonprofit called Save Lafayette. They'd begun as opponents of the 315-unit apartment complex before rededicating themselves to the mission of stopping the 44 houses set to replace it. Years earlier, when Steve pitched the new project as a good compromise that would significantly reduce future density, Michael Griffiths, a software salesman who'd co-founded Save Lafayette, said this was misleading and that the number 44 was not fewer than the number 315 because houses and apartments were apples and oranges.

Another critic was a nuclear engineer named Susan Candell. Candell had quibbled with the project's earthquake study, argued the proposed soccer field was on a too steep of a hill, and in the months before the meeting had sent half a dozen letters about the potential for carcinogenic dust during construction. The dust letters ran for about thirty pages and had charts, maps, air-quality reports, equations, exclamation points, CAPS, and the word "cancer" over and over. Now various people were set to testify that if the project was approved, it could lead to premature death for the students of a nearby high school. Steve settled in by the fire exit and watched as SF BARF and Save Lafayette collided.

BRIAN HANLON: It's a really egregious time to be doing this, given the acute need for new housing, especially for new moderate-income housing.

SONJA TRAUSS: An ordinary political process like a sales tax, both sides have an opportunity to show up and say whether they're for or against it. But when you have a new project like this, where there are 700-plus people who would initially move in, much less the tens of thousands of people who would live in it over the lifetime of the project? Those people don't know who they are yet. Some of them are not even born. So however many letters you got from people who are against it, you have to imagine you are making a decision that will house or de-house thousands of people.

IAN KALLEN: I'm somewhat disturbed by all these parties from outside my neighborhood telling me that I should accept this degradation to my quality of life.

DIEGO AGUILAR-CANABAL: Let me tell you a bit about the quality of life for the heavily rent burdened residents of California. I spend 50 percent of my income on rent. That's an entire paycheck out of my two monthly paychecks.

ROBERT MCKEE: For those people who don't live here, let me tell you, people who live in Lafayette are on the top of their game. To get here it takes a lot of hard work, and to stay here it takes a lot of hard work . . . If you perhaps feel that it's a little too expensive here, there is a large country here and you can move. You don't have to stay here.

LEORA TANJUATCO: Hi, I'm Leora Tanjuatco and I'm one of the young people who can't afford to live here and should just stay away forever.

ARMAND DOMALEWSKI: When I came here tonight I expected to have a reasonable conversation about costs and benefits. I expected to talk about preserving neighborhood character versus building afford-able units. Instead, I heard this—I heard that I was a degradation. I heard that all the people out here who came two hours because they want to live in this community, because they want to have affordable housing, they are a degradation and a cost and a burden. No hu-man being is a degradation. They are a benefit. Let's talk about the economic benefits of adding people instead of simply treating them as costs.

Most of the time, Sonja never seemed to think too deeply about how any particular move or protest fit into a larger strategy, but Lafayette was a rare instance where she actually had a long game in mind. She was coming up on a year of full-time activism, and in that time had demon-strated that SF BARF was a powerful idea that could attract members and patrons. Despite this, it still wasn't clear what exactly SF BARF was. Strictly speaking it wasn't anything. There was no legally recog-nized organization called SF BARF. Its existence was limited to a mail-ing list, a Google Group, and Sonja's GeoCities-grade website. If she was going to build a movement with legs and secure herself more stable employment and a wider swath of donors, she needed to build a real nonprofit with a clearly defined mission that she could pursue and fundraise around.

For this she teamed up with a fellow activist named Brian Hanlon, who, like Sonja, had moved to the Bay Area after dropping out of grad school. Brian was an unapologetic hipster who had a beard and wore skinny jeans and was particular about natural wine and fixed-gear bikes. He'd gotten involved in housing via the typically San Francisco route of going to eviction protests and marching next to people who held signs that said things like "Tech = Death." Then he got into a bunch of disputes with his fellow protestors and the San Francisco Tenants Union over his belief that new development was good and renters' groups were misguided for fighting it, after which he started complaining to friends about his frustration that the left only knows how to critique and conduct purity tests. It was during one of these rants that an old friend told Brian that he knew this woman named Sonja who said a lot of the same things about housing, and so yeah he should totally talk to her.

At the time Brian was working an uninspiring desk job at the U.S. Forest Service whose government hours gave him ample free time for bike rides and extracurricular projects. Soon he was dedicating that energy to reading about housing policy and attending planning meetings, where he often spoke just before or after Sonja during public comment. Frustrated with the glacial pace of politics, Brian also started noodling around with the idea of trying to sidestep the legislative grinder by starting a legal nonprofit that would file racial discrimination lawsuits against exclusive suburbs (something fair housing groups had been doing since the 1960s) in hopes of getting judges to make them build housing.

Then Sonja went a step further, unearthing the Housing Accountability Act, finding a potential case in Lafayette, and raising another $100,000 from Jeremy Stoppelman to hire a lawyer to litigate it. On account of an approaching legal deadline, Sonja wrote the lawsuit herself by copying old Housing Accountability Act cases and pasting in the particulars about Lafayette, then filed it on behalf of herself and SF BARF at the end of 2015. This pushed Brian's fair housing idea to the sidelines and made enforcing the Housing Accountability Act the guiding mission behind the California Renters Legal Advocacy & Education Fund (CaRLA), which was the name of the formally incorporated nonprofit that Brian and Sonja co-founded just before she filed the Lafayette suit. "Thirty-five years of wonky liberals trying to induce localities to build housing has been a complete failure," Brian declared at CaRLA's first public event, which was held in a small classroom in a Mission District community center. "So, why not just sue the suburbs?"

The event consisted of a panel discussion with two lawyers and an economist. Brian DIY catered it with a spread of wine, persimmons, and a blue-gray eggplant dip that came with crackers and an origin story. Toward the end, the panel went over Sonja's Lafayette suit, which alleged that the city had illegally browbeaten Dennis O'Brien into abandoning his original 315-unit apartment project for the 44-home compromise that the city had now approved.

The great irony of Sonja's lawsuit was that nobody wanted her to sue Lafayette less than Dennis O'Brien. O'Brien had spent four years and several million dollars proposing two completely different projects. Now his permit was being threatened by a group that didn't even exist when the process got started, and through some twisted-up logic they were suing the city, and him, on behalf of his old project—in essence, suing him on behalf of him. It got worse. As part of his development agreement with the city, O'Brien had signed a standard indemnification clause assuming legal responsibility for the project. That meant he had to pay to defend the city from Sonja. O'Brien had asked Sonja to stand down before she sued. This had by implication made it clear to her that if she went ahead with the suit it would do little to ingratiate her, a newly minted housing activist looking for support and big donations, to him, a rich and powerful developer who sat on the board of one of the largest nonprofit affordable housing developers in America. Sonja went for it anyway. She was only a developer shill when it served her, and this time the developer was in her way.

It still took her a while to find a lawyer to take the case. There were lawyers who sued cities on behalf of developers, and lawyers who sued cities on behalf of angry neighbors, and lawyers who defended cities from both. Sonja was suing a city *and* a developer, while also inflaming the neighbors, so she faced the near-impossible task of finding someone who knew a lot about land-use law yet had no loyalty to the usual players. Then one day she was at a San Francisco Ethics Commission hearing and heard a lawyer named Ryan Patterson dispute a new disclosure proposal. The content of his disagreement wasn't of interest. What interested her was that during his comments Patterson said his firm sometimes represented developers and sometimes represented neighborhood groups ("played both sides" would be another way of putting it). After the hearing, Sonja walked up to him to say she had a case she wanted to chew over with him.

Ryan Patterson was a San Francisco renter who was sympathetic to the SF BARF cause, as well as a rare California Republican who had interned in the Schwarzenegger administration. He worked for a firm that had a sub-specialty in suing the government and had a muscular view on property rights that was a product of growing up in a conservative former mining town with small-business-owning parents. Sonja's case was intellectually adventurous—and impossible to win. Patterson's job was to convince a judge that Lafayette had unfairly forced Dennis O'Brien to build 44 houses instead of 315 apartments, while Dennis O'Brien sat on the other side more or less going, "No they didn't." The judge predictably sided with Lafayette, but after Sonja threatened an appeal, the city—meaning Dennis O'Brien—agreed to pay CaRLA's legal fees. O'Brien had now argued, and paid for, both sides of the same case.

Even in defeat, the Lafayette case more than served its purpose for Sonja, further raising her profile and generating news articles galore. The following summer, Open Philanthropy, the same nonprofit that funded the YIMBYtown conference, gave CaRLA a $300,000 grant. In the "Risks and Reservations" section of the grant, Open Philanthropy wrote, "Trauss has limited experience running a formal organization, and her public persona presents a degree of informality that we worry may limit her effectiveness as the leader of a more formal institution, though we believe it has contributed to her success drawing attention to this issue in the past." This statement was backed up by a footnote to a *Bloomberg* article about Sonja. Toward the middle of the piece, the reporter wrote that when he asked Sonja for a picture he could run with the story, she e-mailed one picture of herself holding a textbook on zoning law and another of her in a bikini.

Sonja was done with Lafayette, but Lafayette was not done with lawsuits. Steve Falk had walked into that August 10 city council meeting thinking he was about to witness a vote that would steer his city away from an expensive lawsuit and toward what he felt was a reasonable compromise. What he witnessed instead was a promise for several more years of process and the beginning of the end of his career in Lafayette's government. That's because while Sonja was busy fighting Lafayette in court, Save Lafayette had started collecting signatures for a referendum vote to try to undo the council's approval of Dennis O'Brien's new project. When Lafayette tried to argue the referendum was illegal, Save Lafayette sued. Thus, after getting rid of a lawsuit alleging the project was too small, Steve was now dealing with a second lawsuit that wanted to stop it for being too big.

U.S. SUBURBS OFFER two kinds of sprawl. The first is the freeways and tract houses and one-direction traffic that characterize the constantly expanding autoscape. The second kind of sprawl, less visual and less talked about, is the simultaneous sprawl of governments that created Lafayette. To understand how Lafayette became a city and why being a city is important, first you have to understand that cities are a privileged class. The U.S. Constitution talks about the federal government and states. Counties are a step below that and serve as the branch offices of state government. Cities are harder to define than the first three. Legally, they're what you might call an independent governance zone—small, geographically defined places where a state has specifically allowed a government to form and pass laws inside its boundaries. The people who run cities call this "local control," and they are constantly flummoxed to learn that this control only exists to the extent a state allows it.

For the first half of the twentieth century, the privilege of being a city was typically reserved for big and middle-sized places. They weren't all

New Yorks and Chicagos, but they weren't a bunch of Lafayettes either. The suburbs of the time were usually on unincorporated county land, and when they got big enough to even contemplate becoming their own city, a bigger city usually came along to eat them through annexation. That started to change in the 1950s as the postwar suburban boom, and the impulses for racial and economic exclusion that were tied up in it, created a constellation of new subdivisions that wanted to be able to pass their own laws—especially their own land-use regulations—and needed to incorporate as cities to do it.

This created a conundrum. Bound up in the privilege of becoming a city that can pass its own laws and deliver its own services is the responsibility of actually paying for the functions of government, which is hard to do below a certain size. If a community is going to go through the expense of creating its own police force and fire department and building codes, it's going to have to be either rich enough to fund all that stuff or big enough to distribute the cost across a wide area. Postwar suburbs were rarely either: middle class and small in population, with residents who reacted fiercely to the prospect of high property taxes, the housing developments of the 1950s and 1960s had the desire to control their own fate but lacked the ability to pay for it. Then came Lakewood.

In terms of its design, urban history regards Lakewood, CA, as the Los Angeles version of Long Island's Levittown. Lakewood was a 17,500-home megadevelopment that sat on the southern end of Los Angeles County, right next to Long Beach. It was the second of its kind. The Burger King of suburbs. But Lakewood was completely original in at least one way: unlike the unincorporated Levittown, it became a full-fledged city. Lakewood incorporated defensively to stave off an annexation threat from Long Beach, and what was unique about how it did it was that instead of becoming a city the normal way—by passing a bunch of taxes and using the money to hire police and firemen and street sweepers—Lakewood's founders came up with a plan to pay the county government and private contractors to run all but a handful of city services. It was America's first "contract city."

The Lakewood Plan unleashed a kind of municipal technology that lowered the financial barrier of acquiring local control by spreading costs across the county, and over the next few decades contract governments and other incorporation-encouraging policies, such as laws that allowed cities to pass their own sales taxes and control the receipts, acted to shatter metropolitan areas into dozens of suburban fragments. Lakewood became a city in 1954. In Los Angeles County, four new cities had been incorporated by 1956 and twenty-six by 1960. There were thirty-two, with a total of 700,000 residents, by 1970.

Incorporation boosters framed the surge in new cities as a revolution in consumer choice. A whole school of local government theorists, led by a UCLA economist named Charles Tiebout, started pushing the idea that U.S. metro areas were becoming like the shelves of a supermarket. Some families want a city with a lot of parks. Others want a place with a math-minded high school. Some want no frills and low taxes. A region with a lot of individually incorporated cities was a region with a lot of happy and satisfied residents who instead of complaining about their government could simply move to one they liked better.

At least that was the argument. As metro areas broke into dozens of new cities distinguishable mostly by their "Welcome to _____" signs, the middle class and affluent white people who had the option to move wherever they wanted did indeed find that smaller and less service-intensive cities gave them better government for lower prices. But one of the main reasons it worked was that these cities effectively opted out of paying for expensive social services by zoning out poorer people. A city that is run primarily to reduce costs is a city that does everything it can to draw in things and people that generate the most taxes while keeping out people who are likely to need affordable homes or financial help.

To that end, "maintaining local control" was often a euphemism for maintaining control over zoning and land use so that cities could dictate things like the building of apartments versus the building of houses, and set regulations for how big those houses should be and roughly what they should cost—decisions that by and large determined what sorts of people could move where. It's telling that the one function contract cities almost never contracted out, the thing that consumed almost all their business and made up the bulk of their actual employees, was the planning department. "Lakewood Plan cities were essentially white political movements," wrote Gary J. Miller in *Cities by Contract*.

In 1950, Compton was a diverse and well-functioning city with a solid tax base and a spectrum of high-, middle-, and lower-income households. In the later 1950s and 1960s, as higher-income white families fled to Lakewood and higher-income black families to nearby Carson, Compton's poor population jumped. While its neighbors promoted the efficiency of low-tax, low-service governments, Compton was busy providing the Los Angeles region with the higher-density housing that contract cities like Lakewood refused. By 1970, after Compton's tax base had been further eroded by the migration of auto dealers to Lakewood, the city's violent crime rate had jumped by twenty-five times, and its share of lower-income and poor families had grown to two-thirds of the population, from a quarter in 1950. Compton taxes went up. Lakewood taxes were reduced. To believe that shopping for cities is like shopping for groceries is to believe that the reason poorer and nonwhite families settle where they do is that they've gone around their region and surveyed all the available options and after careful consideration decided that a higher-tax city with more crime and crowded housing was the government they'd always wanted.

None of it seemed so sinister to the kids who actually grew up in Lakewood. Steve Falk was one of them. He'd spent his childhood cruising the city's freshly paved streets on a Schwinn Stingray or Bahne skateboard, and when he graduated from Lakewood High School in 1979, Steve was flush with American optimism and a faith that the future would be better. Lakewood families had bought unbuilt houses on unidentified streets in an unknown neighborhood of an ahistoric city with untested schools and social support systems, yet no one had seemed to doubt that somehow it would all work. The mass sameness of subdivisions was visually boring, but it could also be socially inspiring to see everyone living so equally. Steve and his friends all lived in the same-style houses and all went to the same shopping mall and same schools. They also never thought about who was richer, because they all seemed the same, and were never told how this this equality was engineered.

THERE WAS NEVER any sort of plan to return to a city like the one he grew up in. Steve began his career crunching numbers for the Long Beach and San Francisco budget departments, all the while angling for a route to the city manager's office somewhere. It was embarrassing to say, given that he lived only a few miles away in San Francisco, but Steve had barely heard of Lafayette when he was offered an interview for the assistant city manager job. The job was what prompted his first-ever trip through the Caldecott Tunnel that cuts through the Oakland Hills. It was on the other side of the tunnel that he got his first glimpse of the *HOLY CALIFORNIA!* sight of undeveloped hills of oak surrounded by green grass and neon-yellow mustard flowers and a view of Mount Diablo through his windshield. *This* was what Lafayette meant when it said "semirural." It was a perfect place with perfect weather, yet was also just a short ride away from one of the most urbanized places in America. Steve wanted the job and to live there. He got both and was promoted to city manager a few years later, well before he expected to.

Steve Falk spent most of his career serving an exclusive suburb. There was no way around that one. Lafayette was itself a contract city, and his job was to deal with contractors and oversee a few dozen full-time employees, many of them in the planning department that was the city's reason for existence. He still did not consider himself the suburban devil of the YIMBY imagination. Far from it. Steve had been trying to work on exclusion and density long before Sonja Trauss had sued. His proudest achievement was Lafayette's downtown, which had been redeveloped from a strip of half-vacant storefronts into a walkable town center. There were apartments over retail buildings and a seventy-five-unit housing complex near BART. Steve had used redevelopment money to build subsidized affordable housing for seniors and disabled people, a plan that was pilloried by residents who accused him of threatening their property values but still went through. Working on the inside meant pushing a little, then backing off when things got too hot. In addition to making sausage clichés, Steve liked to repeat the quotation that politics is the art of the possible. Dennis O'Brien's apartments were not possible. So he'd worked a compromise for forty-four houses, forty more than the neighbors wanted to accept. According to Steve's change-from-the-inside way of thinking, a good compromise was a good win.

But somewhere in the Deer Hill odyssey, Steve started to sympathize with the activists instead of the place where he'd raised his children and the city he'd given his career to. His son lived in San Francisco and paid too much rent to live with a pile of roommates. His daughter was a dancer in New York. It was hard to watch his kids struggle with rent and not start to think that maybe Sonja had a point.

In mid-2016, Governor Jerry Brown, who was now close to eighty and in his second tour of running the state, affixed that year's budget with a sweeping proposal to allow developers to build urban apartments "as of right"—that is, without cities' approval. This was a threat to local control and the state/city equivalent of a parent threatening to take away a naughty child's favorite toy. Cities like Lafayette were apoplectic. Steve, feeling rebellious, decided to write a staff report recommending the city council vote to endorse the governor's idea to curb their power. "It recognizes that, because no single city perceives that it can impact the affordability crisis (and thus has little incentive to try), the solution must be region-wide or state-wide," Steve wrote to the council about Brown's plan.

This was a heretical position. Steve knew that. There would have been blowback just for writing a memo about it. His next move, putting the report on the upcoming council agenda so that the entire city would have to talk about it in public, was outright apostasy. It would have probably been career suicide if he had done it years earlier when he was new to city managing and Lafayette. Now he was nearing retirement and had an eighteen-month severance package worth close to half a million dollars including benefits, a package that the Lafayette City Council had given him specifically to insulate the city manager's office from election cycle thinking.

Residents were still furious. Susan Candell emailed a letter at 8:47 a.m. on the day of the meeting where Steve was set to present his report on Jerry Brown's housing proposal. "We are a tiny city surrounded by very big cities with very little money," she wrote. "I think our City Manager belongs in another city, one much larger than we are right now, if suggestions like this continue to come." Candell said much the same thing that night at the public comment microphone, followed by various others. "Cannot be trusted," "ineptitude," "disingenuously manipulating the city council," and "should be publicly and explicitly reprimanded" were some of the other things voters had said about Steve.

The council discussed and dismissed Steve's report, Jerry Brown's proposal died, and later that year Steve got a behind-closed-doors talking-to during his annual performance review. A little while later, when it came time for his next contract negotiation, members of Save Lafayette descended on a city meeting to protest Steve's severance package. Nobody ever told Steve how his employment contract became a political sticking point, but Save Lafayette was still embroiled in its lawsuit to allow a referendum vote to undo the council's approval of the forty-four-house compromise, and the court had prevented Dennis O'Brien from starting construction until the suit was resolved. Steve assumed what had happened was that someone from Save Lafayette had started looking into what it would take to fire him and realized the severance would make it prohibitively expensive.

"I suggest you don't just rubber-stamp this one more year," Susan Candell told the council in reference to Steve's contract.

"The city, in the broad sense of the word, has been taking actions that have been upsetting residents across the city," said Michael Griffiths of Save Lafayette, who was the next speaker. "I'm not being personal here, all I'm saying is it's something to consider. Nobody likes to get into lawsuits."

A council member later retorted that it wasn't the city's fault they were getting sued. This was presumably meant to remind Michael Griffiths of Save Lafayette that *Michael Griffiths of Save Lafayette* was currently the one suing them.

"Citizens would not bring lawsuits if they thought there was a good dialogue," Griffiths snapped back.

The following February, the court decided Save Lafayette's referendum vote could go forward. Dennis O'Brien added a campaign consultant to his growing list of development costs. That money was wasted too: The referendum passed that June, and two people associated with Save Lafayette, including Susan Candell, had started running campaigns for the city council. O'Brien did have a kind of insurance policy: The council had never actually voted on the original 315-unit apartment complex that had started the whole fight, which meant he could pick that project up more or less where he'd left it. The thrust of his campaign against the referendum was: "If you vote against the forty-four houses, you will get 315 apartments instead." Save Lafayette members had dismissed this as a bluff. It was not: shortly after the referendum passed, O'Brien resumed work on the original development application he'd submitted way back in 2011. If the city council denied it, he could always sue them under the Housing Accountability Act.

Steve could imagine this consuming another seven years of the city manager's life. But after the referendum to undo his deal with Dennis O'Brien, he decided that city manager would not be him. His bid for compromise had failed, citizens had rejected him at the ballot box, and he was now facing the prospect of having people who wanted him gone being elected to the city council. Friends told him he should stick around hoping to get fired so that he could cash in on that fat severance check. That seemed like a waste of life. He knew it was time to go and wasn't going to drag it out for money.

On the day of his resignation, Steve was uncharacteristically seated at the staff table when the council meeting was called to order. Usually some distinguished citizen or Boy Scout was given the honor of leading the Pledge of Allegiance, so the room could tell something was going on when the mayor asked Steve to do it. After the pledge, the mayor said Steve had something he wanted to say. Steve was already choking up by then. He looked down at the paper in front of him and told the room he was going to read his resignation letter *in part*. The part he read was polite. It was about how he loved the city and was proud of his accomplishments and believed Lafayette was a model of civility and democratic engagement and had a brilliant and professional staff.

When he was done, the room was silent, and the mayor said they would all take a moment to let this announcement sink in. Then the council said nice things and Steve nodded thank you, and it was all so gushy and positive that nobody thought to dwell on the tantalizing detail that Steve had begun with, which was that he was only reading his letter *in part*. The other paragraphs were right there on the page in front of him, and the city council had had the full text delivered to their inboxes several hours earlier. Soon enough they'd be making the rounds on Twitter and prompting reporters to call Steve for interviews. But Steve wasn't there to make a scene, so he left them out and enjoyed the happy ending, knowing it would all come out eventually.

"For a small town, Lafayette's land use, housing, and political challenges are surprisingly complex," he'd written in the full letter. "The City's great schools, quiet streets, easy proximity to San Francisco, and exquisite valley setting amongst the old oak trees make it a perfect place to live and raise a family—so perfect, in fact, that many, many people seek to move here. As a result, development pressures have always been pervasive in Lafayette. Indeed, the City's very raison d'être in 1968 was to preserve its semi-rural character, and Lafayette's animating mission since incorporation has been to use its municipal powers to stave off the Bay Area's inexorable urbanization.

"During the same fifty-year period, however, scientists have learned more about the earth's atmosphere and concluded that human activity and carbon emissions are responsible for climate change. Seas are rising, oceans are warming, the atmosphere is warming, the land is warming, ice is melting, heat emergencies and wildfires and hurricanes are increasing, rainfall patterns are changing, and the ocean is becoming more acidic. The risks and consequences for humanity cannot be overstated.

"All cities—even small ones—have a responsibility to address the most significant challenges of our time: climate change, income inequality, and housing affordability. I believe that adding multifamily housing at the BART station is the best way for Lafayette to do its part, and it has therefore become increasingly difficult for me to support, advocate for, or implement policies that would thwart transit density. My conscience won't allow it."

CHAPTER 6

THE SECOND HOUSING PACKAGE

SCOTT WIENER'S POLITICAL superpower was that whenever he got into a fight, he always seemed to come out of it as the designated adult in the room. Wiener represented the Castro District on the San Francisco Board of Supervisors, the local equivalent of a city council, and his first big rush of media attention, the moment when his name became established throughout the city, was when he proposed a ban on public nudity. People had a lot of fun with that one. Scott *Wiener* wrote a bill that made it illegal for anyone over five years old to "expose his or her genitals, perineum or anal region" on any public street. He'd written the bill because San Francisco's long tradition of having naked men with no tan lines cruise the sidewalks on warm days had escalated into a raucous scene in which nudists had started mass congregating near an intersection that became known as "the buff stop."

This being San Francisco, Wiener's bid to end the shenanigans led to free expression protests and a "nude in" demonstration on the city hall steps. For weeks Wiener was tarred as a conservative killjoy, but really it was just meat-and-potatoes constituent work. Castro businesses were annoyed with the nudists. He was the Castro's elected representative. He dutifully answered the call. After the measure passed the board of supervisors and half a dozen men and women disrobed in the chambers and were escorted away by sheriff's deputies, Wiener sat there in his suit looking like the guy who had just rescued San Francisco from itself.

Wiener was a Harvard Law graduate and prolific legislator who stood six feet seven inches and was thin, with glasses and a comes-and-goes beard. His demeanor was consistently unemotional, and he spoke in a voice that *SF Weekly*, the alternative newspaper, once described as "the monotone of a man dictating his name on an outgoing voicemail message." He'd been elected to the board of supervisors after spending two years of evenings, weekends, and lunch breaks knocking on fifteen thousand doors in his prospective district. In office, he became known for calling his staff at midnight and following up with long text messages at 3:00 a.m. Wiener had dim views of San Francisco's penchant for creating process on top of process and specialized in writing highly technical bills that aimed to strip away bureaucracy, transfer power from voters to city departments, and streamline local permitting and environmental processes so that it would be easier to build things. He passed so many different bills on so many different topics that voters never seemed sure what he was up to, just that he seemed competent and was evidently up to a lot.

On account of his comfort with development and his willingness to take on quality-of-life issues like pop-up nudist colonies, Wiener was what San Francisco politicos called "a moderate." Moderate was a term that meant a lot in San Francisco and absolutely nothing outside it. When it came to national issues, most of the city was some version of what Scott Wiener was: a very liberal Democrat who received 100 percent ratings on union scorecards and was in favor of gun control, higher income taxes, legalized marijuana, single-payer health care, state-sponsored abortions, state-sponsored gender confirmation surgery, windmills, and fracking bans. But none of that really mattered in local elections, first because there was no point of differentiation and second because city politics re-volve around neighborhood arguments that have little to do with the fed-eral government. San Francisco's solution to its political mass sameness was to create two hyper-local factions that warred over hyper-local issues. They were called the moderates and the progressives. The mods and the progs.

The progressive label began as a means of saying "more liberal than the city's already liberal establishment," and the local progressive faction came to prominence after the 2000 elections. San Francisco had just switched to district elections from citywide elections, allowing a group of far-left neighborhood activists who could never win citywide races to secure seats on the Board of Supervisors. Victorious but unsure how to transition from insurgency to leadership, the progressive-controlled board spent the next few years producing only-in-San Francisco legislation (like a bill to ban Happy Meal sales) and only-in-San Francisco characters (like supervisor Chris Daly, who tried to prevent the Blue Angels from flying over the city and once vowed to begin every board meeting with word "fuck") that overshadowed a more tangible set of accomplishments (like establishing inclusionary zoning rules that require developers to build subsidized housing in market rate developments, rules that were considered radical at the time but were now widely accepted).

The progressive faction had trouble holding power because they were made up of an odd mix of unions, neighborhood groups, and city-funded nonprofits that were united less by a belief of where to go and more by their shared hatred of developers and business interests. Pre-dictably, they were swept from office during the Great Recession as unemployment increased and voters turned to politicians who talked about creating jobs. But by 2015 they were surging back to relevance over the city's growing disgust with rising rents, private buses, multiply-ing Ubers, and the politics of Scott Wiener, lover of buildings and hater of process.

The problem, at least when it came to housing, was that it was hard to say exactly what the mod/prog labels actually meant—essentially all

San Francisco politicians would be considered progressive on the national stage—and what sort of constituencies and power structures they stood for. It was roughly fair to say that local progressives tended to favor more government control, but that control was broad enough to put millionaire white preservationists in the same category as Latino tenants' rights advocates. It was also roughly fair to say that local moderates tended to be more favorable to developers, but only if the definition of "favorable" was broad enough to include for-profit developers who engaged in outright cronyism and nonprofits who wanted to make it easier to build subsidized housing in rich neighborhoods.

Wiener disavowed the faction labels and rejected the idea that he was any kind of moderate. Only in San Francisco would a gay man who opposed the death penalty and marched in the local BDSM festival in leather straps have to argue he was truly of the left. Wiener's counter, which became a stock speech in rooms of voters, was that the label had no real meaning and that it was San Francisco's idiosyncratic definition of "progressive"—where rich homeowners who fought for the sanctity of single-family zoning somehow got to be in alignment with poor renters fighting gentrification—that was off. And for the most part he lived up to his professed independence. In 2011, he was the San Francisco Chamber of Commerce's most ideologically aligned supervisor. That is, a classic moderate. Two years later he was middle of the pack. Wiener once simultaneously pissed off both the San Francisco Tenants Union and one of the city's most notorious evictors.

His real game was volume—he wrote a lot of bills and passed a lot of bills—and he played it by chipping away at his issues and pushing things through by isolating the opposition and establishing an angle to adult-in-the-room status. Case in point was a 2015 bill to eliminate the need for a conditional use permit on apartment buildings where 100 percent of the units were subsidized. A conditional use permit is a permit that a developer needs to get when he wants to build something that isn't automatically allowed on a particular parcel, which in essence makes it a permit that requires certain kinds of developments (like chain stores) to beg. Wiener's bill amounted to a statement that affordable housing projects shouldn't ever have to beg.

It was also NIMBY bait. A proposal to eliminate a permit that provided one of the best chances a neighborhood had to kill a new project: How could a preservationist resist going down to city hall to protest its passage? In the case of market-rate housing, a proposal to eliminate a permit hurdle would have an obvious route of attack—"giveaway to developers." Now that attack had been neutralized. In San Francisco, where affordable housing projects were almost universally built by nonprofit developers with union labor and help from the city, Wiener's proposal to eliminate the need for affordable housing projects to seek a conditional use permit amounted to a giveaway to labor-friendly organizations that built homes for people like teachers, social workers, and seniors on fixed incomes.

During one of the bill's early hearings, homeowners showed up to give defensive speeches about how they didn't like the idea but also weren't NIMBYs and had no problem with affordable housing so long as it was built "in the right place." The weird part was that they were joined by The Council of Community Housing Organizations, a politically influential group that was known locally as "Choo Choo" and had branded itself as "the voice of San Francisco's affordable housing movement."

Choo Choo's founder, Calvin Welch, was a gray-ponytail-wearing don of the city nonprofit world and a descendant of the freeway revolts. According to local legend, he'd begun his escalation from Haight-Ashbury commune member to feared political power broker after agreeing, over a joint, to support future Mayor George Moscone during the 1975 election. Since then Welch had become an architect of the local progressive faction and had his fingerprints on virtually every important development battle since the 1980s. This had given him the admirable reputation of being responsible for much of the city's new affordable housing stock, as well as the not-so-admirable reputation of being someone who specialized in extracting money and influence from the mounds of bu-reaucracy known as "community input."

Choo Choo was a powerful coalition that, like the progressive faction generally, was fraught with internal conflict and contradictory goals. Its members included affordable housing developers and tenant organizers who were in theory on the side of making it easier to build affordable housing, but also included a bunch of no-growth neighborhood groups, who very often were not. In practice, the alliance operated on an implicit exchange in which eastside activists got city money to build subsidized housing and nonprofits that espoused *San Francisco values*, while west-side homeowners got their neighborhoods sealed off from new develop-ment, including affordable housing. This was the central hypocrisy of San Francisco politics, and the trade-off of building a coalition of home-owners and tenants' groups.

When it came time for a hearing to discuss Scott Wiener's proposal to make it easier to build subsidized buildings, Calvin Welch was there in attendance and during public comment said he was opposed to the bill and that it threatened to drive apart groups that should be sticking to-gether. What he meant was that Wiener's legislation was so favorable to affordable housing developers that they would be insane not to break ranks with neighborhood groups and support it. This was 1) absolutely true and 2) not remotely lost on Scott Wiener.

Also present at the meeting were a bunch of nonprofit builders, who testified in favor, as well as Pat Scott, executive director of the Booker T. Washington Community Service Center, who urged the bill's passage by describing a hellscape of lawsuits that had added millions of dollars and five years of process to an affordable apartment development her organi-zation was building for kids transitioning out of the foster system (a no-torious pipeline to homelessness). When Welch argued that the Booker T. story was misleading, suddenly you had a situation where it appeared as if the city's left flank was fighting a home for foster kids, while Scott Wiener, the supposed moderate, was trying to help them. This was what it meant to split the opposition, and sure enough the bill got through.

San Francisco politics are an up-or-out affair. Despite having a world-famous name and lots of money and ambitious people, the city has a population of just 880,000, a little bigger than Columbus, Ohio. There are eleven seats on the San Francisco Board of Supervisors, along with one mayor, one and a half* congresspersons, and three seats in the state legislature. With the exception of the main congressional seat, occupied by Nancy Pelosi since 1987, all of the other offices are subject to term limits, so it really is up or out. That means anyone who wants to go somewhere is eventually going to face off against a political ally or old friend. Scott Wiener was an ambitious and well-educated politician who believed he was going somewhere, but for most of his time on the board of supervisors he was serving with David Campos, David Chiu, and Jane Kim, three equally ambitious and educated politicians who were determined to be on the up side of up or out too.

In addition to being up or out, San Francisco politics can also be quite incestuous. Campos, Chiu, and Wiener all went to Harvard Law together, while Kim, who went to the UC Berkeley School of Law, used to be roommates with Chiu. Campos and Wiener had been close friends at Harvard (Campos was also gay, and Wiener was one of the first people he came out to) and once ran a dual campaign for seats on the board of the local Democratic Party. After they both won and Wiener ascended to chair of the party, Campos and Chiu helped vote their old friend out of his seat. Wiener apparently got over that, because he endorsed Chiu when Chiu ran against Campos in the 2014 state assembly race. And Chiu apparently got over his old roommate, because shortly after winning his election, he endorsed Wiener over Kim, when the two of them faced off in the 2016 state senate race.

If Scott Wiener could get himself elected to the California State Senate, that would be a big deal. This was not some rinky-dink local office. California has forty million people and the fifth-largest economy in the world, yet a comparatively small legislature. The state senate has forty

---

* The Fourteenth Congressional District contains a tiny sliver of the city.

seats, so each senator represents about a million people, more than members of the U.S. House of Representatives. It was a potentially powerful position for a politician who was expert at ramming through new laws, and during the early campaign Wiener was already talking about a plan to introduce statewide housing legislation that would go way beyond the little permitting laws he was pushing at the board. But first he had to win.

AROUND THE COUNTRY, in the Bay Area and everywhere else, whenever some cross-political task force of planners and developers and tenant advocates was convened to produce a road map for solving their local housing affordability problem, the same basic plan emerged. First, cities didn't have enough housing in their most popular and transit-rich neighborhoods, so they needed to build more and taller in those places. Second, America didn't have enough affordable housing anywhere, so it needed more subsidies for people who couldn't afford what the private market was building. More housing generally, more subsidies for those who needed them: that two-sided equation constituted the median view of good housing policy. Housing *politics* were another matter. Housing *politics* came down to which side of the subsidies-versus-supply equation a person appeared to represent. According to housing politics, people who spent most of their time talking about subsidies and rent control were affordable housing advocates. People who talked about making it easier to let the private market build housing were developer shills.

Come campaign time, Scott Wiener was either San Francisco's most outspoken proponent of more housing or the city's biggest developer shill, depending on who was talking. He'd earned the reputation through all those years of permit streamlining and a perceived coziness with developers. He was also the rare San Francisco supervisor to push for a big project in his own district. Wiener frequently tried to remind people that even though he was in favor of making it easier to build market-rate housing, he also supported rent control, had done more than most to make it easier to build subsidized housing, and voted yes on pretty much every affordable housing tax. But balance wasn't a trait San Francisco had much use for, so to a good amount of the city he would always be the developer shill.

In 2015, when Wiener started running for the senate, San Francisco politics started escalating into total war. The November ballot had been a de facto referendum on the tech industry, with measures to raise money for affordable housing and to regulate Airbnb rentals. The most contentious idea was called Proposition I, which was being pushed by Wiener's old friend David Campos. That was an initiative to impose an eighteen-month moratorium on all new market-rate housing in the Mission District, which would have shut down essentially all new development in one of the city's most popular and transit-rich neighborhoods. Wiener was against it on the logic that it would only make the supply problem worse and that a moratorium in one neighborhood would be a gateway drug to moratoriums in every other neighborhood. But the measure was popular with renters, who saw it as fortification against tech and a middle finger aimed at gentrification. Wiener spent a good amount of the year getting yelled at and even had a march of protesters congregate outside his condo holding signs that read "Support the Mission Moratorium."

Proposition I ended up failing, but it became a case study in how development politics were just as difficult in cities full of renters—two-thirds of San Franciscans were tenants—as they were in surrounding suburbs. That year on Election Day, while Wiener was out campaigning, a political scientist named Michael Hankinson and a team of forty people were distributing surveys at San Francisco polling places. Hankinson's surveys showed that even though renters agreed that San Francisco had a dire housing shortage, a majority still opposed new development in their neighborhood for fear it would accelerate gentrification. That is, in terms of how they voted, there was little difference between homeowners in Lafayette, who worried nearby development would cause their property values to fall, and renters in the Mission, who worried nearby development would cause their rents to increase. "In short, the long-run benefit of more supply is eclipsed by the immediate, short-run threat of displacement," Hankinson wrote in his paper, which was called "When Do Renters Behave Like Homeowners? High Rent, Price Anxiety, and NIMBYism."

Scott Wiener was all too aware of this attitude, and it wasn't hard for him to see why. All he had to do was look out from his seat in the board of supervisors' chambers to the rows of people who showed up to comment on new housing proposals. Those against would be nice little old ladies and embattled tenants and the usual collection of house owners worried about neighborhood character. Those in favor would be developers. You almost never saw a regular person say the city needed more housing because there simply wasn't enough of it, at least until Sonja showed up, so of course he started encouraging her.

Five weeks after the moratorium vote, on a drizzly Sunday morning in December, Wiener, relieved of his weekday suit and now wearing jeans and Adidas, walked into a Market Street co-working space to speak at a meeting of pro-housing neighborhood groups that Sonja had billed as the first-ever "YIMBY Congress." When Wiener arrived, a bit after 10:00, Sonja was standing by a whiteboard delivering a welcome address to the three dozen people sprawled across mismatched furniture and a carpeted floor. It was a typical YIMBY event, millennial and professional, only a handful of whom had ever been involved in politics beyond voting. "For the first few years I was on the board of supervisors, it was a really lonely place because you had all these self-appointed housing advocates who are really opposed to housing," Wiener told the group. "And now to have a lot of young people engaging in the process. And not because you are wedded to any one politician or any one group, but you are there and talking in an authentic way about 'What is my future in this city? Where am I going to live? Where am I going to be able to raise a family?'"

This was right about the time Sonja started establishing herself as a fixture in local media, and the room's posture was in line with her insurgent and combative tone. CaRLA was just about to file the Lafayette lawsuit, and there had recently been a small news cycle around an attempt by Sonja and others to flood the local Sierra Club with new members so they could elect density advocates to the group's board (the San Francisco chapter of the Sierra Club once fought a sixty-six-unit apartment building with nine affordable units on the grounds that it would destroy a historic radiator shop). "There is a strain of self-described progressive politics in San Francisco that says: 'Lock down the city,'" Wiener told the room. "Just lock down the city, don't build new public transportation, don't make it easier for people to commute in and out of the city. Don't put new transit in because you're going to gentrify neighborhoods, don't build more housing—just lock it down, and maybe if we dig a moat around the city and put crocodiles in it we can just stop people from coming."

The following year, the commotion SF BARF had brought to public meetings started to congeal into something like a YIMBY party. New chapters were spreading down into Southern California and further around the country, while back in the ground zero market of San Francisco, the organizing Sonja had begun with the YIMBY Congress was becoming more deliberately political. This was the work of a woman named Laura Foote Clark, who was originally from Washington, DC, and had come to San Francisco with her Facebook-employed husband. Laura began her time in the Bay Area working sales jobs at tech companies while seeking an angle into local politics. This led her to volunteer for David Chiu's assembly campaign and start working with a crop of young would-be candidates from the next generation. Realizing that housing was a potent and winning issue, Laura started a group called Grow SF and joined Sonja in indignant public comment.

Laura was confident and argumentative like Sonja, but this was not to say they were exactly alike. Sonja's roughness bordered on performance art and she described SF BARF as a "do-ocracy" where anyone could work on anything they wanted, so long as they actually did it. This wasn't just a motivator. It was a means of self-protection that prevented

Sonja from having to endure the emotional labor of organization building by discouraging anyone who wasn't self-motivated from sticking around. Nothing annoyed Sonja more than people who showed up to meetings expecting to be praised for their ideas. She once said she didn't understand why women complained about "mansplaining," not because mansplaining didn't annoy her, but because she would conversationally decapitate anyone who even started down that path so she never experienced it for long and therefore didn't dwell on it. Such was the mind-set she'd designed her club with: On the many occasions that someone told her how to run SF BARF or suggested she change the name, Sonja's response wasn't to argue but to enthusiastically tell the person that if his ideas so excited him, he should feel empowered to leave and do his own thing. Sonja kept things small because she couldn't handle the compromises of being big.

Laura wanted big, or bigger, a proper political club that could be to local housing issues what the Sierra Club was to environmentalism. So while Sonja established herself as the archetypal founder with all the attendant quirks and big ideas, Laura slipped into the role of an operations-minded builder who accepted daily realities like the need to engage in hand-holding and the fact that most people join a club expecting to be told what to do. This was not without its edge. Laura had a person-with-a-clipboard kind of militancy and a rough-bordering-on-abusive vocabulary that was heavy on words like "idiot" and "inept." She also had a tendency to dismiss well-meaning but politically inviable ideas with phrases like "this is nothing but useless virtue signaling."

Laura never appeared happier than when she was clapping a room to attention or commanding someone to stack chairs, and while nobody outright declared this, her organizational drive spelled the end of the name SF BARF. It was one thing to have a politician like Scott Wiener indulge your "Congress" on a rainy Sunday, and another to be regarded as real players and a club whose endorsement got emblazoned on campaign paraphernalia (which, even in San Francisco, wasn't going to happen with "BARF"). Not that a loud tone wasn't useful. Before she met

Sonja, Laura had tried to make Grow SF a mature and restrained pro-housing group, only to see it be completely overshadowed. The lesson Laura took was that whatever club came after it should be a merger between the attitude of SF BARF and the ambition of Grow SF, so that somewhere on the other side was a Goldilocks organization that could be rude enough to keep getting attention but not so rude as to be politically untouchable.

At her core, Laura understood something Sonja was reluctant to acknowledge, which was that it was all fine and good to say you wanted to make it easier to build housing and talk about the importance of supply economics, but in the real world, the political world, you couldn't just clear a hill of enemies and hope for better policy to come from the vacuum. You had to build an army of your own to hold it. Laura made zero attempt to hide her desire to become a power broker in her own right, telling people she wanted to be "the next Rose Pak" (Pak was a feared activist from Chinatown who once posed for a photo in *San Francisco Magazine* holding a bat). And since there was no better way to elevate an upstart organization than to acquire a friend in higher office, that summer Laura directed the group's energy toward the cause of electing Senator Scott Wiener.

This would not be easy. Jane Kim was a member of the local progressive faction who was in favor of the moratorium as well as cooler than Scott Wiener. She did Tae Kwon Do in her campaign commercials, used to play bass in an indie band called Strangely, and was a former community organizer who'd earned a reputation for extracting affordable housing from for-profit developers. The Kim campaign even got Bernie Sanders, whose national reputation had just begun surging, to fly to California and campaign for her. Wiener had more money and better local endorsements, but the Bernie surge was real, and his multipoint lead shriveled, allowing Kim to eke out a win in the summer primary. That would have been it for Scott Wiener in a lot of states, but California has an open primary system in which all voters, not just Democrats and Republicans, vote in the election's first round. The top two vote getters face off in the general election, even if they're in the same party, so all the primary had established was that the general election would be a rematch and that the rematch would be close.

In the final months of the election, Laura and Sonja started an independent expenditure committee called YIMBY PAC that raised about $100,000 to advertise in favor of Scott Wiener and other candidates. This became something of an organizational boot camp where they learned all the boring but necessary stuff it would take to build the pro-housing political operation that would continue after the election and be called YIMBY Action. They had to learn how to raise money online and properly report the donations. To find a printer to produce the glossy palm cards that volunteers handed out to voters. To learn what disclaimers had to be where and in what font size. To find voter rolls and software to decide who was mostly likely to be receptive to the YIMBY message. Laura also started a semiweekly newsletter and started hosting boozy happy hours that acted to turn local housing politics into something that young professionals of the sort who normally avoided city hall and couldn't name their representatives wanted to be a part of.

They had eighty volunteers in the streets on Election Day, all the women leaders and their "hoodie caucus" of young guys, many of them software engineers, who took the day off work to knock doors, flyer handles, and wave signs at Muni stops until the polls closed at 8:00. Later at Scott Wiener's party, which was at a bar called Beaux, people watched the national returns on TV and received yelled-out local updates from campaign staffers. Wiener's results were promising and YIMBY world appeared to be on the cusp of having a considerably more powerful friend. But that was suddenly hard to focus on. That's because according to the overhead screens, Donald J. Trump was poised to be elected president of the United States of America. People started talking about a hypothetical Sophie's choice in which they could sacrifice a Scott Wiener loss for a Hillary Clinton win. By midnight the bar was quiet as hundreds of bewildered people stared into their phones trying to process what it meant that Donald Trump would, like, actually for real be the president. One of Scott Wiener's friends said that winning his senate race that night would be like having your birthday on 9/11.

Eight days after the election, when San Francisco was still in a kind of post-electoral grieving, Sonja and several other YIMBYs arrived at a board of supervisors meeting to urge the city to approve a 157-unit project in the heavily Latino Mission District instead of voting for an appeal. Neighborhood groups had argued the impact on gentrification had to be studied before it was approved. That was an argument San Francisco neighborhood groups had made and lost several times before, and in the previous months a strong majority of the board of supervisors, including several from the progressive faction, had voted against similar appeals. Even David Campos, who represented the Mission and had been the public face of the moratorium campaign, was widely expected to vote for the project.

It was with this likely approval in hand that a software engineer named Vincent Woo, an enthusiastic YIMBY member, walked up to the microphone during public comment. "The only thing we can do to stem the actual tide of gentrification is to build places for rich people to live, because otherwise they're going to do what I did—I muscled out some guys for a basement unit in the Mission," he said. "If we don't build units for people with money to go into, we all know what's going to happen. They're going to compete with the existing stock for middle income housing residents, and we know who's going to win, the people with more money." Woo's comments went down in semi-infamy among anti-gentrification groups but were immediately overshadowed by Sonja, who walked to the microphone four seconds after he left it.

Sonja began her own short speech by noting that earlier in the meeting someone had objected to the project on the grounds that it would bring "strangers" into the neighborhood. "In Trump's America we're already disturbed by nativism everywhere," Sonja said. "And when you come here to the Board of Supervisors and say that you don't want new, different people in your neighborhood, you're exactly the same as Americans all over the country who don't want immigrants. It is the same attitude. It is *exactly* the same attitude"—audible gasps in the crowd, cries of "come on"—"so basically you can be the kind of person that's ready to have new people come into your neighborhood or you can be the kind of person who wants to keep people different from you out of your neighborhood."

David Campos was born in Puerto Barrios, Guatemala, in 1970. When he was eleven years old, with the economy in tatters, his family made their first attempt to cross into America. They burrowed under a fence at Mexicali and later that evening hid in a cemetery while a helicopter flooded the ground around them with light. They found the coyote shortly after and were on their way to life in America when Immigration and Naturalization Service agents pulled them over on the suspicion, correct, that the low-riding car was packed with illegal immigrants. Campos and his family were detained in a cell and later sent back, but they tried again four years later, crossing successfully at Tijuana. They settled in South Los Angeles, where Campos's father, who was a meteorologist in Guatemala, started a new career as a carpenter. David Campos graduated at the top of Jefferson High School, then went to Stanford and Harvard Law, where he became friends with Scott Wiener.

So there Campos sat, one week after Donald Trump's election, the elected representative of San Francisco's Latino Cultural District, listening to Sonja compare a woman who was complaining about incoming techies to a president-elect who had campaigned on building a wall to keep out Mexican "rapists." Campos had gone into the hearing intending to vote against the building's appeal, just as he had voted against various other, similar appeals. Then it came time to vote. "For those of you who always wondered 'Does public comment make a difference? Does public comment change minds?' I think this hearing is a perfect illustration that it does," he said. "And I specifically want to thank the representative from BARF for helping to change my mind today." Campos continued to say that he didn't even think the appeal was very good and found the legal logic suspect, but now, purely because of Sonja's comments, he was going to go ahead and vote for the appeal.

Lost in all the talk about the housing shortage and supply and demand was a concept called power. When Sonja sued Lafayette or YIMBYs showed up screaming at public microphones in Silicon Valley, it fit the comfortable narrative of a fight against the powerful. In gentrifying areas, however, they represented the very sources of power that neighborhood groups were fighting against. YIMBY members had good-paying jobs at tech companies and were highly organized and well educated. They got funding from millionaires and billionaires, and all they'd had to do was show up at a few meetings and in the space of a few months they'd amassed more media and political attention than decades-old housing groups had gotten in their entire life spans. Encoded in that ascent was an age-old American message, which is that problems are only problems when they affect white people.

That didn't make the supply argument wrong. The Bay Area had continued to create far more jobs than housing, so the shortage was only getting worse. David Campos would later say he regretted being behind the Mission moratorium and that he agreed, in principle, with much of what YIMBYs said about the city needing vastly more housing (unbeknownst to a good amount of the gasping crowd, Campos had a cordial relationship with Sonja in the marble hallways outside the public hearing brawl). But the exchange was a neon example of why development politics were so contentious, and why housing could never really be as simple as a two-sided equation with some subsidies on one side and some development on the other.

Sonja and David Campos had something of a makeup session a few months later. One night Sonja and Laura were sitting on Sonja's couch looking at their phones when they came across an article about how Palantir Technologies, a big data firm backed by Peter Thiel, the billionaire tech investor and libertarian Trump supporter, was building surveillance software that tracked phone logs and criminal records to help ICE find and deport people. As it happened, Sonja knew where Thiel lived. A few months earlier, when the idea of Donald Trump being president still seemed preposterous, she'd gone there to have breakfast and talk about a donation (Thiel agreed to give her some money, then recanted). After reading the article, Sonja and Laura decided they'd rustle the growing list of contacts they'd amassed during the election and organize a group protest on Peter Thiel's doorstep, and invite Campos to come along.

And so it was that on a bright Saturday afternoon, Sonja, Laura, David Campos, and fifty other people gathered in front of Thiel's nine-bedroom, $25 million house. "The reason we're here is to call upon the people who are complicit in what Trump is trying to do," Campos said, through a megaphone. "If your company is complicit, it is time to fight that," Laura said later. "What happened to being a libertarian?" Sonja yelled toward one of Thiel's windows. "What happened to freedom of movement for labor?" Later, after the group chanted, "I am human, I am not data," Sonja, Laura, Campos, and the dozens of other people they'd gotten to join them, posed for a photo on Thiel's stoop.

THE YEAR BEFORE Scott Wiener arrived in Sacramento, Governor Jerry Brown, who in terms of housing was right back where he was in the '70s, proposed a failed piece of legislation that left a blueprint of what he wanted from the legislature on housing. What Brown proposed was that he would sign a budget that replenished some of the affordable housing money he had cut in the lean years after the Great Recession, but only if the legislature approved a streamlining measure that would allow projects that conformed to local zoning codes and had 10 to 20 percent of their units reserved for people making below the median income to sidestep city councils and planning commissions. Such projects would also be immunized from environmental lawsuits. (This was the idea Steve Falk wrote a memo in favor of, leading neighbors to call for his ouster.)

As the proposal made its way through the capitol, cities, environmental groups, and construction unions all rose up against it. Each of these groups wanted different things—cities wanted more say over what could be built where, environmentalists wanted more environmental reviews, and unions wanted a prevailing wage guarantee that favored their workers—but what united them was a fear that if building was easier, they would lose their leverage over projects. That was why housing law was so hard to streamline: A complicated process was full of political profit. Negotiations broke down, and the governor's proposal died. Nevertheless, Brown had established the framework of a potential housing deal: legislative Democrats could get back some of the affordable housing money he had cut if they delivered him some kind of streamlining bill.

The next year California legislators introduced something like 130 housing bills. Disasters always created bills. There were water bills during droughts and fire bills after fires and earthquake bills after earthquakes. Now housing costs were a state disaster. Given how many housing bills the legislature had introduced, it was all but guaranteed that by the end of the session it would end up passing something having something to do with housing. The question was which bill or bills would be signed. Democrats were already writing various affordable housing funding bills, which legislators like David Chiu had been pushing for years. But Jerry Brown had made it clear that he wasn't giving out money until someone gave him a streamlining bill, otherwise the state would just be throwing new taxes at a broken and expensive process.

Scott Wiener introduced just such a bill on the day he was sworn into office, and in doing so had put himself in the enviable position of having written a piece of legislation that his colleagues would have to pass to get the money they wanted. Wiener's first draft of the bill was just a couple sentences of streamlining language combined with some stipulations that would guarantee higher wages for the unions who had killed Brown's attempt from a year earlier. He still had to write an actual real-live bill that could end up on the governor's desk, and he had to write it in such a way as to anticipate the various special interest kill orders that would inevitably emerge during the session.

This was the first job assigned to a legislative aide named Annie

Fryman when she arrived in Sacramento. Annie was a YIMBY. She'd grown up in Kentucky and had a tobacco-farming father, then moved west to go to Stanford and after graduation found herself living in San Francisco and trying to be an architect and to afford rent. She'd helped Laura start Grow SF almost solely as a means of pushing through a duplex she'd designed and was trying to get approved, then got so involved with politics and so enraged with the amount of process it took to get something built that she left architecture to take a job in Scott Wiener's Board of Supervisors' office. She'd never worked in government or even really had a desire to do so, and now, at twenty-four years old, she was helping to write a big new piece of housing legislation for the nation's largest state (and trying to find a new apartment).

Annie started by making a spreadsheet of every group that had opposed Jerry Brown's year-earlier streamlining proposal next to a list of the reasons why: mayors (local control), Greens (environmental review), affordable housing advocates (zoning review), unions (wages). Her job was to make each group happy enough to support Wiener's bill or at least not try to kill it, yet to not make them so happy that whatever streamlining got passed turned out to be useless.

Normally this process would begin with a legislative aide calling the various right people to try to persuade them to give support, but because she was new to the capitol and politics, Annie had to make a first round of calls to figure out who the right people actually were. The next months were meetings with labor unions, affordable housing groups and the governor's housing office, and lots of calls to cities. She got coffees with aides and legislators and had rectangular walking meetings at Capitol Park. When the bill was drafted and needed some tweaks, Annie made a second round of "technical assistance" calls to YIMBY-friendly attorneys and cities' planning staff. "Technical assistance" was a euphemism for getting bureaucrats to help you seal up potential loopholes. Around the state, city planners, the sorts of people who worked for Steve Falk, had become so frustrated with the degree to which NIMBYism determined how they did their jobs that they were now all too happy to stealth advise

Wiener's office on how to write its bill in such a way that mayors and city councils couldn't ignore it.

Wiener's approach to legislative warfare was to telegraph the message that he could outwork anyone who didn't go along with him. He met with opponents regularly and would try to wear them out by keeping spreadsheets of their concerns and plugging little holes, then asking big questions, reframing the argument, plugging more little holes, asking more questions, reframing some more, forcing them to listen to his droll voice, quickly answering their emails after their meetings, sending back long and technical counterproposals, until finally the opponent and their staff were too exhausted to keep protesting.

This was how Wiener got what he wanted while also maintaining a reputation as a nice guy who didn't get into gutter politics. He never got nasty. He wasn't big on threats. He overwhelmed people with attention and made it clear that anytime you said no to him, he'd try so hard to make you say yes that the very act of denying him was tantamount to asking for your office to be buried in work. Wiener had no obvious personal life, and his staff was mostly single with no children. His long hours and seven-day workweek almost seemed to tell the capitol, I dare you to drive your staff as hard as I do. I dare you to ignore your kids. I will. I don't have kids.

Wiener's strategy of using work as a cudgel was never more evident than when someone tried to attack. When Choo Choo came out against his streamlining bill and wrote a letter to the senate that Wiener felt was dishonest, he had Annie draft an eight-page response. The letter's tone was don't mess with me, but the letter's message was, I dare you to sit down and write me something longer. When the League of California Cities said SB 35 would exempt wealthy coastal communities, Wiener had Annie spend two days drafting a ten-page response, then get it printed on sturdy color paper and bound like a star student's book report. The next Friday afternoon she spent the day walking to 119 assembly and senate offices to drop off each packet in person.

Over the course of that summer, the state capitol became a sort of YIMBY graduation ceremony. While Annie Fryman was running around building support for Wiener's streamlining bill, Brian Hanlon was trying to push a different kind of housing bill through a Berkeley senator named Nancy Skinner. That bill was called SB 167, and it was a law that would update the Housing Accountability Act in such a way as to make it easier for Sonja and him to sue cities. By now, Sonja was well on her way to losing the case against Lafayette, and Brian, newly emancipated from his job at the Forest Service after being hired as CaRLA's second full-time employee, was spending a goodly amount of his time riding the train from Oakland to Sacramento with a Japanese fixed gear that he called Sparkle Pony. In terms of the actual text, 167 didn't change the Housing Accountability Act all that much, but by changing words like "substantial" to "preponderance," it would make it far harder for cities to beat CaRLA in the future. It also imposed harsh fines on cities and forced them to pay the other side's lawyers' fees if they got sued for downzoning a project and lost, which was intended to cow cities into not putting up a fight.

Senate leaders wanted Wiener's bill, so SB 35 flew through its first committee hearing. No drama there, although a contingent of San Franciscans drove up to provide entertainment value. Laura Foote Clark, the newly professional face of the newly professional YIMBY Action, got her own graduation moment when she was invited to testify before the meeting as a "renters advocate" and got to sit at a special table at the front instead of having to join the public comment cattle call as she did in San Francisco. Not that the cattle car wasn't there. The chamber behind Laura's front table seat was packed with bearded members of the hoodie caucus and a man wearing a dress and Easter bonnet. The scene caused Scott Wiener's fellow senators to start sending texts that asked him why he had teleported San Francisco into Sacramento. Wiener texted back that they should feel lucky because in San Francisco each public comment lasted two minutes. In Sacramento the crowd only got a few seconds each. When the first YIMBY stepped to the microphone and began a circular anecdote in which he compared the statement "I'm not racist, but . . ." to the statement "I know we need more housing, but . . . ," the committee's impatient chairman cut the guy off and told the crowd that he wanted the speakers to limit themselves to saying who they were and what their position was, thank you.

The chairman of the second committee was from the notoriously NIMBY Marin County and therefore was never going to vote for it. That was okay. He was just one vote. But there is a protocol among senators that they try to be polite to each other by deferring to the chair's vote instead of having the other members gang up to vote against him—this was called rolling—so before the hearing Wiener had to go through the gentle business of telling the chairman he was going to be rolled and persuading him to be okay with that. This was a case of picking battles within battles. Just as junior senators like Scott Wiener had to be careful when and when not to roll chairmen, chairmen had to be careful about when to not deliver senate leaders something they wanted.

But then along came the union bosses, the same people who had killed the streamlining bill the year before, threatening to get their people to kill this next bill unless they got some training funds in addition to the prevailing wage stipulation Scott Wiener had already shaken hands on. Unions from around the state subsequently sent Wiener's office a bunch of multipage letters that said his proposal to build housing at a slightly faster pace in California's major cities could lead to mass extinction. Unions were close to all-powerful in Sacramento, and the bill seemed to be headed for an early death late into the evening the night before the final senate committee vote. Then, around 11:00 p.m., an angel in Jerry Brown's office came down to tell the union bosses to chill out, at which point they decided that the housing their members would get paid to build wouldn't lead to mass extinction after all, and the bill made it out of committee.

Once it was clear that a bunch of bills were going forward and legislators would have to compromise and swap votes so that the affordable housing money could be replenished and Jerry Brown could have his streamlining, other senators and assembly members started slipping their own bills into the mix. The once-straightforward combination of money and regulatory pruning grew into layers of funding and loan programs and tax credits until finally there were fifteen bills that Sacramento called the housing package. That kind of girth made final passage something of a self-fulfilling prophecy by giving a dozen or so legislators something to claim and making them all want to root for each other and go home to an "I'm solving the housing crisis" speech. The large number of bills also meant that opponents got distracted trying to figure out which bills they wanted to fight. Fifteen housing bills was a lot of paper to argue against, and as Annie Fryman well knew, it took the better part of a day to drop by each of the offices in the capitol.

The housing package passed on the last day of the session. It wasn't easy. David Chiu had to hold a climate bill hostage to get Assembly Democrats' assurance that the housing bills would be passed. Over in the senate, a number of actually moderate Democrats were reluctant to vote for the increased taxes that would create a new funding source for affordable housing. Arms were twisted, sweeteners were added, and all fifteen bills were sent to Jerry Brown for a signature. That night Laura sent YIMBY Action members a congratulatory email full of superlatives and exclamation points and invited them to celebrate in the back room of a loud Caribbean restaurant in the Mission. Scott Wiener and David Chiu agreed to come and bask in their applause.

They arrived late, as politicians do, but it was just as well because that gave the crowd lots of time to rev up on sangria and chicken wings. Laura excitedly relayed text updates on Scott and David's ride to the bar. *Coming soon. Almost here. About to pull up.* When finally the announcement came that the YIMBY heroes were outside, the crowd rushed to the back room's entrance and watched Scott Wiener's six-foot-seven head bob above the bar crowd as he and Chiu glad-handed their way toward the "yeahs" and "woos" in the back room. Once inside, they stood halfway up a staircase to address the mass of drunk YIMBYs.

"Are you feeling good tonight?" Chiu asked the room.

Chiu was infamous for a hype-man routine that was heavy on questions like, "Are there any *X* in the house?"

"All over the state there have been folks who have said you know we need more housing but not in my backyard—fuck that," Chiu said. "What do we say?"

"Fuck that!" the crowd yelled back.

"Fuck that," Chiu agreed.

Scott Wiener rarely cursed in public. A year earlier when he visited the YIMBY Congress, his most unguarded expression of outrage was the abbreviation "BS." That night he began his victory speech with the now well-worn anecdote about how years earlier when he was on the board of supervisors, the only people who came to advocate for new housing were the developers. And now look where they were. They'd started a real movement. The speech seemed to be heading down the road of yet another one of Wiener's nice-uncle pep talks full of pragmatic guidance and warm encouragement and far too many "uhs." Then something changed. Maybe it was the excitement of victory or the heat of the room or the sangria, but as the speech neared its conclusion, Wiener raised his voice and started to compete with the amped-up David Chiu by air punching the crowd with staccato promises that this was not over, that this was just the beginning. "We have momentum, we have the wind at our back, and we are going to go back over and over and over until people can actually afford *to fucking live here.*"

A month later, in September 2017, a crew of YIMBYs including Sonja and Brian and Laura got VIP invites to watch Jerry Brown sign all fifteen housing bills on the lawn of an affordable housing complex that looked out on the San Francisco Bay. They showed up in suits and dresses and before the event mingled among politicians and news cameras and expressionless bodyguards with little white wires in their ears. There was a stage and a lectern with the gubernatorial seal, and just off to the side sat the little wood desk that the governor's office carted around the state for ceremonial signings like this one. The downside of having so many housing bills became apparent after the event started and the moderator proceeded to invite *fourteen* people—senators and assembly people and union bosses and affordable housing advocates and the mayors of San Francisco, Oakland, and Los Angeles—to come up and fondle the microphone.

"Tents." "Encampments." "Displacement." "Supercommuters." "The California dream is in danger."

"Solutions." "Solving problems." "Action." "Stepped up." "Rolled up his sleeves." "Get this done." "Across the finish line." "Dedication and leadership." "Historic."

"Beginning." "First step." "We look forward to building on this momentum." "I've got some bills for you next year."

"Thank you." "Thank you." "Thank you."

"I want to thank." "I want to thank." "I want to thank."

"I hear we have one minute each, but if we cross Bakersfield this morning, we get two."

"Let's hear it for housing."

"How are we feeling today?"

"Do we have any housers in the house today?"

By the end of the ceremony, Laura was crying. Jerry Brown was not. Brown had been governor of California twice and had been through a housing affordability crisis twice. In the month after the housing bills were passed, newspapers were full of headlines like "Out with California's NIMBYs and in with the YIMBYs." However amazing that seemed to a thirty-year-old like Laura, Jerry Brown might have remembered signing a ten-bill housing package seven years before Laura was born. He might have thought that when Scott Wiener went onstage and declared it a new day for housing, it sounded a lot like the new day described in a 1980 *Los Angeles Times* op-ed that said Governor Brown's focus on affordable housing had sent a message to local governments that if they didn't take steps to build more housing, "the state of California will." After the fourteen previous speakers had burned their microphone minutes, when it was finally the governor's turn to speak, the fire of jubilation and self-congratulation that had been roaring all morning was doused with one of Jerry Brown's loopy and philosophical speeches.

"I can't add anything because it's all been said, but I just can't help but add this one note," Brown said. "We talk about digging a ditch. No, it's not a ditch. It's not a ditch. Look. All of these rules were passed by people like *you*. Let's face it. City and state people did all this good stuff. Energy efficiency, better insulation, more this and more that, you name it. It's all good. But, as I always say, too many goods create a bad. So now you're trying to clean up some of the bad, but it is a lot of good, too. So that's the paradox. We want to achieve safety and aesthetics and the right kind of neighborhoods, and all the rest of that stuff, and we get a lot of rules. So now we gotta figure out a way to streamline, and we're doing that in these bills. And we need to fund, because this capitalistic system. I mean, it is powerful. But it's so powerful you can't control it. And when people make a lot of money 'cause they have all these apps, they start spending it and bidding up the price of housing. And there we are. So, I know none of you want to cut the value of people's homes they struggled to buy. So we're not talking about lowering the prices, in one sense. Although we are. So there it is. Plenty of paradox, plenty of complexity."

There is a fine line between a movement that is gaining momentum and a movement that is smoking its own supply, and in the weeks after the housing package, the YIMBY world started veering into the latter. At the end of the year, Laura hosted a YIMBY Gala where several hundred well-dressed people gathered in a banquet hall to eat buffet food and drink too much while an awards ceremony that David Chiu ("Are there any YIMBYs in the house?") described as a kind housing Oscars played out on the stage. Some of the awards were serious, like "Best Housing Legislator," which went to Scott Wiener (of course). Others were less so, like "Worst Public Comment," which went to a woman who had shown up at a Berkeley planning meeting shaking a tiny zucchini as proof of the damage done by excessive shadowing. The zucchini lady wasn't there, so a man in a dinosaur mask accepted the award on her behalf.

CHAPTER 7

THE OLD WAYS

IT WAS A SURREAL THING to see in a housing crisis: dozens of rect-angular apartments scattered across a parking lot twenty-five miles northeast of San Francisco. They had windows and doors on the outside and kitchens and bathrooms inside. Ready-to-go shelter, but for now each unit was hoisted on stilts and wrapped in white plastic, sitting be-hind a chain-link fence. This was both an experiment and Rick Holli-day's latest housing project. The project was a 316-unit development that if all went well would be approved by the end of 2018 and soon after that would house low-income tenants and formerly homeless peo-ple in Oakland. The experiment sat a few hundred yards away in a warehouse where World War II workers used to build submarine peri-scopes. Now it was a house factory where buildings glided off an assem-bly line in pieces as if they were new Fords.

The scent of fresh-cut lumber touched every corner of the space. There was a staccato thud of nail guns and the stop-and-start screech of table saws. The concrete floor was covered with sawdust, spare nails, and 150 or so workers in hard hats who toiled on eleven-by-twelve-by-seventy-foot cuboids that slid around the room on gliders and pulleys, acquiring pipes and walls and fixtures until finally there was the outline of an apartment.

Rick was sixty-five now, officially a senior citizen and maker of the joke that he was the Forrest Gump of housing. He was in the back of his parents' station wagon during the great California migration. He was there in 1980 when Jerry Brown had a private breakfast with home builders to discuss what would become the first housing package. He cofounded one of the largest affordable housing organizations in the nation, helped start the live/work loft craze in San Francisco, and was the first developer to reinvest in West Oakland. Rick's story also included a massive heart attack that would have killed him if not for the stranger who called 911 after finding him sprawled on the ground next to a bicycle, and the crushing sudden loss of Don Terner, his teacher, mentor, friend, and business partner, who died in a 1996 plane crash with the U.S. commerce secretary, Ron Brown, during a trade mission to Croatia.

Lots of years and lots of twists, and yet so much of life's basics remained pretty much the same. Rick met his wife, Nancy, in high school and married her before he could drink, and they were still together and lived just a few miles from their childhood homes. He also still liked building things. And California was also still in a housing crisis. Protests against gentrification, demands for more housing, cries for expanded rent control, stories of the middle class fleeing to Texas, declarations that the state was over and unlivable: substitute angry millennials for angry boomers, and a shortage of city apartments for a shortage of suburban tract houses, and it was a mirror to his twenties. The really eerie thing was that Jerry Brown was even governor again.

For a while Rick entertained a vague plan of retiring to the mountains. Instead, he went on a late-career detour to start the house factory where he now spent most of his time. It was less a project than a gambit that revolved around a centuries-old question, which is whether it was possible to build most of a building indoors, and in doing so make construction radically faster and cheaper. Rick was an efficiency bug who had become a combination of alarmed and disgusted as a steady rise in building costs threatened to dig California even deeper into crisis. He told Nancy he couldn't bear to retire with the industry so fucked up.

Maybe that was true. He was also a lifelong wheeler-dealer and like every real estate developer was in possession of a terrifying optimism that he could dream things out of the ground and navigate every bank, permit, and protest that stood in the way of his mind's concept. That was the addiction he came into as a child building tree forts: the belief that he could will something to work out. Rick had spent his life applying that optimism to new buildings, and now he'd transferred it to an attack on rising construction costs. Win or lose, riches or bankruptcy, the building of a house factory would form the end of the movie and be his final project.

If you were to ask Rick to reduce his career to a single moment, one crucial inflection point from which all the other things followed, he would say he needed two. The first was the day he walked into Don Terner's Berkeley classroom as a graduate student in 1977. The second came a few years later, when an anonymous donor gave $600,000 to help solve the local housing problem, money that was ultimately used to create a nonprofit developer called BRIDGE Housing. The money got batted around by consultants for a few months before its overseers went looking for a person to run the organization that would be seeded by it. Rick, who was then running Eden Housing, decided that person should be him and applied for it.

Trouble was, Don Terner was finishing up his run as Jerry Brown's head of housing and community development and about to be out of a job, so he applied for it too. When Rick met with one of BRIDGE's board members to talk about the position, the board member told him there was no way some twenty-nine-year-old was getting the top job and anyway a more experienced housing expert named Don Terner was probably going to take it. Then he asked Rick if he knew Don. Rick said he knew Don well. And that's how Rick and his old professor became co-founders of BRIDGE.

One of Don Terner's last acts as Jerry Brown's housing chief was to produce a sixty-seven-page report called "101 Steps to Better Housing." Like so much about California housing in the 1980s, the document is full of "the more things change . . ." suggestions like building homes near jobs and transit and using the higher authority of state law to make it harder for localities to block new development. The report also spent an entire chapter dwelling on ways to reduce the cost of building and financing new homes, and those were the pages that formed BRIDGE's spiritual founding.

Rick and Don didn't want to emulate other housing nonprofits, which tended to be baby organizations that were inefficient and neighborhood focused. They wanted to create a large regional developer and took their inspiration from for-profit players like the Lincoln Property Company, the Dallas-based builder of walk-up garden apartment complexes that were predictable, comfortable, and cheap. BRIDGE's mantra was "quantity, quality, and affordability," and the founders lived it by employing the efficiencies of standardization and replicability to build subsidized apartments at market-rate scale.

They wielded the nonprofit halo the way a businessman wields financial power. BRIDGE's first project was a 166-unit development in Livermore in which 60 percent of the units were market rate and 40 percent were affordable. The way that worked was BRIDGE partnered with a for-profit developer, then used its do-gooder status to persuade the city to upzone a plot of land so that the money from the market-rate rental units would subsidize the lower rents in the affordable ones. California had a whole program for redeveloping underutilized school sites, and there again BRIDGE would pair up with for-profit developers, trading entrée to sites that nonprofits had first dibs on for the ability to use corporate scale and funding to reduce the per-unit cost and stretch the number of affordable apartments.

Each of these deals rested on a fact that is obvious but sometimes oddly hard for government officials to appreciate, which is that most of land's value is tied up in the rules for how much you can build on it, and government makes the rules. In the case of that first 166-unit development, all it took was some meetings and a vote, a stack of paper and some political will, and suddenly the land was valuable enough to support 66 units of subsidized workforce housing for middle-income families. In essence, BRIDGE was showing California governments just how expensive overzealous zoning regulations had made developable land, then persuading them to unlock free affordable housing money by changing the rules to allow more density, although nobody ever talked about it that way.

It was good and important work, but the fact that the work was necessary, that there was even a need for a nonprofit to take care of people whom regular market-rate developers used to take care of, exposed a hole in the housing system, and helped to move the focus away from the actual poor. While BRIDGE was building middle-income apartments for the teachers and firefighters who were being pushed out of California by high housing costs even back then, a shocking new form of poverty was starting to emerge on city streets.

Researchers described it with phrases like "homeless" and "literally without shelter," because in the 1980s the word "literally" was still necessary. Until the late 1970s, when people described skid row–style poverty, they were almost always referring to the haggard old men who squatted in abandoned buildings or lived in boardinghouses and scary hotels. Many were severely disabled and chemically dependent and mentally ill, and yet they were all mostly housed—housed in places that were frequently inadequate and dangerous but still had beds and bathrooms and were shelter. Now there were multiplying panhandlers and men sleeping on park benches and "shopping bag ladies" pushing grocery carts through the night.

The initial explanation was the deep 1981 recession. When the subsequent recovery failed to dent the problem, new theories multiplied and tended to fall along partisan lines. The right blamed social isolation, falling marriage rates, and drugs. The left blamed President Ronald Reagan, whose deep cuts to the safety net prompted housing advocates to refer to the first half of the 1980s as "starving time." The explosion of street homelessness was accompanied by a simultaneous explosion of street homeless research, and the collective tone of social scientists and books like *Over the Edge* and *The Homeless* was that it was hard to blame one thing when the real answer seemed to be everything. Good-paying factory jobs were shriveling. Unemployment spells stretched from months to years. A surge in minimum-wage jobs in big-box stores and elsewhere helped to create a vast new underclass of adults who worked full time but still had trouble paying utilities and needed help from food stamps. Those at the very bottom fell lower: "deep poverty," people whose few-thousand-dollar-a-year income put them more than halfway below the poverty line, grew throughout the 1980s and by 2018 accounted for about half of poor households.

Poverty has always been with us, and poor people have always had a hard time living near good jobs. The colonial era had itinerant workers and "sturdy beggars," while the post–Civil War urbanization was marked by crowded and unsafe tenements that were documented in books like *How the Other Half Lives*. Then the Great Depression, with its dust bowl itinerants and Hoovervilles. The difference between those cataclysms and street homelessness is that they could be by and large explained by the ups and downs of the economy. That is, when job opportunities improved, housing conditions did too.

This new thing, this literal homelessness, seemed to have little to do with the number of jobs or the level of interest rates or foreign wars or bank runs, and instead served as the most extreme example of how brutal and unstable America was becoming. It was as if the country had started specializing in creating new ways for people to be and remain subsistent while jettisoning the programs designed to help. The concurrent growth of single-occupant households and the newfound ease of procuring hard drugs—a hit of crack could cost as little as $2.50 in the 1980s, bringing the fleeting excitement of cocaine to people who previously couldn't afford it—weakened the family tethers and made it easier to fall to the depths.

From the beginnings of the homeless problem and continuing to today, there has remained a persistent narrative that the civil rights era's "deinstitutionalization" movement, which emptied out state mental hospitals but failed to give patients anywhere to go, can explain most of the people living in the streets. The narrative is a convenient one because it shifts the blame from society and the economy to individual brains, quelling the public guilt by assuring us that this isn't a housing problem, or even a poverty problem, but something different and out of our control. Many of the earliest studies of homelessness were all but designed, with the Reagan administration's encouragement, to reinforce the mental health story.

It's an easy story to sell, because the most chronically unsheltered people, who represent a small fraction of the homeless but a high fraction of what not-homeless people see, appear out of sorts and suffering. And yet, while there's clearly an association between mental health problems and homelessness, study after study shows that deinstitutionalization cannot explain all or even most of the phenomenon, and beyond the most extreme cases it's hard to delineate when mental problems cause homelessness and when homelessness causes mental problems.

In 1979, when two Columbia University graduate students performed what was probably the first study of people sleeping on the streets and coined the "homeless" label in hopes of moving the public conversation away from phrases like "bum" and "vagrant," many of the people they found sleeping on subway benches and the halls of Grand Central Terminal had lost their source of affordable housing. Various other studies in Los Angeles, Boston, and elsewhere have found much the same thing.

In the 1960s and 1970s, when cheap housing was plentiful and cities were a refuge for listlessness, it was possible to be an unskilled and slightly off-kilter day laborer with a drinking problem and still find a nightly place to sleep. But the same redevelopment programs that demolished black neighborhoods around the country also destroyed thousands of rooming houses and "cage hotels" with single-occupant dwellings and shared bathrooms, removing a crucial supply of last-resort shelter. In the decades since, the combination of urban renewal, housing discrimination, and the conversion of bargain rentals to condos and co-ops has left the country with a deficit of seven million fewer affordable units than households who need them.

For decades the archetypal homeless person was a white man with a drinking problem. Now it's as diverse as the country: women, families, wayward teens, and many more nonwhite people fill the surveys of shelters and outdoor encampments in California and elsewhere. The more dire the housing crisis gets, the more "homeless" means "poor." By 2018, about 550,000 people were homeless in the United States, and about a third of those were unsheltered people living in parks, under bridges, or in cars.

California has about 130,000 homeless people, by far the most in the nation. It also has about half of the unsheltered population and a whole bunch of stories that are hard to find anywhere else. The vagabond rows of trailers that line the streets near Google's headquarters. The dozens of people in Sacramento who lived on the banks of the American River in makeshift rafts so they and their belongings would remain above water when the winter floods came. The sleeping woman in Modesto who was crushed to death by a front loader when the California Department of Transportation came to clear her encampment.

A few lots over from Rick Holliday's office in West Oakland, a mile-long homeless camp stretches across a stripe of undeveloped dirt that sits between a frontage road and a freeway. It's a dense little neighborhood made from campers and blue tarps and has a micro economy of social security checks and late-night scrapping and copper-stripping jobs. There are amenities like wash bins and clotheslines and a fire-heated bathtub that is periodically drained and refilled with water from a nearby fire hydrant. During the day the camp is mostly quiet and has the peaceful ocean sound of distant cars passing at 70. At night it lights up with lamps and TVs that have been rigged to pull electricity from the freeway lights.

There's some stories out there. Meth habits. Old weed arrests. Abandoned children. Years on the lam. Also: Mass layoffs. Foreclosed homes.

Abusive husbands. Crippling strokes. A career moving furniture followed by a back injury followed by $1,300 a month in disability followed by an eviction, and suddenly you're on a couch in a dirt lot at 11 a.m. drinking a beer next to a barking dog and broken appliances.

A remarkable statistic lies inside the camp and others near it: Many of the occupants were born between 1955 and 1965. Tommy Goodluck, 1964. Regina Richard, also '64. Andrew Aramburo, 1958. These people and others like them, the homeless who are becoming senior citizens on the streets, all belong to a cohort of late-stage Baby Boomers who entered adulthood during the brutal back to back recessions of the late 70s and early 1980s, which was followed by the decades long depression in working class wages and a run-up in housing costs.

Since the very beginnings of modern homelessness in the 1980s, people from this birth cohort have accounted for the largest share of the homeless population and are three times more likely to be homeless than would be expected by generational size alone. None of them is perfect and bad life decisions abound, as they do in every generation. But because they were born at the wrong time and entered the economy during an unstable period, those decisions have had harsher consequences and deeper financial repercussions at every stage of life.

That homelessness is so concentrated among a single group whose lives have been on the wrong side of each recession is yet another example of how a good amount of homelessness can be explained not by drugs and mental illness—though it is certainly exacerbated by them—but by the economy running out of good jobs and affordable places to live. That and a politics that has decided that when the economy is low on opportunity it's OK to take the most vulnerable people in society (trans people, disabled people, and adults over fifty are all over-represented in the homeless population) and simply throw them out. Homelessness is often described as complicated, and individually it is. But the deepest question, "How can this happen in America?" has the simplest of answers: Because we let it.

When something in society goes so wrong, that something is often a product of one very large agreement instead of the various small disagreements that consume the political sphere. Looming over the fights about which administration is to blame for housing becoming so unstable and what percentage increase this or that program is entitled to sits the inconsistency of America spending about $70 billion a year subsidizing homeownership through tax breaks like deferred taxes on capital gains and the mortgage interest deduction (MID), which allows homeowners to deduct the interest on their home loan from their federal income taxes. Together these tax breaks amount to a vast upper-middle-class welfare program that encourages people to buy bigger and more expensive houses, but because their biggest beneficiaries are residents of high-cost cities in deep blue redoubts like New York and California, even otherwise liberal politicians fight any attempt to reduce them. These programs are also entitlements that live on budgetary autopilot, meaning people get the tax breaks no matter how much they cost the government.

Contrast that with programs like Section 8 rental vouchers, which cost about $20 billion a year, have been shown to be highly effective at reducing homelessness, and cost far less than the morally repugnant alternative of letting people live in tents and rot on sidewalks, consuming police resources and using the emergency room as a public hospital. That program has to be continually re-upped by Congress, and unlike middle-class homeowner programs, when the money runs out, it's gone. This is why many big cities either have decades-long lines for rental vouchers or have closed those lines indefinitely on account of excess demand. The message of this dichotomy, which has persisted for decades regardless of which party is in charge and despite the mountains of evidence showing just how well these vouchers work, is that America is willing to subsidize as much debt as homeowners can gorge themselves on but that poor renters, the majority of whom live in market-rate apartments, are a penny-ante side issue unworthy of being prioritized.

IN MARCH 2017, Dr. Wilma J. Wooten, the public health officer for San Diego County, got a call from a staff epidemiologist telling her that hepatitis A was spreading through the local homeless population. Outbreaks are a function of poor hygiene and tight quarters and are often traced back to prisons, dorms, classrooms, and other crowded areas. That year about nine thousand people in San Diego County were homeless, and the most desperate of them lived in shanties built from tarps and bungee cords or assembled off the road in out-of-sight communities that formed in ravines and riverbeds. An outbreak was a matter of time.

The county identified twenty-eight new hepatitis A cases that March. The number jumped to fifty-one the next month, eighty-six the next, and by the end of the summer the county was seeing close to a hundred new cases a month, in a region that normally sees no more than a few dozen a year. Crews of nurses and outreach workers scrambled to the fringes in vans to deliver 121,921 vaccination shots. Street cleaners started bleaching the sidewalks, and the city installed pop-up handwashing stations across downtown.

As cases piled up in the hundreds and twenty people died and worried parents called the county health line and news reports multiplied and the tourism industry got shaken, local businesspeople funded the construction of three puffy tent structures that were run by a housing nonprofit and sat right off downtown, a short walk from the Padres' baseball stadium. Inside they were lined with bunk beds and had rows of nearby sinks and portable toilets. There were closets and picnic tables and wheelchair parking and TVs and refrigerators for medication and places to put prosthetics. It wasn't a tent most people would want to hang out in. Face tattoos, trash bags of belongings, foul smells, shuffling, tattered shoes, the occasional scream. It was still at least a statement that this was what had to be done—*now*. Temporarily, at least, the delusion that a city full of people could live side by side with destitution and not have it affect them had been lifted.

In the absence of an emergency, people had a tendency to get caught up in big intractable issues like mental health and drug addiction that loom over the homeless question, but once a city was in triage, they quickly came to the conclusion that homeless advocates had spent decades trying to convince them of, which is that mental treatment can only accomplish so much, that society has never been very good at curbing the temptation to lose oneself in chemicals, that people who've lost their self-worth need someone to care before they can find it, and that programs to accomplish these things work better when patients aren't in a daily battle to figure out where they will spend the night.

The same realization seemed to be setting in across the state. In 2016, Los Angeles voters overwhelmingly passed a $1.2 billion bond measure to build ten thousand supportive housing units—apartments with on-site counseling and other services—for formerly homeless people. Then came the 2017 housing package, with its $4 billion affordable housing bond. Homeless activists in San Francisco started preparing a ballot measure that would tax big companies to double homeless spending in the city, and there would be more city and county housing bonds and more state homeless funding, all coming in the offing. Together it amounted to a broad and statewide acknowledgment that the bargain apartments of the past had to be replenished if homelessness was ever going to be solved, and that the feds weren't coming, so it was up to state and local governments to mend the nation's worn and tattered safety net.

Except now there was a new problem: The money was being consumed by steadily rising construction costs that would almost certainly force cities to drastically reduce the estimates of how much housing they could build with the money they were raising. According to the analysts, California needed to build 3.5 million homes to even think about solving its housing crisis, and statewide it cost about $425,000 per unit—roughly double the median home price in the nation—to build a 100-unit affordable housing project. This sort of math could make a joke of any new funding effort.

Take, for instance, the $4 billion raised with the 2017 housing package. That represented about $12 billion in housing once it was paired with money from private sources. Twelve billion dollars divided by $425,000 per unit equals 28,235 units, or 0.8 percent of the goal. The entire California budget was $200 billion. Two hundred billion dollars divided by $425,000 per unit was 470,588 units. That was 13.4 percent of the goal. The figures grew worse each year as construction costs kept rising, and were even more damning in big cities like San Francisco, where it cost $850,000—often more—to build a single unit of afford-able housing.

Rick Holliday left BRIDGE in the late 1980s to become a for-profit developer. He was no less immune to rising construction costs, which by 2018 were so high that private developers were selling off parcels they'd bought only a few years earlier—not because they couldn't get a building permit or were muddled in legal hell (although there was plenty of that too), but because even $3 million condos and $4,000-a-month rents weren't enough to cover rising costs elsewhere. "It doesn't pencil." "The numbers don't work." That was how developers talked about it.

It was a non-penciling project in Truckee that had led Rick to his late-career detour to the house factory. Truckee is a little mountain town near Lake Tahoe that sits between Reno and Sacramento, about fifteen miles away from the Nevada border. Years earlier Rick had bought an old railyard that sat next to Truckee's two-story-high down-town, and he'd spent a decade planning a cluster of several hundred apartment and condominium buildings that would sit just beyond the main street retail strip. Then the numbers stopped working, and he went looking for a better way.

Nobody was going to feel sorry about Rick's not making a profit, but in the symbiosis of the housing market his problem was everyone's prob-lem. For-profit or nonprofit, building a building is building a building. The forces that had caused Rick's project not to pencil were the same forces that made the state's $4 billion affordable housing bond a relative joke. The subsidized and for-profit housing worlds were further tied together by development fees that used the construction of new condos and apartments to finance a good deal of cities' affordable housing ef-forts, and inclusionary zoning ordinances that required market-rate de-velopers to set aside some of their units for renters making below the median income. The first hundred units of Rick's Truckee project were scheduled to be affordable units reserved for local service workers who held up Truckee's economy but couldn't afford to compete with the wealthy second-home buyers who drove the mountain city's real estate market. Those units wouldn't get built unless the rest got built too.

There were two big drivers behind the surge in construction costs. One was a short-term gash and the other a long-festering wound. The short-term gash was the Great Recession, which flattened the construction industry, prompting younger construction workers to find new professions and older workers to unintentionally retire. When demand came back, the workers didn't come with it: a decade after the recession, the number of construction workers was a quarter below where it was before the recession, and the number of specialized tradesmen like plumbers and electricians—the people a project could not go forward without—was down 17 percent. With the demand for housing high and the supply of labor short, builders had started bidding up wages for the few remaining workers. This exposed the long-festering wound, which was that construction was one of the world's least efficient industries.

Rick spent a lot of time complaining about all the different ways government made housing more expensive, and they weren't hollow complaints. California was one of the hardest states in the nation to get a building permit, and the typical California city charged developers about $20,000 per unit to build new apartments and about $25,000 to build a single-family house. That was three times more than the national average. But it's not as if the construction business were a model of creative thinking. There was an old joke among builders that they now used nail guns instead of hammers, except it wasn't really a joke. Construction workers did in fact use nail guns, and not much else had changed. Latex paint. Longer-lasting roofs. Slightly better Sheetrock. These were the sorts of things Rick thought of when he thought about what had changed in forty years of building.

It used to be possible to say housing developers were innovative. When Levitt & Sons started building Levittown and kicked off the postwar subdivision boom, the company's regimented production techniques were so much more efficient than rival builders' that in 1948 *Harper's Magazine* reported that Levitt undersold competitors by as much as $1,500 per house and still made a $1,000 profit.

That was also about the time building innovation stopped. From 1945 to 2016, sectors like agriculture, retail, and manufacturing saw their productivity rates—how much work is accomplished for each hour an employee puts in—jump by 1,500 percent, according to the McKinsey Global Institute. Over the same period, the construction industry's productivity rate was flat. In other words, over the past seventy years, while the rest of the economy was supercharged by the introduction of new machines, computers, and robots, the construction industry was no more efficient than it was when Levitt was still at work.

Rick didn't need a report to know this or a McKinsey consultant to tell him why. He explained it to laypeople like this: If a car company built cars the way a real estate developer built housing, the way it would work is that the developer would hire a contractor to come over on a Monday with four tires. The next day a subcontractor would bring four rims and wrap the tires around them, then wait for a subcontractor whose job was to put the wheels on the car. The next day the transmission would show up, and a new crew would weld it together. Finally, after two years of piecemeal assembly, there would be a $600,000 car in the driveway.

History said it did not have to be that way. The past was full of moments when America needed more housing than it had workers to build it, and it always seemed to get solved the same way: by building indoors. In 1624, Massachusetts settlers arrived in ships full of ready-to-go walls and roofs that had been hauled over from England and were nailed together upon landing. British colonists to Australia, Africa, and India did the same thing, and over the next few centuries new versions of the idea seemed to pop up anywhere people needed to build lots of homes in a hurry—during the California gold rush, after the Chicago fire, and through America's westward expansion. California was now living through another such situation, and the success of Europe and Asia, which both had well-established modular construction companies that built buildings like Legos, had long-ago demonstrated that a more efficient way was possible. So Rick decided to follow the lead of other countries and his construction industry ancestors by building the Truckee project elsewhere, then driving it up the hill and putting it together on-site.

Truckee was a symmetrically appropriate place for Rick to start something new. The first time he saw the town was shortly after his family crossed the state line during their move to California way back on his tenth birthday in 1963. Five decades later, he woke up in town one morning and retraced his family's drive from Tahoe to the Bay Area, with a brief stop at a Sacramento company called Zeta Communities that manufactured modular apartments like those in Europe and Asia. As it happened, that day Zeta's very first unit was coming off the assembly line, so Rick arrived to speeches and bubbly wine and the site of an apartment inside a box that would be hoisted onto a truck and driven to a construction site in just the manner he needed.

Soon Rick was making an excited phone call to his longtime contractor, a gruff and chain-smoking former army man named Larry Pace, during which Rick told Larry they were going to try out this modular thing, and Larry told Rick that that sounded like a fiasco and he didn't need that shit in his life. Rick persisted, Larry relented, and they performed something of a test run by using Zeta modules to build a smaller project in San Francisco. It cost 20 percent less than budget, and they built it in half the time, which was both good and bad for Zeta. Rick and Larry decided they were going to keep building with modules, and also to start a housing factory of their own.

They called it Factory_OS, which Rick credited to Nancy and, depending on how he told the story, stood for either "Off-Site" (because they were building off-site), "Operating System" (like the operating system in a computer), or "Oh, Shit" (because two guys in their sixties were becoming start-up founders). It began as an idea and an empty warehouse that was three football fields long and inside was crossed by a skeleton of metal beams that looked like the backdrop of a *Terminator* movie. Rick was the schmoozer who rounded up investors and secured an early order from Google, which was trying to develop housing near its headquarters. Larry was the operator who went about designing a U-shaped assembly line that employed the use of large pneumatic disks that turned the warehouse into a giant air hockey rink, allowing a handful of guys to slide an entire building from one station to another.

It took twenty-two steps to build an apartment. Station one was the floor, which sat on a raised platform flanked by a pair of gangways so that one set of workers could install pipes through the underbelly while another was up top laying down flooring. From there the floor went around the room, where more workers added toilets, walls, a roof, electrical outlets, windows, sinks, countertops, and tiling, until men and women in hard hats were walking around a 245-square-foot studio with gray faux-hardwood floors and a galley kitchen. The final step was to wrap the future home in white plastic and stamp it with the Factory_OS logo.

Behind Rick and Larry's factory was a bet not only that housing could be built differently but that the industry's financial structure could be changed too. Developers like to imagine themselves as workingmen, and during drives around town they point out the window and say "I built that" whenever they pass an old project. Actually, they don't build anything, and their employees don't either. The job of developers is to buy a piece of land, find something useful to put on it, then persuade a bank to give them money and the government to give them permission. When it's time to actually build something, however, the bank money gets passed to a general contractor, who passes it to subcontractors, who pass it to even more subcontractors.

When you ask people in the chain to explain why they go through this elaborate handoff, the answer is that they are "brokering risk." What they mean is that while everyone has promised to build his piece of the project for a set amount of money and in a given amount of time, none of them are sure they can actually do it. They broker the risk of failure by paying someone else to do it for them, minus a small fee. By the end there can be a dozen or more subcontractors on a site, most of whom are paid a percentage of a steadily rising price that nobody wants to go down. Factory_OS was trying to invert this structure. Instead of off-loading the risk of building, it assumed all of it. Instead of sending jobs to subcontractors whose workers the company didn't have to be responsible for, it hired workers of its own. And instead of making profit by taking a cut of rising construction costs, it was trying to emulate Levitt and other postwar builders who made their money on a margin and worked mercilessly to lower costs.

A house factory was an obvious answer that came with an obvious question: If it was such a good idea, why did the building industry always seem to default back to the standard, site-built construction methods that Rick had made his career on? The thesis of production line manufacturing is to efficiently make products whose designs are so standard, and their sales so regular, that it's worth it to spend gobs of money on large machines and large electricity bills and hiring a small army of workers to man a line from whistle to whistle. The corollary is that whenever sales plunge—an unavoidable fact of housing, which sits high on the list of the economy's most boom/bust sectors—your once-efficient factory will become a sinkhole of rising costs, and you'll have to turn off the power and lay everyone off, then do nothing while waiting for the economy to recover, and after that decide, when business finally comes back, if you want to go through all that again or default to the less efficient but financially safer method of hiring project to project and building outside.

Just as history was replete with examples of factory-built housing helping solve housing crises, it was also replete with examples of U.S. housing factories going bust because they couldn't generate enough business to keep their lines running efficiently. During the housing boom in the mid-2000s, Pulte Homes, one of the country's largest builders, opened a prefabrication plant that aimed to revolutionize how houses were built. The company closed it during the housing bust. Zeta Communities, Rick's inspiration for Factory_OS, went out of business shortly after he and Larry completed their first project with it.

Rick's answer was to center part of the business on affordable housing, which was as much a financial strategy as a statement of higher purpose. The billions of dollars cities and states were passing to build subsidized apartments represented a recession-resistant revenue stream that could help smooth the economy's lumpiness and keep the line running through the inevitable next downturn. This also amounted to a bet that the housing crisis wasn't going away anytime soon, and that the construction industry was now so expensive and out of whack that it really was time for an overhaul. It was a bet Rick was far from alone in making.

In the time Factory_OS got started with a relatively puny $10 million from investors, venture capitalists had plowed several billion dollars into construction technology companies that were using 3-D printing and machine learning and milling their own components, convinced that one of the world's oldest trades, home building, would be the next big industry to be disrupted by tech outsiders. Rick could dream about him and Larry hitting late-career gold and becoming the new Levitts. He could also see them getting squashed by the multiplying number of better-funded and potentially smarter and more technologically advanced competitors. What he couldn't see was the industry continuing as it had throughout his career, because the old way wasn't working anymore.

The biggest vote of confidence seemed to come from construction unions, which spun into a turf war before Factory_OS was even operational. Rick and Larry had secured an agreement with the Northern California Carpenters Regional Council to staff the factory with its members, which in turn prompted the head of a plumbers' union to write a letter to the City of San Francisco urging it not to use the company for city-funded projects (like affordable housing). The issue wasn't wages or health care, but that carpenters represented everyone in the factory, which was similar to how industrial unions like the United Auto Workers organized auto plants.

Rival construction unions considered this a declaration of war. A typical big construction site had different unions representing carpenters, plumbers, electricians, boilermakers, and the various other trades. At

Factory_OS, one employee could work on everything from electrical wires to pipes to windows to plaster, and the training was easy enough that the assembly line had stereotypically handy guys working next to people who used to be movers and waitresses—a setup that, were it to take off, would obliterate the old trade structure. After the second housing package was passed, the umbrella organization for California construction unions threatened a lawsuit to prevent Factory_OS and other modular builders from using Scott Wiener's streamlining law, prompting counter legal threats from the carpenters. The more popular modular construction became, the louder this fight would get.

It was out of fashion to believe you could do well and good at the same time. Too many scars from the financial crisis, too many tech monopolies, too many flippers who evicted entire buildings then used a coat of paint and some tile to rationalize doubling the rent. Too many rent-seeking schemes that portrayed a capitalism that had lost its way. Rick still believed it. He'd spent his life jumping between the worlds of do-gooding and moneymaking and had come away believing that each needed the other for progress to occur. Governments had good intentions and lofty ideals, but they always lost their way on costs and in the case of housing seemed unable to actually accomplish the things taxes and legislation set out to do. It was a well-known absurdity of the affordable housing system that it frequently cost more per square foot to build no-frills nonprofit apartments than it did to build high-end for-profit condos. The public sector had too much going on, too many political mouths to feed, to make an even semi-serious attempt to address it.

If cities couldn't get this housing thing right, people would get cynical again. Behind each new affordable housing bond and the additional billions for homeless services was a public who thought they were being generous, when really the new taxes were nothing in comparison to a problem that was getting worse faster than cities could deploy the money. Cities like Los Angeles and San Francisco were entering an ominous moment in which they were spending hundreds of millions more a year on homeless services, only to have to annually update the public that the number of homeless people was increasing by double-digit percentages. There was a quiet dread among affordable housing advocates, at least the more prescient ones, that when the public found out how brutal the statistics were and how little each new influx of money accomplished, the appetite for new taxes would start waning.

Neither Factory_OS nor any other company was going to outright solve this. Even if it managed not to become another entrant in the long line of modular builders that began with a lot of fanfare and died just as quickly, there were still land costs, government fees, and NIMBYs to contend with. There was still so much else driving the bill besides construction costs. And in the case of affordable housing you still needed public money and public will, because this was a societal problem, not a business one. But that was the sort of stuff that depended on who the president was and which party controlled Congress, which was way beyond where Rick was operating. Who knew, maybe one day there would be some wildly ambitious national building program. Until then, faster and cheaper construction could help to do more with what was there, and like any new technology it held the power to open the public imagination to the idea that big problems could be solved.

Rick was so eager to demonstrate this that the first boxes off the line were for the formerly homeless. The project was called the Phoenix. If it got approved, there would be a new cluster of 316 apartments in West Oakland that would include 50 affordable units for working-class earners and 51 supportive units for people coming off the streets. Rick lined up two well-known nonprofits, Abode Services and the East Bay Asian Local Development Corporation, to run and service the affordable and supportive units. The nice way to describe it was to say it was "a mixed-income community," and the realistic way to describe it was to say it was a bunch of studios and one-bedrooms for yuppies next to apartments whose residents would be one step removed from a homeless encampment. It was a bold, utopian-sounding idea, the sort of thing cities badly needed and wanted to say yes to (and the sort of thing Factory_OS could point to as a success and drum up new business with).

Most of the financing for the Phoenix would come via a federal tax program worth $10 billion a year called the Low-Income Housing Tax Credit (LIHTC), which was a product of the Reagan administration's 1986 tax overhaul. The way LIHTC works is that the federal government gives tax credits to states that give them to affordable housing developers (some nonprofit, some for-profit) who transfer them to banks and corporations in exchange for equity stakes in low-income rental buildings, at which point the banks and corporations use the credits to offset their future tax bills. It's convoluted and complicated, but that's what makes it safe. Unlike the old public housing programs, which tended to grow during Democratic administrations and shrink during Republican ones, LIHTC allows conservatives to say America is using private markets to solve public problems while allowing liberals to steer housing money to localities. Since 1987, LIHTC credits have funded the construction and rehabilitation of some three million subsidized units. It is, in effect, our national public housing program.

The tricky thing about the credits is that they are usually paired with other sources of money. A typical affordable housing project has to get half a dozen or more local loans and grants to augment the money it gets through LIHTC. Each funding source has its own peculiar rules and applications. Its own deadlines to receive funding. Its own deadlines to spend the money before it has to be returned. Most of the time developers can't get money from one source until they have money from another.

This is part of the reason why affordable housing can cost more than market-rate housing: nonprofit developers can spend years, years that they aren't building, trying to find the perfect overlapping window to get all the money pots lined up. The process is expensive and time consuming, but it is also an opportunity, because deadlines are pressure, and pressure is politics, and politics allow a developer to show up at a city meeting and say if you don't approve this now, we won't get the other money we need to build the *affordable housing* you say you want, which was roughly the pitch Rick made when he showed up at the Oakland Planning Commission to seek approval for the Phoenix.

It was a homecoming of sorts. Rick hadn't built something like the Phoenix since he'd left BRIDGE, and like the old days he was back in the strange position of having to show California governments that they could essentially print money for affordable housing if they wanted. He'd bought the land for the Phoenix from the California Department of Transportation, and now he was before the Oakland Planning Commission asking for a zoning change to build it. That is, he bought land from the state and was now trying to persuade a city to change its land-use rules, to change its own rules, and use the value of density to help build housing for homeless people.

People had asked a lot of questions in the six months since Rick had filed his development application with the city—state questions, city questions, county questions—but the biggest question was the one nobody asked, which is why it was necessary, at a time when cities and states were struggling to find enough money to solve their homeless problems, to have a developer persuade them to unlock value that they could at any point just unlock themselves.

Across California, city and state legislators were talking about the boldness of spending single-digit billions on new affordable housing programs, but outside a handful of cases they did it while ignoring the untold hundreds of billions (maybe more) in land and buildings that state and local governments already owned. All the open land by train tracks. All the dingy government office complexes that could be redeveloped into new housing and office space. All the government parking lots that could have parking and housing.

This was a far more radical idea than a house factory, and with a little creativity there could be a bunch of Phoenixes everywhere, for very little public cost, if governments and voters could just somehow find the will. That was the sort of high-minded thing Rick talked about at the bar, where the power of imagination could outdo the realities of politics. But that night when he was in front of the planning commission, he kept it simple and focused on the little victory of getting his buildings approved.

"It's a project that focuses on homeless housing, where we as a community will take our responsibility to get a homeless project approved, in our neighborhood, next to us, and we do it enthusiastically, with open eyes," he told the commissioners when the proposal came up for a vote. "We have our reservations about what this may bring in terms of difficulties, but we are ready to take them on."

It was amazing how easily you could get a city to vote your way when you helped it solve a problem. During public comment there was one woman, one, who protested the Phoenix on the grounds that the market-rate units would accelerate gentrification. Later, planning commission members asked a few probing questions about whether local residents would be prioritized for the affordable units (yes) and whether the formerly homeless people would have access to the same outdoor lawns as the yuppies in the market-rate apartments (yes). Mostly it was words like "impressed," "exciting," "appreciated," and "awesome."

"I'm sensitive to one of the speakers who talked about how new development can sometimes lead to displacement, or at least rising rents in the area, which has a ripple effect on displacement, and this project is in my mind particularly different because of the number of affordable housing units it provides, and supportive housing for homeless folks, which we almost never see come before the commission," the chairwoman said before the vote. "So I'm really grateful for this type of project and I think it will have a different impact on the neighborhood and on Oakland than other projects do."

Even when you were building studios for the homeless, you couldn't be a developer without optimism and a taste for risk. Rick was so confident that the meeting would go the way he wanted that the factory had actually already built the fifty-one supportive housing units that would be the first phase of the project. And so as everyone sat there discussing the need for homeless housing, the units they were all talking about sat twenty-five miles away in a parking lot, behind a chain-link fence, on stilts in white plastic, waiting to become homes.

CHAPTER 8

THE VALUE-ADD INVESTOR

THE WAITRESSES AND shopkeepers were somewhere between bored and worried. It was Saturday afternoon and overcast, but the threat of rain was not so great as to explain the lack of customers along Middle-field Road. The jewelry shop had already gone out of business. The Christian bookstore had also closed. That afternoon the taqueria was open and empty, the piñata store was open and empty, and Recuerdos Mex was open and empty. Carina Escorza worked at the jewelry shop before it closed and was now employed by Recuerdos Mex.

Recuerdos Mex sold *quinceañera* dresses and baptism bootees and white suits for tots—special occasion religious items that people were willing to splurge on when they weren't splurging on much of anything. Escorza found this to be a safer line of business than selling silver rings and gold necklaces as she had at the now-closed jewelry shop. Religious items were selling better, if not well, than most of anything else in her store. Recuerdos Mex had shelves full of crosses and baby-faced angel dolls. It was having more sales and stocking more religious items. More sales on religious items.

The problem was rent, not for stores, but for their customers. As the numbers outside the stores went one direction, the numbers inside the stores went the other. The numbers outside the store were numbers like a salary of $15 an hour and rent that went from $1,500 a month to $2,800 a month. Numbers like a family of four in a one-bedroom or three jobs and a 120-hour workweek. People who lived in trailers had an effective rent of $1,500 a month: one $50 ticket per day times thirty days.

That afternoon, Omar Osorio, the lone clerk at Piñata Surprises, sat alone with the crowd of piñata princesses, piñata fish, piñata trains, piñata Batmans, and piñata Wonder Women that hung from the ceiling on wire hooks. Money had never been easy for Osorio, but working three jobs used to allow him to take his family to an average sit-down restaurant once or twice per month. Now, on account of rising rents, it seemed as if everyone just stockpiled ham, bread, a bucket of beans, a quart of rice, and some eggs. He was not in the position or mood to buy a piñata. He understood why customers weren't either, and while there was plenty of money being spent by the Facebookers who congregated near the company's headquarters a few miles away, it wasn't as if Piñata Surprises or any of the nearby taquerias, *panaderias, paleterias, joyerias,* salons, bodegas, and coin laundries were going to change course and start selling $10,000 bikes and gluten-free muffins.

In their 1987 book *Urban Fortunes,* the sociologists John R. Logan and Harvey Molotch described neighborhoods like Middlefield Road as cross-fire victims in a battle over land and profit. According to Logan and Molotch, how cities look and operate is defined by the never-ending tension between land's economic split identities. There is the business of profit and the business of life. Everyone is doing a little of both, a little living, a little profiting, but poor people do the least profiting, by definition, and therefore tend to settle in places where the value of life, meaning the value of place and community, is highest. An affluent family can use money and a spreadsheet to answer questions like private school tuition in the city versus public school property taxes in a ritzy suburb. Low-income renters like Sandy Hernandez, who lived a short drive from Piñata Surprises when she and Stephanie were displaced from their apartment, survived on the nonmonetary income of place.

For Sandy and her family, the stress cost of living with four people in a one-bedroom apartment was offset by the benefits of being near a Latino community they knew, of having friends and the Siena Center to lean on for child care, of having the kids be able to walk and take buses to school. Those amenities of place were worth more than Sandy could make in dollars if she worked every single hour of every single day, and rising rents disrupted it. The more tenants like Sandy spent on rent, the less money they had to support the surrounding community, the fewer piñatas and baptism bootees were sold, and the less the place was the place. Rents went up, friends moved away, child-care options shriveled, and slowly the connections weakened. "Indeed, efforts at urban 'revival' are often schemes to break, through either wholesale land clearance or selective destruction, just this chain of complementary relationships within poor areas," Logan and Molotch wrote.

A mile away from the Middlefield Road retail strip, the old Bucking-ham Apartments, the building whose clearance had inspired Coach Ra-fael to start the rapid-response team and make Stephanie a teenage activist, sat renamed and rebranded. Gone were the Buckingham Apartments at 180 Buckingham; in were the "180 Flats." A raw-lumber fence emerged along one side, and the standard black address numbering had been re-placed with a neon red-orange "180" in sans serif font. The subterranean garage had Audis, and the outdoor recycling bins were stuffed with dis-carded LaCroix cans, cartons of almond milk, and Apple product boxes.

Sister Christina's office was still across the street, so she watched the daily renovations and from her window could see displaced tenants carry their belongings out of their apartments. Later, when someone from Trion told Sister Christina that tenants would have the option to come back, she told him not to treat her like a fool and asked how he slept knowing that he was putting people with nowhere to go on the streets.

The stock answer was that they were doing something good by making the building better. And the building was indeed nicer. Fresh paint. New fence. To the eyes of an investor, things that looked better were better. Sister Christina did not see the same things they did. She saw lipstick on an ugly process and a violation of the "moral mortgage" that comes with owning someone else's home.

Sister Christina grew up in Pasadena and was an undergrad at UC Santa Barbara in the 1970s when she left to volunteer with a group of Catholic nuns and decided that instead of getting married she was going to become a Dominican sister and dedicate her life to service. Her order was conceived to be teachers, and she was the superintendent of Catholic schools for the Diocese of Monterey, where she spent most of her time meeting with bishops and lawyers and doing ordinary desk work that kept her far from the mission of uplift that had prompted the abandonment of her old life. So she left to take over the St. Francis Center, which at the time was a little house with a food and clothing program.

Over the next two decades she built it into a powerhouse nonprofit that served immigrants and Latino families in and around North Fair Oaks and Redwood City. The needs were always changing, but housing was always up there. During the financial crisis it was the foreclosures. Then the explosion of rents and the influx of flipper investors. Sister Christina could see the effects of gentrification reflected in the scope of her food and clothing program. A decade after the Great Recession it was half the size of what it used to be. This wasn't a sign of diminishing need but an indication of poorer residents leaving the area for cheaper housing far away.

The residents who moved into the Buckingham Apartments after it was bought by Trion were not exactly rich. There was at least one cook. Also some grad students and game developers who did fine but couldn't afford an apartment in Mountain View or Palo Alto. A handful had lived there before and stuck around after the renovations, but many of the new residents didn't seem to get what sort of neighborhood they'd moved into. One new resident complained about the common patio on the back of the building, which looked at an old train yard and a house with a broken-down car in the yard. A Yelp reviewer noted the Norteño graffiti that had been spray-painted on the new raw-lumber fence. Yelp was full of people describing gentrification without fully realizing it.

"No loud sounds that keep you up at night. Although there is an ice cream truck that comes around every once in a while and the noise can stick with you if you have the windows open."

"I've reported a girl who does not leash her collie."

"YES YOU HEAR THE TRAIN."

Across the street at the St. Francis Center, people had started regarding the building like an old friend who'd been possessed. That didn't seem right to Sister Christina, because it wasn't really the new tenants' fault. The St. Francis Center's motto was "Compassion, not judgment," so when a young woman who had moved into the building shortly after renovations went to the center to inquire about joining the local garden, there was no mention of what had happened. Later Sister Christina had her staff go through the complex distributing leaflets that invited the new neighbors to become part of the community.

Nevertheless, the newly renovated building represented a direction that was very much a threat. Unlike the previous residents, the new people were for the most part not going to be partaking in the laundry, clothing, schooling, and immigration counseling services that St. Francis had located across the street to provide. They were probably not going to buy piñatas on Middlefield Road or otherwise reinforce the chain of complementary relationships. Sister Christina's calling was to keep that chain intact, and it was in service of this mission that she had become a multimillion-dollar apartment investor herself.

As executive director of the St. Francis Center, Sister Christina presided over a portfolio of ten buildings with eighty-seven apartments whose value on the open market would be well into the tens of millions. But they weren't on the open market. Sister Christina bought them with money from foundations and corporations and loans and rich people, then set them aside, worked down the debt, and deed restricted them as affordable forever. She had in a sense removed them from capitalism. The St. Francis Center first got into housing in 1997, buying a twenty-four-unit apartment complex back when Silicon Valley was swelling with new techies during the dot-com boom. Sister Christina kept expanding it, another building here, another building there, then backed off for a short while to focus on building the Siena Center. People had started telling her they needed a safe place for kids to go, so she listened.

Now housing was back to number one. The St. Francis Center developed housing and bought housing, and Sister Christina operated inside real estate's twisted web. She got money from the same tech companies that her tenants accused of being the agents of gentrification. She got loans from the same banks that financed investors like Jesshill Love. One of St. Francis's board members was also on the board of the California Apartment Association, the state's biggest landlords' group and a fierce opponent of rent control. As always she followed the Center's motto—"Compassion, not judgment"—and didn't dwell on the institutional hypocrisies, which would only distract her from the mission of expanding her portfolio and insulating the neighborhood from rising rents.

There was, in general, a certain kind of building Sister Christina was interested in. You've seen them. They were the blocky walk-up apartment buildings enclosed by metal grates, the stucco duplexes resting on poles above a carport. The worn old buildings that exist in every city and are supposed to be a foundational piece of the low-wage economy but in California were being consumed by investors seeking higher rents. After she got them, Sister Christina rented her buildings to people like Sandy and Stephanie's family—the St. Francis Center owned the one-bedroom where they'd moved after being priced out—at heavily subsidized rates. Morality was a competitive tool. Sister Christina found many of her buildings by enlisting her business-minded board members to persuade local property owners to sell apartment buildings to the St. Francis Center in quiet, off-market transactions instead of auctioning to the highest bidder. Her sales pitch was "It's the right thing to do." And with the right owner, it worked.

In the real estate lingo that she now spoke as fluently as any broker, Sister Christina was an "opportunistic buyer." Go slowly. Don't covet. Find deals. Such are the rules of value purchasing, and most of the time she followed them with the discipline of a careful investor. But there was one building she wanted more than any of the others. Sister Christina was obsessed and willing to volunteer that she wanted it so badly she could taste it, and would pay whatever market price. It was the building that sat right outside her window, 180 Buckingham Avenue, now the 180 Flats. Three times she tried to buy it. Three times she failed. The first time was in 2015, when it sold for $13.1 million. The second time was a year later, when Trion bought it for $15 million. Shortly after Trion's purchase, Sister Christina tried to buy it back. Trion refused and started renovating.

WORDS LIKE "HOMELESS" do not appear in investor newsletters or the various how-to books and blogs and podcasts that surround the apartment investing industry. The language is of math and euphemisms. Run-down old buildings are "vintage," and renovating them is "value-add" investing. A building with families headed by low-income nannies and construction workers who can easily be replaced is "an underperforming asset." Handing out eviction notices is "re-tenanting" and raising rents by 50 to 100 percent is "stabilizing." The trade press routinely writes number-choked articles about floating mortgage rates and the "professional management practices" that allow an investor to buy an old building and double its value and operating income in a few years, without ever once mentioning what happens to the people who lived there.

Trion Properties was founded in 2005 and named for a fictional beast. One co-founder, Mitch Paskover, went to the University of Southern California, home of the Trojans. The other, Max Sharkansky, went to Loyola Marymount, home of the Lions. Trion = Trojan + Lion. Sharkansky and Paskover were childhood friends who both worked in real estate. Sharkansky was working as a broker in the San Fernando Valley and had become tired of being a middleman. He wanted to run his own buildings and started with what he knew, buying small properties in the Valley that he financed with friends and family equity and what he once described to an interviewer as "high-octane debt." Debt was a dangerous word in the mid-2000s, as the world economy was about to be undone by it. But Trion fortuitously unloaded most of its portfolio before the 2008 financial crisis.

For anyone who could find cash, the Great Recession was one of the greatest real estate buying opportunities in the history of time. Trion was a bit player compared with the private equity firms and hedge funds that would end up buying hundreds of thousands of single-family houses and building new publicly traded companies like Invitation Homes from a once mom-and-pop industry. Still, the partners found their openings, got foreclosure deals, and were able to build a business by keeping things basic and steadily raising rents. Even though the economy was in tatters and unemployment hit 10 percent, people still needed a place to live. A rush of new college grads and people who'd lost their houses to foreclosure were both out looking for rentals, while the strict post-crisis credit standards had people who had been considering buying a house staying in apartments they already had. Rents flatlined during the recession but never really fell. With all the pressure for space, when the economy started to recover and job growth picked up, prices resumed their steady rise.

This created a new business opportunity. During the downturn, when rents were stuck, investors' general business plan was to buy a building and get it leased up quick. Whatever rehabs they did were in the name of making things habitable and clean. They turned a profit by buying low and holding the line on costs. But as the foreclosure stock cleared and the demand for rentals grew, investors shifted from fire-sale bargains to buying "value-add" buildings where they could make money by renovating and significantly raising the rents. The business logic is thus: The higher average rents go, the easier it is to find someone to pay the area average. The easier it is to find someone to pay the average, the easier it is to make money by replacing tenants who pay less than average. Commercial real estate brokers describe older complexes as "primed for rent hikes" and will very clinically lay out how affordable buildings with easy-to-evict tenants promise the biggest returns.

"The current in place rents are below market," Trion wrote in an investor presentation before purchasing the Buckingham Apartments. "As such, there is significant value-add opportunity. . . . Upon obtaining title to the Project, it is anticipated that the Company will begin adding high-end interior finishes and strategic common area improvements to attract the high income demographic living in the area."

The best way to execute this plan is to find affordable buildings in fast-growing cities near high-paying employers. Trion's website was full of blocky apartments with concrete walls and outdoor staircases of the sort Sister Christina was always looking for, and they resided on the peripheries of some of the nation's hottest rental markets: San Diego, Los Angeles, the Bay Area, and Portland. Trion operated an apartment building near Tesla's manufacturing headquarters in Fremont and another in Beaverton, Oregon, near Nike. In 2016, about the same time Trion was renovating 180 Buckingham, the company bought the thirty-six-unit former Walnut Tree Apartments in Tigard, Oregon, outside Portland. The company cut down the eponymous walnut tree, renamed it Tigardville, and proceeded to double the rent after renovations.

"We've been able to find a tremendous amount of value in East Bay, in Portland, and in more high-growth gentrifying markets," Sharkansky told a podcast hosted by RealCrowd, an online platform where investors raise money to buy commercial real estate.

———

YOU NEED A bit of money to become an apartment flipper, but the industry is by no means exclusive. Trion's website had a fill-in form where anyone professing to be worth at least $1 million could sign up and view investment opportunities, while crowdfunding sites like Real-Crowd acted as middlemen, allowing doctors, lawyers, and other ordinary rich people to buy shares in about-to-be-flipped buildings for as little as $10,000. Real estate celebrities recruit fans through blogs and social media and invite them to invest in new projects, where they are promised a stream of passive income without ever having to see more than the returns, project timelines, and milestones that are spelled out in neat infographics. One of the investors Trion found through Real-Crowd was an anesthesiologist who gave Sharkansky's wife an epidural when she was in labor with their first son.

RealCrowd operates like the high-end-landlord version of online shopping. As with Trion, their prospective investors have to certify $200,000 in annual income or a net worth of at least $1 million, and after that can toggle between retail, industrial, and multifamily properties. There are apartment buildings in Marietta, Georgia, storage units in Las Vegas, strip malls in California exurbs. Users filter out buildings by minimum investment or business strategy, and it costs nothing to browse or submit an investment. Instead, RealCrowd charges companies like Trion a $15,000 listing fee plus a varying rate processing fee whenever someone gives them money. By welcoming anyone with a decent-sized savings account, RealCrowd positions itself as something of a democratizing force in commercial real estate, a boring but reliably lucrative industry. It's the same vaguely idealistic "we promote economic empowerment" pitch given by finance start-ups across the Bay Area, perhaps because RealCrowd is itself a product of Silicon Valley.

The company's CEO, Adam Hooper, went to Penn State and brokered commercial real estate deals in Sacramento before entering Y Combinator, the famed "accelerator" that serves as a kind of exclusive boot camp for start-up founders, in 2013. A year later RealCrowd raised $1.6 million in seed funding from investors including Initialized Capital, a San Francisco venture capital firm, and Paul Buchheit, a former Google engineer who created Gmail and is credited with suggesting "Don't Be Evil" as the company's former motto. Fawning industry articles and Q&As often position young executives like Hooper and Sharkansky as innovators who cater to the desires of millennial tenants by buying in cool neighborhoods and outfitting their units with the right consumer tech. "I recently visited one of our properties in West LA and one of the tenants ran up to me to tell me how excited he was about the Nest Thermostat and that was the amenity that sealed the deal for his lease," Sharkansky said in an interview with a blog called *A Student of the Real Estate Game.* "It's a thermostat that costs two hundred bucks!!"

The blue pop-out information windows at RealCrowd never really say what happens to the people who already live in the buildings on the site, but the gist is clear enough: "STRATEGY Heavy Renovations / Major Re-tenanting." Value-add buildings are "typically characterized by lower occupancy or significant near-term tenant expirations," RealCrowd explained to users. Every now and then one of the investor-seeking landlords on the site will drop the facade of jargon and use a phrase like "evict and gut" in their online explainers. The risks of value-add investing usually relate to swings in the economy or the condition of a particular building. Pipe problems, foundation problems. But as displacement became rampant and activists like Coach Rafael and the Rents Too High team started making noise, protestors joined the list.

"Some of the surprises that you see outside of physical can be legal, you know, you have some tenants," Sharkansky said on the RealCrowd podcast. "There are some areas that are very sensitive like parts of the Bay Area where people don't like to be displaced and they will raise a big stink and a PR nightmare can ensue. So that's another thing that can cause some cost overruns and we've had that happen. The way that can cause a cost overrun is you've got low-paying tenants in their units much longer than you expected and you've got a loan where you're negative cash flow so you've got more negative cash flow than you anticipated, so your interest reserve winds up going up pretty significantly."

"And I mean that's again, that's part of the nature of the beast, right?" Hooper said.

"That is," Sharkansky said.

"When you're coming in to add value, naturally, you're going to be raising rents and that's just part of the process," Hooper said.

"Yes, it doesn't sit so well with everyone," Sharkansky said.

After Trion purchased the Buckingham Apartments and put out its forthright investor presentation talking about the money to be made with gentrification and its specialty in re-tenanting, Daniel Saver's non-profit filed a federal fair housing lawsuit that prompted a quick and undisclosed settlement. Six months after Jesshill Love's rent increase pushed Sandy and Stephanie out of their apartments, Saver and a few dozen other protestors were marching in front of the San Francisco headquarters of First Republic Bank—which had financed Love's purchase of the building—holding signs that said things like "Hold Banks Accountable" and "First Republic Finances Serial Evictors."

Protests could make flips more expensive, but not nearly by enough. The demand for housing was there, so banks and investors were lining up behind it. In the presentation it laid out to prospective investors, Trion estimated that once it raised the Buckingham building's rents by 40 percent and charged tenants more for utilities and trash pickup, it could sell the $15 million property for $22 million. Given the financial reality, the only real solution for tenants would be for someone to do what community land trusts had been doing for decades, which was to get the properties off the market.

SISTER CHRISTINA HAD always let it be known that when Trion was finally ready to flip the 180 Flats, she would still be an eager buyer. Her portfolio of former trap houses and small apartment buildings didn't

yield much cash, but as homeless camps multiplied and Bay Area housing costs spiraled into a political crisis, institutions and wealthy donors
were becoming much more generous and had vastly expanded the St.
Francis Center's buying power. Once the 180 Flats had gotten an exte-
rior paint job and the gray faux-wood floors and track lighting had been
installed, online rents for the studio, one-, and two-bedroom apartments were listed in the $2,000–$3,000 range. That was enough to rationalize a purchase price of $21,750,000, and in September 2018, the
St. Francis Center paid it. The price was steep but the apartments were
now back in community hands, and Sister Christina finally had the
building outside her window.

The deal was its own kind of math problem, and it pulled Sister
Christina ever deeper into the capital web. Private donors led by the
foundation of John Sobrato, a billionaire Silicon Valley developer, gave
$10 million. An arm of the Facebook-backed Catalyst Housing Fund
committed a $4 million loan. The San Mateo County Board of Super-
visors agreed to help pay down some of that debt with a second loan.
The balance came from a loan extended by First Republic Bank, the
same bank that had financed Jesshill Love's purchase of Sandy and
Stephanie's building, the same bank that had been named the Bay Area's No. 1 displacement financer by the California Reinvestment Coalition, the same bank that Daniel Saver, who sat among the crowd of
clapping people at the ceremony to celebrate the St. Francis Center's big
purchase, had picketed six months earlier. Saver had his own blurry alliances: the nonprofit he worked for had just gotten a big donation from
the Chan Zuckerberg Initiative.

Buckingham's new neon "180" address sign was still there during the
grand re-opening, but the name "180 Flats" had been replaced with a
black block-lettered sign that read "La Casa de Sobrato." It was a sunny
fall day, and the St. Francis Center's supporters sat in neat rows of metal
folding chairs to watch John Sobrato and people from Facebook's community relations team participate in the big ribbon cutting. The street
was lined with foreign-model sedans and a Tesla Model 3. There were

two sheriffs' SUVs nearby. They weren't there to carry out any evictions but rather to block the intersection for the big party.

Aside from the new name, the building looked the same as it did under Trion. Same raw-lumber fence, same drought-resistant landscaping, same black-and-white paint job accented by pops of neon orange around a few windowsills. The fake cacti in the entryway had been removed, and that afternoon, during the reception, the faint sound of guitar-heavy Latin music passed through the glass front door, which was propped open by a rock.

Outside there was small talk and the smell of *al pastor* on a grill. Trion had installed wooden outdoor seating and a gray-and-white geometric rug and succulents in terra-cotta pots that looked as if they had been transported fully assembled from a display at the Ikea down the freeway. But now there were Sheriff's deputies sitting on the benches eating tacos. Sister Christina was nearby in a knee-length brocade jacket mingling with board members. After the party, Coach Rafael led clean-up with a group of kids in burgundy-and-white Holy Family uniforms who shrieked with kid enthusiasm as they carted folding chairs and other communal resources back to the Siena Center.

Once it had acquired the former Buckingham Apartments, the St. Francis Center owned 135 rental units in eleven buildings. The plan was to add Buckingham to its portfolio of deed-restricted housing for low-income renters, but Sister Christina had also made a vow never to evict anyone, and that included Trion's new higher-rent tenants. It was the moral thing to do, and morality, like everything, had a price. Were they to immediately reverse Trion's business plan and to clear the building of higher-income renters and fill it back up with lower-income ones, the St. Francis Center would get access to about $250,000 in annual property tax breaks for buildings where at least 90 percent of the tenants were low-income. By refusing to evict new tenants, the center estimated it would take about four years of attrition to reach that 90 percent threshold. In the interm it would have to spend an extra $1 million in taxes—money that could be going to other low-income buildings, and now wouldn't. This is what Sister Christina meant about the moral mortgage.

Early the next year, Trion sent out its 2018 investor letter. About halfway down the letter, after a discussion of the housing market and the "light value-add business plan" it had for a new property outside Portland, the company talked about two buildings it had profitably sold, one of which was the 180 Flats. It "delivered a project-level IRR of 18.02%," Trion said, leaving out the bit about two years of protests and a social justice-minded nun being the purchaser. Trion also told investors that on account of rising building prices, it had started buying raw land entitled for development: "We determined that although the development pipeline is robust, there remains strong demand for multifamily housing in California, and given the state's draconian and primitive land-use policies, oversupply seems nowhere in sight."

CHAPTER 9

SONJA FOR SUPERVISOR

THE 2017 HOUSING package had been a victory of incremental compromise. It was a real step, but a small step, and a small step wasn't enough to solve a decades-old housing crisis. It wasn't even enough to keep the crisis from getting worse. The best you could say about what the legislature had accomplished was that they had shown the public and themselves that the appetite for action was there, and that there was probably appetite for more.

The next year would be dedicated to finding out how much more. Scott Wiener would introduce a bill to essentially rezone California. There would be a statewide ballot measure to radically expand local rent control laws. San Francisco homeless advocates would push a big new tax on companies with more than $50 million in annual revenue to build more supportive and affordable housing. All the while Gavin Newsom, the ex-mayor of San Francisco, would cakewalk his way to replacing Jerry Brown as governor and campaign on a promise to more than triple the state's pace of homebuilding. Incrementalism was out, big ideas were in, and it was during this new and more extreme moment that Sonja Trauss, the original YIMBY, started running for a seat on the San Francisco Board of Supervisors.

Life comes at you fast. That was one of Sonja's stock phrases in the months after the housing package passed. She was cresting the arc of her thirties and had acquired a ring on her finger (Scott Wiener had married her to her husband, Ethan, earlier that year) and a bump in her belly (she was due in November). Were she to also win her election, she would have in the space of four years gone from a struggling math teacher delivering economics lectures at the public comment microphone to a new mom and San Francisco supervisor. It was a lot of work and a lot to process. Sonja tried to be blasé about it. *Why shouldn't I produce in two venues?* was her reply to people who suggested that campaigning for office with a newborn might be difficult. *That's what they say* . . . was what she said to the many people who thought it was clever to tell her that a new baby would make for a nice political prop.

There was a lot of sameness in running for office. Fund-raisers had red and white wine and some sort of cheese/fruit/meat plate. Sonja began her meet and greets by saying how happy she was to be wherever she was, then transitioning into a biographical spiel about how she was a math teacher who got into housing politics, was now running for supervisor, and was full of ideas and optimism for how the city could be better. Cue an hour of questions. Housing. Parking. Transit. Bike lanes. Homelessness. Petty crime. Crosswalks. She had answers for all of them, although at the beginning, when the baby was pushing on her diaphragm, the answers were physically difficult and she ended the Q&As with a red face and gasping.

The tension of those early events would be the tension of the campaign, which was that Sonja was now the symbol of a big national issue yet was vying to represent a small, local district. She'd moved from Oakland to San Francisco nine months before declaring her candidacy, and whatever name recognition she had was based purely on the press she'd received as a housing activist. She got endorsements from Scott Wiener and

David Chiu and hired a consultant who lent her a few blazers and told her to start wearing makeup and asked her to cut her hair (which she refused to do). Sonja learned how to say "no comment" in interviews, and descriptors like "caustic" and "divisive" became pitches like "passionate" and "a person who tells it like it is." But even as she started looking like a candidate and sounding like a candidate, when she sat in voters' apartments or did after-work chats at offices, there was usually one question about what she stood for other than housing, and another about how she'd go from being a bomb-throwing activist to a politician in the system.

People were suspicious that she was running to promote a platform instead of running to help the district, because the district needed help. Sonja was running to represent District Six, which was the unofficial repository of San Francisco's biggest problems and a symbol of the third-world-grade inequality the American economy had become. On one side was the Tenderloin, a neighborhood that had the country's largest concentration of single-room occupancy hotels and was the site of open-air heroin use and blocks of people with tattered clothes and shredded shoes sleeping on sidewalks smeared with human shit and orange needle caps. On the other side was South of Market, which had towering glass condos and the headquarters of Salesforce and Airbnb. It took about ten minutes to walk between those scenes.

Eight weeks after delivering a boy named Anton Kazimir, Sonja emerged from her $3,000-a-month one-bedroom in a black dress and plaid wool coat pushing a stroller on her way to her official campaign kickoff. Nearby, a very strung-out man who appeared to have slept in the alley was completing a battle with a kiddie vacuum cleaner that he'd found on a doorstep and smashed on the ground until the orbs of colored plastic were rolling across the asphalt. After a short walk past scenes of wealth and misery, she arrived at a community auditorium that was full of smiles and cheers. The fifty-or-so-person crowd was a mix of family and friends and YIMBYs. Scott Wiener was there. So was Jeremy Stoppelman. And also her dad's cousin Myrna, the reason Sonja had moved to California in the first place.

Taking a page from the "make strength from a weakness" theory of campaigning, Laura kicked everything off by talking about the virtues of being obnoxious and not caring if people disagreed with you and thought your style was rude. Sonja walked onstage with a speech hand-written on sheets of notebook paper and asked the room to join her in singing the theme from *San Francisco*. She emphasized the second verse, which, she explained, was a metaphor for the campaign:

> *San Francisco, open your Golden Gate*
> *You'll let no stranger wait outside your door.*

MOST PEOPLE DON'T pay attention to local politics, and the few who do don't tune in until a month or two before Election Day. Sonja's kick-off was in January, ten months out and early enough that the full field of candidates hadn't even been established yet. So once the event was over and everyone had taken their pictures, the collective focus of the housing world shifted back to Sacramento, where Scott Wiener had seized the attention by introducing yet another big housing bill.

This one was called SB 827, and it was a proposal to allow developers to build four- to eight-story apartment buildings within half a mile of California rail stations and a quarter mile of high-frequency bus stops, regardless of what local rules said about height and density. Wiener could be competitive about legislation and would often tell his staff they needed to introduce X or Y big bill before someone else did it first. SB 827 was a bid to jump way ahead of the conversation with what amounted to a wholesale rezoning of all the major metro areas of the nation's largest state. If it read like a YIMBY bill, that's because it was. With the success of the previous year's housing package, Brian Hanlon had started a new statewide lobbying group called California YIMBY, and presented SB827 to Wiener as the organization's first bill.

Wiener framed 827 as a climate change bill on the logic that it would reduce sprawl, which made sense but also represented a huge political test. There was no question that people who lived in denser communities and took public transit had a much smaller carbon footprint than people who drove everywhere in a car, and that if the world was ever going to slow the pace of rising temperatures, then a vast urban and suburban retrofit would have to be part of the program. That was why pretty much every environmental group had some version of "build compact communities along transit lines" among their bullet-point list of green policy proposals.

This didn't make the politics any easier, however, because unlike solar panels or electric cars, which do not fundamentally change how cities operate or what neighborhoods look and feel like, 827 was asking for a degree of sacrifice that even liberal-minded Californians, whose state was proudly leading the nation on things like conservation and renewable energy, were unwilling to embrace. This was a well-known glitch in climate politics. Various polls and California's own experience showed that voters were willing to support climate action only to the degree that "these initiatives do not demand a significant alteration of lifestyle," according to one survey.

People who politely hated 827 referred to it as "heavy handed." Some other phrases were "insanity," "hydrogen bomb," and "an undemocratic power grab" that would make neighborhoods of bungalows "look like Dubai." The mayor of Berkeley called it "a declaration of war against our neighborhoods" while an anti-gentrification protester compared it to the Trail of Tears. Wiener often referred to crises as opportunities. Droughts were an opportunity to build new filtration systems and mandate conservation measures that would drive down long-run water usage. Fires were an opportunity to talk about climate change actions that the state should have always been talking about. And the housing crisis was an opportunity to start thinking about how America was going to undo half a century of sprawled development patterns whose environmental and infrastructure costs were becoming unsustainable. Wiener's feeling was a big bill would ignite debate, and 827 certainly did that, if not in the way he'd intended.

He'd done no more than introduce the legislation when it became a campaign issue in the midyear primaries. Across the Bay Area, local debates frequently featured a version of "Do you support SB 827?" and the bill became a focal point in an unplanned mayoral election in San Francisco. Late the year before, Ed Lee, San Francisco's mayor, had collapsed and died of a heart attack in a grocery store. This led to an immediate three-way race between a former state senator named Mark Leno along with London Breed, the president of the board of supervisors, and Jane Kim, who was months away from being termed out of her own supervisor seat.

Breed became something of a YIMBY hero by becoming the only candidate to support the measure, while Kim all but framed her candidacy as a referendum on the bill, staging an anti-827 rally on the city's low-density West Side and running commercials that said the legislation "would allow unlimited luxury condo high-rises." Wiener's greatest successes had been marked by neatly crafted legislation, like the affordable housing permit streamlining in San Francisco or the money/streamlining compromise at the center of SB 35, that cleaved the imperfect alliance of archetypal NIMBYs worried about views and anti-gentrification activists worried about displacement. But there was nothing careful about 827, which was designed to be a headline grabber and only brought his opponents closer.

Two of the bill's fiercest critics were a Beverly Hills city councilman named John Mirisch and a South LA anti-gentrification activist named Damien Goodmon. Mirisch described 827 as "the urban planning love-child of Vladimir Putin and the Koch Bros." Goodmon called it war and referred to YIMBYs as colonizers. It was a common view among YIMBYs that NIMBYs from rich cities used the auspice of social justice to defend policies that kept wealthy neighborhoods low density and exclusive, and there seemed to be no better example of this than the curious alliance of Beverly Hills and South LA. This view was superficially fair but also made perilous assumptions about who was using whom.

Damien Goodmon ran a small nonprofit called the Crenshaw Subway Coalition that was based in Leimert Park, a historically black neighborhood that held a special and symbolic place in LA history. In the years after World War II, most of the city's African American families were sequestered into crowded and dilapidated housing in South Central and Watts, prompting white people from the east coast to remark that Watts looked like a village version of Harlem. Which was the point: Black people who moved to Southern California after the war didn't want to live in Harlem. They'd gone west in search of the same vision of spacious homes and yard space as white people had, but instead got crammed into neighborhoods that, in the case of Watts, were as much as three times as crowded as greater LA.

In the 1950s, that started to change, gradually, as African American homebuyers, with help from a growing community of black real estate agents, black mortgage lenders, and black-owned financial institutions like the Golden State Mutual Life Insurance Company, began to filter into nearby neighborhoods like West Adams and Leimert Park, which sat on the very western edge of South Central. There they found better housing, better schools, and a piece of the Southern California dream that had to that point been denied. Three-quarters of a century later, a typical Sunday for Goodmon was to throw on some shorts and walk from his apartment through the local retail strip, past Jamaican restaurants and a jazz museum, to Leimert Plaza Park, which on weekends filled up with drum circles and pop-up merchants selling African jewelry and natural remedies and paintings of Thurgood Marshall. This was where you found suit-wearing men from the Nation of Islam distributing copies of the *Final Call*. It was the place where neighbors gathered to mourn black men killed by police.

The arc of gentrification in black neighborhoods often goes something like this: Lovely and solidly built former white neighborhood becomes a lovely and solidly built largely black neighborhood until the necessity of rising housing costs prompts young white homebuyers to return to blocks that racism had caused previous generations of white people to abandon. South Los Angeles was starving for investment after the 1992 riots (rebellion) that followed the acquittal of four police officers who'd been filmed beating, kicking, and clubbing a motorist named Rodney King, and the boulevards leading to Leimert Park were speckled with the abandoned storefronts and liquor stores and check cashers that follow disinvestment.

Once you got off the main roads, however, you found the same quaint streets of bungalows and small apartment buildings that 1950s African Americans had left Watts for, and financial capital was returning in the form of new shops, new restaurants, and a new subway stop for LA's expanding rail system. Goodmon's group fought for the subway stop, and he was plenty eager for new amenities—so long as Leimert Park could remain a center of black culture, which didn't seem likely after home values doubled to a little under $800,000 after the Great Recession while the median household income stayed stuck around $40,000. When the city started remodeling Leimert Plaza Park as part of a beautification project tied to the new subway line, he interpreted it as an attempt to make the area more palatable to incoming white homebuyers by discouraging the revolutionary culture that had long defined it.

It was an inescapable fact of economics that something like SB 827 would have to happen if California was going to tame its housing crunch and regain even a modicum of affordability, and it was a little-talked-about detail that the bill would have made it drastically easier to build the affordable housing that every constituency claimed to want (some more honestly than others). Scarcity helped no one, and if housing scarcity persisted, it would lead to more gentrification, not less. Scott Wiener was right about that. The politics were in where and how the scarcity got filled in, and who had a hand in leading it. At least in its initial drafting, SB 827 put the onus of new development on places like Leimert Park and gave them essentially no say in how it went. According to one analysis from researchers at UC Berkeley, most of the transit-rich areas that would be affected by the bill were already gentrifying or at risk of being gentrified soon, and low-income neighborhoods would see about two-thirds of the potential demolition of existing housing, meaning the housing that was most likely to be affordable and rent-controlled.

This wasn't by nefarious design, but a combination of green logic (build near existing transit) and a reflection of what sorts of neighborhoods buses and train tracks have historically run through. Nevertheless, the bill's pitch basically consisted of a stack of economics papers and the words "trust me," to which Damien Goodmon had answered: Why should I? Trust required believing that this new pitch wouldn't be the same old story, like the 1960s redevelopment program that had begun with promises of new and improved affordable housing that existing residents could move into, or the Reagan-era pitch of better government and widespread prosperity from de-regulation and lower taxes.

In the argue space of Twitter, Goodmon veered from statements of pure rage to playfully antagonistic GIFs. In person in Leimert Park, he was a dreamy and optimistic organizer who espoused a sort of socialist utopianism where you had neighborhoods full of Sister Christina–style land trusts and cooperatives and local work requirements and government programs to allow tenants to buy their own apartments—"a real shared economy, not the screwed-up definition of shared economy where your apartment is now a hotel and your car is now a taxi." Civil Rights icons like William Byron Rumford had fought for equal opportunity to a capitalist system that they still basically believed in. Damien Goodmon did not believe capitalism was capable of being equal opportunity, so instead of fighting for access to the suburbs, he was fighting, in essence, to keep the suburbs out.

In this sense, exclusionary zoning, whatever its racial history, was seen as protection against what people were now calling "exclusionary displacement." Land-use rules were one of the few tools gentrifying neighborhoods had to assert some semblance of control over capital that came from outside city and even national borders. It was a way to have a say in a system that allowed for little say. Goodmon wasn't just going to hand that off to Sacramento the way neighborhoods had during redevelopment, and he was adept at making strategic alliances, even with Beverly Hills, to help keep it.

Two weeks before SB 827 faced its first senate committee vote to advance or kill the bill, the San Francisco Board of Supervisors had a vote on whether the board would support it. Everyone knew the board would vote no so YIMBYs decided to go to city hall to protest the press conference. That morning, before the rally, Sonja, Laura, and others made pro-827 signs that had images of tall buildings next to short buildings. The anti-827 protesters had similar signs, but whereas theirs portrayed apartments next to houses as a monstrosity, the YIMBY versions said things like "More Please" and "Go Big or I Can't Go Home."

Laura walked to the city hall rally holding one of her big-apartment-next-to-a-small-house signs and got there expecting to see members of predominantly white single-family-house neighborhood groups, and indeed many such groups were there to protest. But the no side also had various tenant and neighborhood groups whose members were largely black, Latino, and low-income Chinese, and they made roughly the same arguments as Damien Goodmon as they spoke from a podium at the city hall steps. The YIMBY protest crew stood below on the sidewalk shouting over their speeches and chanting "Read the bill!" People on the other side yelled "Shame!" Sonja waded into the opposing crowd and waved her protest sign, then was escorted away by a sheriff's deputy. All of this was heavily denounced and documented on Twitter and would haunt Sonja throughout her run for office.

Wiener tried to reconcile concerns that the bill would accelerate gentrification by amending 827 with tenant protections and anti-demolition measures, but by then it was too late. He walked into that first committee hearing knowing his bill was going down. Goodmon was in the hearing room holding a sign that said "Wiener's Upzone Is an Uproot of People of Color." John Mirisch from Beverly Hills was nearby, ready to speak against it. It's hard to succeed in Sacramento if you don't have the support of LA. A four-hundred-mile concrete river flowed down the center of the state in testament to this fact. Imminent loss notwithstanding, Wiener gave a dutiful presentation about how the status quo wasn't working and in a nod to anti-gentrification groups noted that Richard Rothstein, the author of a book on segregationist housing policies called *The Color of Law*, had signed a letter endorsing SB 827. During the debate, Wiener's colleagues talked about the dire housing crisis and how it required bold action and told Wiener how much they "appreciated" him for having the guts to push the debate. Then they killed his bill.

After the committee voted, Brian Hanlon walked over to one of the bill's Sacramento opponents and said maybe they could work together next year. In his mind he'd already won. California YIMBY was all of a few months old, and in that time the organization had sponsored its first bill, gotten Scott Wiener to introduce it, generated five hundred news articles, and reset the housing conversation in California, all before a single vote. New donations were flowing in and Brian had moved to Sacramento and now wore ties to work at the capitol. Two weeks after 827 was killed, Stripe, an online payments start-up then valued at $9 billion, made its first-ever corporate donation in the form of a $1 million check to California YIMBY.

The timing was no coincidence and telegraphed to the broader political world that Silicon Valley was starting to more forcefully insert itself into housing fights. The donation also hardened the perception that California YIMBY—whose views on housing aligned with the views of major tech companies and their associated philanthropic arms like the Chan Zuckerberg Initiative—was now a wholly owned subsidiary of big tech. And these suspicions were generally fair. The YIMBY movement had proven that it was possible for a determined group of people to force a change in the political priorities, but no constituency could deny the unbreakable rules about politics requiring money.

BY SUMMER THE campaign season was officially underway. Voters weren't really paying attention, but candidates were at least trying to get them to. Sonja's calendar was stacked with fundraisers, endorsement interviews, and weeknight and weekend canvassing. There were Sonja for Supervisor bike rides and Sonja for Supervisor bar crawls. Visits to police stations, firehouses, and marijuana dispensaries. Meetings with teachers, construction unions, and Realtors. Speeches to local political clubs like the League of Conservation Voters, SF Young Democrats, the Alice B. Toklas LGBTQ Democratic Club, the Brownie Mary Democratic Club, and the Sex Positive Democratic Club. The joke that Sonja's baby could be a campaign prop ended up not being a joke. She canvassed with Anton in a baby carrier and once during an afternoon visibility trip had to attend to the small emergency of him eating part of a campaign flyer. Sonja breastfed before, during, and after events. She worked lines about new motherhood into her plans for clean sidewalks and safer streets. "In a year and a half, he's going to be walking," she said at one fundraiser. "I need to feel like he's not going to pick up needles or pick up poop or run into a four-lane street with people going 45 miles per hour."

The reps paid off in the form of bigger smiles, fewer "ums," and a newfound capacity to talk glowingly about herself. Activist Sonja made self-deprecating jokes about how she was a crazy person who stumbled into the right issue at the right time. Candidate Sonja was a visionary leader who had birthed one of the biggest political movements in San Francisco. Activist Sonja sued the suburbs. Candidate Sonja was the executive director of a nonprofit that enforced housing law. Suddenly there she was wearing a black dress and pearl earrings in the living room of a Nob Hill penthouse laying out her plans for more housing and bike lanes to a room full of women in furs and men in sport jackets.

District Six was a strange platform for a housing activist. In addition to having the city's worst homeless problem, the district had most of the tall buildings and new apartments. This was on account of two decades of redevelopment that had turned San Francisco's industrial quarter into a bloom of new high-density neighborhoods near the waterfront. Sonja's big promise to voters was that *when* she got elected supervisor (candidate Sonja had to learn to say "when she got elected" instead of "if she got elected"), she would force other districts to take on more of the new housing burden, which made her sound like a NIMBY.

Far from the libertarian shill of her reputation, most of Sonja's plans sounded straight-up socialist. One of her pitches was to build homeless shelters on top of parking garages and empower city departments to develop their own land and office space into mixed-use housing projects that would create a new supply of social and affordable housing as well as a new source of revenue that didn't require taxes. It was a practical and financially sound idea that in Europe was being touted by economists and world leaders, and which people in San Francisco regarded as impossible bordering on batty when it came in outsider packaging.

Her other big idea was to introduce legislation to open up more of the city to subsidized affordable housing. It was a little-known fact that San Francisco, for all its liberal good intentions, prohibited affordable housing in most of the city. This was a feature of the old east side/west side land pact that Sonja was now running to blow up. "There's not enough affordable housing, because you can only build affordable housing in 20 percent of the city," she told the crowd at a soup kitchen one afternoon. "In the rest of the city, you can only build single-family houses or duplexes. Affordable housing developers are completely cut off from the rest of the city. It's not fair! It's not fair, because we don't have as much affordable housing as we would otherwise have and because it shuts people out of neighborhoods they might want to live in."

WHEN SHE STARTED campaigning, the District Six race was Sonja, now an official San Francisco moderate, versus a school board member named Matt Haney. Haney was technically aligned with the progressive faction but had done plenty of outreach to mod-leaning tech employees and was clearly in pursuit of a long political career, so he did not present as a cartoon ideologue the way many of the more locally minded progs did. During fundraisers, Sonja described Haney as a "greeting card candidate," which was fair. In addition to being a Stanford Law graduate who had worked on the Obama campaign, he was tall, looked like Tom Brady, and had a manicured Instagram account that featured pictures of him with babies, dogs, old ladies, union members, and bicyclists, pictures of him speaking at rallies with rolled-up sleeves, pictures of him looking pensively over the San Francisco Bay at dusk. Haney was also a really nice guy that people naturally wanted to vote for, and he'd fortified those built-in advantages with a stack of endorsements from important unions, tenant organizations, political clubs, and big-name Democrats like Senator Kamala Harris and soon-to-be governor Gavin Newsom. It was just assumed that he would win.

Then an awkward third candidate entered the race: Christine Johnson, a former planning commission member who had long been making the same pro-housing arguments that had propelled Sonja's candidacy. Johnson was an awkward addition because she was so YIMBY friendly that two years earlier Sonja and Laura had encouraged her to run. When she demurred, Sonja ran instead. Then Johnson had a change of heart, and now here they were competing. Temperamentally, the differences were as bright as could be. Johnson had an engineering background and had worked as a financial analyst, and she hewed to the math-nerd-turned-policy-wonk stereotype by laying out detailed proposals and speaking with encyclopedic knowledge of the San Francisco planning code. She also grew up in New York City and had eight addresses before she was eighteen, so had a story of housing insecurity and during the campaign talked about her belief that if San Francisco built more, it wouldn't just help maintain the diverse population already there but could attract a more diverse group of migrants, including African American families like hers.

This made Johnson something of a housing bridge: She knew the burden of rising rents on working-class families yet was also an economics-minded professional who was as versed as anyone in the supply problem and had also lived the frustration of moving to a new place for a good job then struggling to afford a home and raise a family there. Nevertheless, you had two young women, both new moms, both running as mods, both with backgrounds in housing, both talking about the need to build lots more of it, and both lacking the union support and establishment backing that had blessed Matt Haney.

Similar candidates are normally a problem, because similar candidates split the vote. In San Francisco, similarities were an opportunity because of something called ranked-choice voting. Instead of voting for a single candidate, local voters rank their top three choices. If one of them gets a majority, he or she wins. But when no one gets a majority, which happens often, the city performs an instant runoff in which the candidate with the fewest first-place votes is eliminated and his or her second- and third-choice votes are redistributed to the other candidates until someone gets a majority. That means the second-place candidate can win the race if he or she collects more of the third-place candidate's votes than the first-place candidate did. This encourages the underdogs to run joint campaigns designed to topple the alpha candidate, which is eventually what Sonja and Christine Johnson did. There were joint rallies and joint appearances, and an independent expenditure committee backed by tech donors sprung up to sell voters on a one/two Sonja and Christine ticket. The two also got a joint endorsement from now-mayor London Breed.

"People talk about building more housing, but when the decision comes down the pipeline and a small group of advocates protest moving housing forward in their backyard, these candidates say 'yes' time and time again," Breed said in her Christine/Sonja endorsement speech. "And I get that people love their communities. I love my neighborhood too. But I grew up in the Western Addition. I saw my friends leave San Francisco. I saw the significant decline of the African American population. I lived in it. I saw the mistakes of redevelopment and other things that happened to unfortunately destroy neighborhoods and communities. And the only way that we're going to build a better San Francisco is if we make the hard decision to build. More. Housing. All. Over. Our. City."

Breed grew up in public housing and still lived in a rent-controlled apartment as mayor, so her full-throated support for the YIMBY message had, depending on one's perspective, either clouded or given political cover to the YIMBYs-are-agents-of-gentrification narrative. It at least showed how hard it was to reduce a brutally complicated issue to an easy, lazy story about hordes of incoming techies and their victims. The story of District Six was the story of a diverse and unequal place that was trying to make a broken system work. It was the story of California, America, the world. The person who could unite the voters was the person who could accomplish the impossible task of figuring out how to allow more people to benefit from the vast wealth being created by the tech industry while dealing with the collateral damage of punishing rents, putrid streets, and the growing humanitarian crisis of homelessness that commuters walked by daily as if it were completely normal.

Race was the backdrop, the history, of the housing and inequality story. But there were now so many generational, migratory, and economic crosscurrents, so much actual diversity, that it had become all but impossible to make it fit inside a strict identity politics framework, not that that kept either side from trying when it seemed convenient. You had immigrants who were janitors and struggled to pay rent and immigrants who were engineers and bought new condos. Poor renters who displaced poor renters and wealthy homeowners who complained about gentrification. The alliance of wealthy white homeowners who wanted to preserve exclusionary zoning and poorer black and Latino neighborhood activists who wanted to prevent exclusionary displacement. As Jerry Brown would say: plenty of paradox, plenty of complexity.

To watch San Francisco politics is to watch a pair of twins argue passionately about which is better looking and has superior DNA. Over the course of three friendly debates, the District Six candidates traded phrases like "I agree" and "Picking up on that." Aside from a few comments by Matt Haney that he wouldn't get into ideological fights on Twitter or shout people down from the city hall steps, there was never a real punch. Everyone was for affordable housing and better transit. Everyone had an idea for regulating Ubers and scooters. Everyone said they wished San Francisco politics weren't so petty and factionalized.

Elsewhere in the election, the most contentious issue on the ballot was Proposition C, which was the name of the new tax on firms with more than $50 million in annual revenue to support homeless housing and services—a proposal that, were it to pass, would be the largest tax increase in city history and raise about $300 million a year. And yet even though the local Chamber of Commerce was predictably arguing no, the measure's biggest backer was Marc Benioff—the billionaire founder of Salesforce, which was the city's largest private employer—and everyone in the District Six race was for it.

There was some differentiating personality stuff. Matt Haney framed himself as the stick-to-the-basics localist who would focus on the district and the district only ("I'm a doer, not a talker"). Christine Johnson was the brain who knew everything about policy so could be trusted to find the way ("I'm running because we have a real opportunity to work with our budget, to change our codes, to actually change our experience on the streets"). Sonja asked voters to believe that if they wanted a different sort of direction they'd have to vote for a different sort of candidate ("This district needs an activist"). The real competition seemed to be who could act more shocked at the scale of the homeless problem and how dystopian District Six streets had become, so most of the exchanges consisted of quotes like "I see everyday people walking around in their hospital clothes," and "Safe injection sites are really exciting," and "There are needles on the street, poop on the street, and cars getting broken into" and "We have to ask ourselves, 'Why is it this bad? How did things get this bad?'"

After the first debate, a dozen or so Sonja supporters collected on barstools to rehash the previous hour of politics and talk about how

Christine and Sonja's wonk represented a gleaming example of two women forcing a real conversation full of specific and detailed proposals that cut a stark contrast from Matt Haney and his milquetoast *I'm for more housing so long as it's affordable* positions. They also made fun of Haney for his "doer not a talker" line and having the temerity to open the debate with an anecdote about his grandfather being a "close confidant" of Martin Luther King Jr.

A political scientist might have interjected with some harsh facts about how voters don't really care about the ins and outs of policy and that elections are won with vague pronouncements about shared values and compelling personal stories that are irrelevant to the job of governing and also get votes, but that voice wasn't present so the group continued to talk about their favorite moments and feel good about Sonja's performance and chances.

Later, Laura noticed Matt Haney and his crew sitting at a table across the bar. She waved and bought them a round of drinks. Haney and his crew waved back and bought a round for the rival table in return.

CHAPTER 10

THE RENT IS TOO DAMN HIGH

ONCE SCOTT WIENER'S up-zoning bill was dead, Damien Goodmon turned his attention to passing a statewide rent control initiative. That measure was called Proposition 10, and it was so confusing that it's already weak prospects—rent control proposals rarely went far in state politics, and landlords planned to bury this one with money—were further weakened by the fact that many voters couldn't understand what voting yes or no meant. Voting yes on Proposition 10 meant voting yes to repeal a state law that prohibited certain forms of local rent control, but didn't add anyone to rent control, just allowed cities the option to do so. So: Vote yes to vote no, so that city legislators may vote yes, or no, on some theoretical future rent control proposal, assuming that proposal is ever introduced (which it probably won't be). It was still a huge moment. That renter groups were even in a position to goad landlords into outspending them said much about how far the tenants' rights movement had ascended in just a few years.

Across the state and country, tenants were forming unions, coordinating rent strikes, and descending on statehouses to protest that the rent was too damn high. In California, a handful of local groups had gotten rent control initiatives on the ballot in half a dozen Bay Area cities, and this had started to create the beginnings of a slightly more organized network of volunteers, nonprofits, churches, unions, and eviction lawyers like Daniel Saver, who in his crusade to prevent the displacement of people like Sandy and Stephanie had become a de facto legal consultant to ballot drives around the state. Nannies were going door-to-door after work with clipboards to collect signatures. Secretaries were sitting at fold-out tables handing out voter pamphlets and swapping stories ("mine went from $3,400 to $4,600"). Unions were giving organizing classes and using voter registration software to target renter-sympathizing neighborhoods.

Most of the early measures lost and were countered with millions of dollars in countercampaigning by the California Apartment Association, but a handful had won, including a rent control measure in Google's hometown of Mountain View, and more would be coming. By 2018, tenants were gathering signatures in Sacramento, Santa Rosa, Santa Cruz, Pasadena, Glendale, Inglewood, Long Beach, Santa Ana, Pomona, National City, and San Diego. Those cities had a total of 3,614,386 people, or about 9 percent of the state population. The California Apartment Association responded by organizing whack-a-mole-style rent control repeal drives and sending out internal warning letters emblazoned with cartoon "Wanted" signs that implored its members to quit with the "aggressive" rent increases of more than 10 percent, lest they make the renter backlash even stronger.

Given how much tenant anger there was, landlords were expecting some sort of state rent control fight, but they did not expect anything as big as Proposition 10. That's because statehouses were where landlords ruled. State legislators are inevitably more conservative than city council people, which, combined with heavy lobbying from apartment owners, is why a healthy majority of states prohibit their cities from passing rent control entirely. California wasn't one of them, but it still had a law called the Costa-Hawkins Rental Housing Act that limited the scope of what sorts of rent laws cities could pass. Costa-Hawkins prevented cities from applying rent control to single-family houses and condominiums and any apartment built after 1995 (or whatever year the city passed its rent control ordinance, which in San Francisco was 1979). It also freed landlords from rent regulation whenever a tenant moved out, allowing them to raise the rent back to the market price.

Were Proposition 10 to somehow pass, tenants' groups would have accomplished the feat of moving the rent control fight back to the friendlier confines of cities, where they could push laws to bring newer apartments under rent control and expand regulations to condos, single-family-house rentals, and even vacant units. That ambition had its risks. A ballot run on Costa-Hawkins was the political equivalent of a ground assault on enemy headquarters. It could work. The moment could be just right. Still, the cost of failure was high enough that a number of local tenants' groups—still tiny organizations that were barely a step removed from building to building fights—were worried it could distract them from the steady progress they were making in cities, and inspire an onslaught of new spending from landlords' groups that would make future rent control battles even harder.

Which is just about what happened. When Proposition 10 qualified for the state ballot, California instantly became a national battlefront in a tenants' movement that was spreading around the country. Big investors and private equity firms like the Blackstone Group plowed tens of millions into the "no on 10" campaign to protect their single-family-house portfolios from being pulled into broader rent laws. The campaign was further seen as an opportunity for landlords to make it clear to other states that they would spend mightily to defeat anything even resembling rent regulation. Publicly traded apartment companies started using their conference calls to reassure investors that they were working against the Costa-Hawkins repeal, which they called "an existential threat to the industry." "We'll fight very hard at this level, and we will continue in every other place that talks about having rent control—we'll fight at that level as well," the head of Equity Residential in Chicago said at an investor conference that fall.

The backstory of how things had gotten that far that fast, of how Prop 10 made the ballot and the money behind it, was even more complicated than the measure. California voter initiatives are billed as a way to return politics to the people, and in the case of local rent control drives, where Democratic power was defined by angry tenants with clipboards, the billing was entirely accurate. Statewide initiatives are different because California is big and big elections are expensive. In 2018, getting an initiative on the statewide ballot required the signatures of 600,000 registered voters, which realistically meant a million to compensate for duplicates, nonregistered voters, and the various other names ("Beavis M. Butthead") that the state would deem ineligible.

You could do it like Howard Jarvis and spend a decade building buzz while assembling a volunteer army, but the faster method was to pay people to stand in public squares and outside supermarkets haranguing eligible voters to sign a petition. It cost single-digit millions to pay people to gather enough signatures for a statewide ballot drive, and tens of millions in advertising money to run an even semi-competent campaign. That's corporate money, not tenants' money, and in the case of Prop 10 it came from an odd source: a Los Angeles nonprofit called the AIDS Healthcare Foundation (AHF), which had partnered with a community organizing group called the Alliance of Californians for Community Empowerment, and hired Damien Goodmon to manage the campaign.

AHF is the country's largest nonprofit provider of HIV medical care and a corporation in all but name. In 2018, it had close to six thousand worldwide employees and was on pace to generate $2 billion a year in revenue by 2020. Most of that revenue came from a chain of nonprofit pharmacies that participate in a federal program called 340B. The point of 340B, which was set up by Congress in 1992, is to incentivize hospitals and other health-care organizations to treat poor and uninsured AIDS patients. It does this by requiring pharmaceutical companies to sell discounted drugs to health-care organizations that provide a significant amount of care to low-income patients, then allowing those providers to get reimbursed by government and private insurers at the drugs' full cost. The difference creates a revenue stream that health-care providers can tap to pay for services for underserved patients. But given how numerous and expensive HIV drugs are, the program makes AIDS patients a kind of nonprofit profit center by generating billions in "excess revenue"—nonprofit profits—that organizations are also free to spend on advocacy, including California ballot initiatives (which are technically nonpartisan, so don't run afoul of federal rules prohibiting nonprofits from engaging in political activity).

Armed with a growing pot of "excess revenue," AHF's president, Michael Weinstein, had become a prolific funder of wandering and quixotic ballot initiatives that aimed to lower drug prices and regulate pornographers, before turning his attention to real estate developers. Weinstein was a notorious character in LA. He was a sixty-six-year-old former Trotskyite from Brooklyn who had a history of radical politics and early in his career founded a gay-friendly Marxist organization called the Lavender and Red Union. Now he ran the largest AIDS nonprofit in the country, yet had become something of an outcast in the gay community because unlike public health researchers and pretty much every other AIDS activist, he had opposed pre-exposure prophylaxis (PrEP), a once-a-day pill that virtually eliminates the risk of contracting HIV. News articles described Weinstein as a "thug," a "bully," and "Satan." He described himself as "gum on your shoe" and had become a fixture in local media and state politics thanks to his go-for-the-jugular political tactics and a shock-driven safe-sex campaign that had plastered LA and other cities with billboards that said things like "SYPHILIS EXPLOSION" or had the image of a line of cocaine and a shot glass followed by: "You know why. Free HIV test."

In 2016, Weinstein funded and lost a state initiative that would have required condoms in pornography, and also funded, and also lost, another initiative that would have reduced the price that the State of California could pay for pharmaceuticals. During the condoms-in-porn campaign, AHF sent out mailers that basically implied that Scott Wiener, who came out against the measure and was already a target of Weinstein's after earlier opposing an AHF pharmacy in the Castro, was a pervert. The next year, when AHF funded a Los Angeles initiative called Measure S, which would have put a two-year moratorium on apartment and condo towers (including affordable housing), there was a new round of controversial mailers. Those were designed to look like eviction notices, alarming tenants who thought they were real and prompting the LA County Sheriff's Department to demand that AHF-funded organizations stop sending them.

Weinstein framed himself as a crusader against luxury development and greedy developers. He also had a long history of what many people would describe as textbook NIMBYism. In the 1990s, when he ran for a seat on the LA City Council, he'd sent out mailers decrying apartment buildings in neighborhoods that were "more suited for single-family homes." And as part of the Measure S campaign, AHF had founded a pretty explicitly anti-development organization called the Coalition to Preserve LA, and later partnered with an antidevelopment group called Livable California, whose founder lived in Marin County.

All of this put tenants' groups in a strange position. They'd been itching to slay Costa-Hawkins for decades, had watched repeal attempts fail in the legislature, and now had a chance to try the same thing at the ballot box. And yet, in meetings, at bars, and in anonymously sourced news articles (sourced anonymously because tenant organizers liked AHF's money too much to berate Weinstein on the record), they chafed at taking orders from a man they described as an "egotistical billionaire."* A number of organizers, particularly those in the Bay Area, were worried that Weinstein and AHF were starting to take over what was supposed to be a grassroots movement. They also had reservations

---

* It is an erroneous but commonly held view that Weinstein is a billionaire. His AHF salary is about $400,000, but the foundation's financial might gives him the power to spend like one in the political arena.

about being aligned with a guy that a good portion of the LGBT community would never forgive for his stance on PrEP.

Another complaint was how the money was being spent. AHF would go on to spend about $22 million on Proposition 10, and some organizers felt that if that money had instead been put toward local rent control campaigns, where landlords only spent tens to hundreds of thousands of dollars, it would have all but guaranteed a few wins. This might have given potentially hundreds of thousands of new tenants some degree of price protection. There was also a belief that a string of small victories would help galvanize the movement and create momentum that would be needed if they were ever going to make long-term progress. And yet, Costa-Hawkins. The old beast. The fight was here and they had to join it.

Whatever anyone thought about Weinstein, Proposition 10 was the most significant state housing initiative in years. In California, where anyone willing to spend enough money on signatures could get pretty much whatever they wanted on the ballot, a rich enough organization could always at least float a big idea. And now that it had been floated, YIMBY Action would have to decide whether or not they would endorse it.

Suddenly the answer meant something. YIMBY Action had swelled to more than two thousand members and now sat among the top handful of local political clubs in San Francisco. Laura had built a small machine of pro-housing volunteers and organizers and instituted a dues structure that brought in a few thousand dollars a month. This, combined with donations and events like the YIMBY gala, was enough to rent an office and hire an employee. The group's continued efforts on behalf of subsidized housing (and the fact that Laura had gotten so consumed by local politics that she was now on her way to being divorced and in a new relationship with an affordable housing developer named Sam Moss) had started to open up new lanes and new alliances. Local radicals and the Prog establishment didn't exactly like them, but they had at least started to accept that the YIMBY thing was building power and wasn't going away soon.

It was a consequence of that power that there was now a constant internal battle to define what YIMBY meant. The group started with a simple message: build lots of housing. It still meant that, but the world of politics came with questions about what kinds of housing and where, who their allies were, and what was and was not a good look. There were questions like whether it was worth it to speak in favor of luxury condo projects or if that was unnecessary and counterproductive. Some members wanted YIMBY Action to get involved in social justice issues like policing or advocating for a universal basic income. Others thought it should remain focused on housing. Even the narrow view came with lots of debates about government versus private building and the role of capitalism in land generally.

Victoria Fierce was a purple-haired trans software engineer who had started showing up at city meetings with Sonja in the earliest days of YIMBYism. Ever since, she had been trying to move the YIMBY mantra further left. The main group she belonged to, East Bay for Everyone, an Oakland-based YIMBY offshoot, endorsed Prop 10 and had made expanding rent control an explicit part of its platform. Victoria had been there at the original Boulder YIMBYtown trying to get people to talk about what role rent regulation could play in a national YIMBY platform. A year later she hosted a leftist roundtable at the second YIMBY-town in Oakland. Where YIMBY Action stood on Prop 10 meant a lot to her, and now there were a lot more Victorias: YIMBY Action had a whole sub-group called YIMBY Socialists made of people who were focused on affordable and public housing. They were the YIMBY opposite of another sub-group called YIMBY Market Urbanists, whose members were rooted in the free-market thinking espoused by economists like Ed Glaeser. And no issue split them, or the club, more than rent control.

When YIMBY Action members gathered at the office to discuss the 2018 endorsements, the pressure of how the Prop 10 vote would turn out, and what that vote would say about the direction of the club, hung heavy over the meeting. They'd already become enthusiastic backers of Proposition C, the big homeless tax. This had helped YIMBY Action tiptoe beyond its base of techie millennials and demonstrate something like independence because the Prop C endorsement ran counter to many of its funders and allies: Scott Wiener and London Breed both came out against it, while tech companies like Stripe, million-dollar funder of California YIMBY, had donated to the no campaign. Should the YIMBYs go hard for Prop C and also endorse Prop 10, it would put them pretty solidly in alignment with tenants' groups, who remained highly skeptical of the YIMBY message.

Some YIMBY Action members were urging a Prop 10 endorsement on the logic that even if you disagreed with the policy, the benefits of potential coalition building should outweigh them. Single-family-house neighborhoods dominated local politics—in the Bay Area, around the state, around the country—and they would continue to dominate local politics for the foreseeable future. The only way to challenge that in any sort of meaningful way, the only way to truly organize the unorganizable, would be to cleave the alliance of anti-gentrification groups and homeowners in such a way as to freeze out the true NIMBYs. Aligning with tenants' groups on rent control wouldn't be some righteous kumbaya moment, but it might at least help.

The three dozen or so people who came to the endorsement meeting (the club voted online so only a handful showed up at the IRL discussion) all knew that rent control was a special test. But they also weren't sure about Prop 10, which was a potentially radical measure and came with all the AHF baggage that even a number of tenants' groups were leery of. After packing into an oval of chairs arranged around a table of salty snacks and beer, the group spent two hours debating the city and state ballot—bonds for seawalls, higher marijuana taxes, and a proposal to change to daylight savings time—knowing that the real debate, the emotional debate, would be Proposition 10.

When finally the meeting's moderator began the rent control discussion, he allotted twice as much time for debate and reminded the room to "respect your fellow humans." Proposition 10 was by now well on its way to becoming one of the costlier initiative campaigns in California history. The total tab would run about $100 million (landlords accounted for about 80 percent of that), and there were many hours of talk radio and many pages of newspaper copy dedicated to hashing out the sober pros and cons. But here they would go through them again by having two people, one from YIMBY Socialists and another from YIMBY Market Urbanists, present the yes and no cases.

The logic behind rent control rests on what seems like a simple idea: If prices are going up too fast then the best way to solve that problem is to pass a law that forces businesses to stop raising them. Behind this thinking is an implied belief that high prices mostly just exploit people who can't pay them. But prices have a big and vastly underappreciated role in society, which is to tell us what sorts of things we need more of. At the highest level, that's what a market economy is: A system in which we allow supply and demand, as expressed by prices, to tell people what things should cost and by extension what sorts of jobs they should be doing. Before market economies this power largely fell to tradition (you did the work your family did) or a king (you did the work the king told you to do).

Markets aren't perfect, but they are mostly better than feudalism, which is why economists, even liberal ones, tend to look down on any policy that disrupts the message prices are trying to send. This is not to say economists oppose policies to tax the hell out of rich people and use the money to provide things like food, housing, education, medical care, and a dignified retirement to people whom the market has left out—lots of economists are in favor of all of those things—just that economists are in favor of using taxes, not price controls, to make those things affordable. And that's because they're worried price controls will turn society into one big Bay Area, which had become willfully deaf to home prices that were screaming: MAKE MORE OF THIS!

In the case of rent control, various studies, meaning pretty much all of them, show that cities with strict price caps end up with less rental housing and higher rental prices. According to the theory, developers build fewer rental buildings, especially fewer affordable ones, because there's no profit in it for them. And existing landlords exit the business by selling rental homes and apartments as owner-occupied housing. The proof that rent control prevents developers from building apartments is tenuous, largely because the few American cities with strict price caps don't apply them to newer buildings (something Prop 10 sought to undo).

But the proof that rent control prompts existing landlords to exit the business is all around. One of the more well-cited studies of rent control was by a team of Stanford economists that looked at apartments across San Francisco and concluded that rent caps had probably accelerated gentrification, by pushing investors to flip affordable apartments into high-priced condos and co-ops, a phenomenon that no one who has spent time walking around the Mission would refute. Anyone who has lived in San Francisco or New York could also verify economists' claim that rent control encourages people who are higher-income and even rich to park themselves in fixed-rate apartments long after they can afford to move out, and in the most egregious cases use their savings to buy second homes elsewhere.

What these studies don't tally or consider are the costs a society bears when people go homeless or a child gets so pulverized by the stress of displacement that her hair falls out in clumps and she misses a month of school. According to economic theory, flippers have almost no productive role in society other than "price signaling"—telling us what we need to make more of. The practical question for California was what if anything the government should do to protect the potential victims of displacement when local politics refused to listen to what prices were telling them, and even if they had listened had to contend with a forty-year supply hole that it would take decades to dig out of. The answer an economist would give you is that society should pass some broad-based tax and give lower-income people a voucher or credit to help them afford the rent, which is a great, humane, and already-proven idea that would cost a hundred-plus billion a year to work on the level it is needed, and unfortunately wasn't happening anytime soon. That left rent control, a tool that is blunt and highly imperfect, yet can also work: The same Stanford study that concluded rent control probably accelerated gentrification also found that it shielded people from displacement, and that the people who benefitted the most were disproportionately older, poorer, and non-white.

Inside the rent control discussion lies one of the most basic questions of society, which is what role the government should play in shielding people from rapid change. America has broadly decided that stable neighborhoods are so important that it is willing to vastly subsidize homeownership and create a market for fixed-rate mortgages so that the monthly cost of owning a home doesn't go up faster than people can adjust to it. In that sense, rent control is little more than a call for tenants to get something that homeowners already get (at huge government cost). The price of California housing had risen so far, so fast, that it was having natural disaster–grade consequences of displacement and homelessness. It was the all bad kinds of disruptive, and the idea that some sort of rent control was needed was broadly starting to win.

Even market-oriented housing researchers were now talking about a statewide anti-gouging law, rent control in all but name, that could end the careers of speculators whose business model was predicated on eviction and massive rent increases. The tough conversation in the YIMBY meeting mirrored the tough conversation in society, which is how you come up with a policy that stabilizes people who are being evicted *now* without pushing a policy that is so radical it makes the problem worse in the long term. Building more housing does nothing for renters being evicted today. Rent control does. Capping rent prices does nothing to solve the underlying problem of a housing shortage that is the root cause of displacement. Building housing does.

Proposition 10 did not chart a pathway here, but instead would hand vast new powers to cities so they could have more leeway to experiment with local tenant laws. The optimistic version of what would happen if it passed is that cities, freed from state rent control restrictions, would become laboratories of regulation and promptly get busy on all sorts of carefully thought out local policies to stem displacement. The pessimistic version of what would happen is that nothing would change in most places, since there was no reason to believe that the vast majority of California cities that didn't already have some minimal form of rent control would pass a stricter version once that was allowed, and that a handful of cities like San Francisco would pass draconian regulations that would shut down construction, inspire even more landlords to flip their rentals into condos, and make the housing situation that much worse. Everyone in the YIMBY meeting knew the vote was going to be divisive and that whatever that vote was it would cause one group or the other to question their role in the club.

"We're talking about the rights of long-term tenants to have stability in their homes and remain in the community that they helped to create," said a member of the YIMBY Socialists during a presentation on why they should endorse yes.

"We give a voice to people who aren't even here today, and this undermines our ability to protect those people," said a member of the YIMBY Market Urbanists during a presentation on why they should endorse no.

"I am for expanding rent control, especially statewide, especially to some places that don't have it, like for single-family homes that are owned by large landlords," Laura said during her presentation on why they should vote not to endorse one way or the other. "But what I think the repeal of Costa-Hawkins sets all of these communities up for is ten years, at least, of perpetually having arguments about the minutiae of rent control policies. San Francisco will descend into madness, where we spend ten years fighting with each other about very small pieces of rent control, pretending that we are arguing about our housing problem when in fact we are rearranging deck chairs on the *Titanic*."

Then, the debate.

"The no campaign on Prop 10 is going to spend like ten times more money than the yes campaign, which is predominately by tenant organizers who have been working on this issue as their pet project for decades, so I think that our voice could be a powerful one outside of that bubble that could lend more credence to this movement."

"I mostly agree with Laura's argument that no endorsement is the right answer for this organization. I think it's the right answer for this organization because I think we're going to be very split."

"It's incredibly challenging to get tenant protections through the legislature . . . We want rent control in our arsenal of policies that YIMBY can use—this is the way forward."

"I think it's important for all of us to vote how we feel about this one and not shy away from conflict."

In the end the yes and no votes were split, resulting in a no endorsement position and exposing an ideological rift that would eventually cause several of the group's more leftist members to leave.

YIMBY ACTION'S OFFICE was about twelve hundred square feet, or about the size of a small single-family home, and it sat between two marijuana dispensaries on Mission Street, a short walk from city hall. By the fall, the storefront windows were covered with blue "Yes on Prop C" signs and pink "Sonja for Supervisor" signs. Inside was an open-floor office/hangout center stuffed with couches, worktables, a photocopier, and a mini-fridge of beer. The space doubled as the CaRLA office and tripled as Sonja's campaign headquarters. The tables by the door had stacks of voter registration forms next to Sonja posters, Sonja flyers, Sonja buttons, Sonja stickers, and Sonja door hangers. Anton, a regular presence, was closing in on his first birthday and now learning to stand, so the office was also littered with toys and had a Jumperoo on the carpet.

On the last Tuesday in October, the whiteboard above the snack basket read "7 Days." That morning, Sonja came in looking like a mix of the old activist and the new candidate. She was wearing a skirt and a blazer over a black T-Shirt that said "Build Housing" in the jagged font of the metal band Slipknot. Shortly after wheeling her bike through the door, she told everyone who would listen that she didn't want a single flyer left over in the office and then began half dictating/half editing an email that one of her consultants was about to fire off to supporters. Everyone agreed that the subject line should be "There is no next time." Beyond that, it was consultants yet again trying to turn activist Sonja into candidate Sonja. "People thought I was too much of a nut to win," Sonja said to a typing consultant, who nodded and wrote something else completely. "I don't want to talk too much shit on the opponents, but why not?" she continued.

Laura jumped in on the editing.

"The *establishment* didn't believe in this campaign," she suggested.

"Yessssss," Sonja said.

Laura leaned over and sat with her elbows on her knees looking intensely at the computer screen. Sonja sat across the table, unable to see the email. As she continued dictating her thoughts to the typing consultant, she drew a picture of a man crying in pain while blood spewed out of his ear. It read "END THE SIREN." The day before, when she'd been out canvassing voters, Sonja had walked by a Tenderloin building that was armed with some sort of screeching machine that went off whenever someone neared the steps. This was to prevent people from sleeping on the stairs or hanging out on the stoop. The screeching annoyed Sonja and escalated into higher-level thoughts and complaints about how installing a piercing noisemaker outside of a building was a violation of the public's right to peacefully use a sidewalk.

And so, Sonja being Sonja, she'd decided right there, in the home stretch of campaigning, that she would start rallying people to end it. She was always and forever an activist. When she saw a problem that bugged her, she went after it totally. As the consultant put final touches on the campaign email, Sonja used markers, tape, and scissors to turn her drawing of the guy with the bloody ear into a DIY flyer that had wobbly block lettering and read: "I pledge to END THE SIREN that is plaguing your block. This loud, irritating sound is illegal and unacceptable. Vote for a candidate who knows your issues and cares to fix them. Sonja Trauss and Christine Johnson #2." Later she walked over to a Xerox machine and made a bunch of copies of the END THE SIREN flyers and left to hang out by the loud stoop, where she introduced herself to voters and tried to rally them around her latest cause.

Two days later, the *San Francisco Chronicle* ran a big Election Day curtain-raiser that had photos of Laura in the YIMBY offices and carried the headline "Housing, by Any Means Necessary." "This week, the YIMBYs' pro-housing revolution is facing perhaps its biggest test," the story said. "Its agenda is all over the Nov. 6 ballot. YIMBY-bred candidates are running for office in San Diego, Mountain View, Palo Alto, Oakland and other cities. YIMBY-supported measures will be voted on in dozens of cities across the state." There was no YIMBY without controversy, so the *Chronicle* article also laid out a catalog of YIMBY fights, quoted Sonja calling neighborhood character "a cancer," and accused Brian Hanlon of showing up at a neighborhood meeting and telling a resident, "We can't wait for you to die and rip those pretty Victorians down" (which Brian denied having said).

It was an A1 piece and an unofficial marker, the good and the bad, of how far they had come. CaRLA, which began with a lawsuit Sonja wrote herself, had filed several new Housing Accountability Act cases since Lafayette, and was now actually winning. Sonja was running for office, and Laura had two thousand YIMBY members. Brian Hanlon had raised $4 million for California YIMBY and was building a ten-person-and-growing lobbying operation in Sacramento, while Annie Fryman was helping build support for SB 827's eventual successor, which California YIMBY was sponsoring and which Scott Wiener planned to introduce later that year.

Across the Bay Bridge, East Bay for Everyone was embedded in the campaigns of several well-established candidates who had been brought over to the YIMBY cause. There was Lori Droste, a Berkeley city councilwoman who was running for re-election and had been encouraging YIMBYs to show up at Berkeley city meetings. And Buffy Wicks, a political veteran who'd worked in the Obama White House and was now running for the California State Assembly. Toward the beginning of her campaign Wicks had contacted East Bay for Everyone to say she had looked them up online, liked what she saw, and asked for help developing a housing platform. Then she supported SB 827 during the primary and talked about increasing density in the wealthy parts of North Oakland, something that had previously been considered a major political no-go. YIMBYs had so infected the narrative that even candidates who didn't agree with them were defensively using some version of "build" in their pitch.

Growth had its challenges. Four years earlier, it was a do-ocracy called SF BARF that consisted of Sonja and a few friends showing up at public meetings. Housing was just a fun way to rabble-rouse and use politics as a means of meeting other people who were new to the Bay Area. Now Sonja was yelling at campaign consultants in high-pressure moments, prompting other consultants to pull her behind shut doors to say, "You can't do that." Sacramento political operators had to tell Brian that he wouldn't go far in the capitol if he kept doing things like Tweeting a cartoon picture of the California flag in which the state's iconic grizzly bear emblem was being stabbed in the back with a knife bearing the name of a Marin County assemblyman that he considered to be overly NIMBYish.

Laura got in trouble over her tendency to overreach for political baubles. Looking to get in on the initiative game, early in 2018 she'd spent several hundred thousand dollars of YIMBY Action's money on signature collectors for a proposal to rewrite the San Francisco city charter to make it easier to build affordable housing . . . then failed to collect enough signatures, in the process alienating donors like Jeremy Stoppelman, who'd put $100,000 toward the effort, read about the failure online, and was unhappy that nobody had thought to tell him that his money had basically been burned in a trash can.

In terms of their destructive potential, the outward fights and missteps were nothing compared to the battles that were raging internally. The job of holding together YIMBY Action's membership had become complicated enough that a working group had started drafting an internal code of conduct, and there was an ongoing effort to impose order and decency on an internal Slack channel that was getting derailed by the vicious infighting that befalls every online forum once it gets enough users. Meantime, Brian's success in Sacramento had become alienating to Laura, who felt he wasn't doing enough to coordinate with local groups like YIMBY Action and regarded his ability to mint money from the tech industry as yet another example of bros helping bros while women did the unglamorous organizing on which the YIMBY brand was built. "There's no 'we' anymore" was the way it got put in a venting session.

Exactly who "we" were was confusing enough that Laura got a round of congratulations when California YIMBY, technically a separate organization, raised $1 million from Stripe. Then there was the time Twitter accidentally routed a $50,000 check to YIMBY Action that it had meant to send it to California YIMBY, and an ensuing dispute over the money. It is a fact of nonprofit life that every nascent political movement faces some sort of existential personality drama eventually, so there was probably no better marker of the YIMBY movement's arrival than the time Sonja hired a couples' therapist to conduct a session with her, Laura, and Brian.

In the final stretch before Election Day, Laura acted out the part of a hopped-up campaign junkie, with all the attendant cursing and whiskey drinking. She veered from high-minded proclamations about integration and meaningful work to sudden fits of tears to disputes with idiot rivals and idiot allies and idiot vendors, to the point that one evening Sonja, of all people, said to her, "Well if you keep calling them idiots. . . ." Mostly it was the raw desire to win. According to some questionable polls—local districts are notoriously hard to poll, and District Six, with its split population of rich and poor voters, notoriously harder still—Sonja was neck and neck with Matt Haney. Despite these warnings, and the fact that the poll's first conclusion was that voters didn't feel strongly about anyone, the numbers were a psychic lift that had Laura talking about Sonja's "surge." Even Matt Haney wrote an email to supporters about the "scary news" of close polls.

Sonja was not so convinced and remained privately dour on the subject of actually winning, but was also relaxed and free, because whatever happened, the grind would at least soon be over. The fundraising was mostly done and she was back to wearing sneakers and T-shirts with cut-out necks, and she'd stopped using the tubes of lipstick and makeup brushes that lined the office sink. Earlier in the race her accountant had made the catastrophic, campaign-rocking error of forgetting to check a single box on a form to request city-matching funds and in doing so had lost her $150,000 in campaign money. Now Sonja made jokes about how she was going to start telling voters that, unlike Christine Johnson and Matt Haney, the annoying mailers she was sending them hadn't been paid for by taxpayers.

Aside from a morning meeting, her days were mostly a series of long walks around the district to flyer poles and chat up voters. She stopped into bars and delis. She caught the closing doors of locked apartment buildings and took the elevator to the top then went down the fire stairs one floor at a time, knocking. She stopped people on the sidewalk to explain she was running for office, accepting it when they brushed her off, and further accepting it when she got roped into diversionary side conversations about drug problems, shitty husbands, vigilantism, and the many other things people will just tell you. A couple of guys told Sonja they would vote for her because she was hot. Uh-huh.

About fifty people were standing inside YIMBY headquarters on Election Day. They arrived at 5:00 a.m. in darkness. Outside, homeless people slept on the sidewalk in cardboard boxes. Blinking bikes and beeping trash trucks dominated the sparse traffic. Inside, a highly caffeinated crowd listened to Scott Wiener give a rah-rah speech. Let's get out there and win. Every vote counts. After the applause, Wiener, never one to skip the grunt work, spent an hour walking through the morning cold dodging needles and poop while hanging pink and blue "Sonja for Supervisor" placards on door handles and security grates. He and Sonja spent the rest of the morning touring polling places where he'd done well two years earlier, while YIMBY HQ became a rotating series of people leaving for flyering trips while other people returned for naps and bad food choices. There was also a brief and official moment when the office energy quieted and every side conversation ceased as London Breed and a guard walked in for a mayoral appearance and get out the vote texting session that would spend eternity on social media but in real life lasted about five minutes.

Late in the day Sonja left the office on one final canvassing session, heading in the direction of the Tenderloin and stopping every few feet to talk to voters and hand out pink and purple "Legalize Affordable Housing" flyers that laid out her plan to allow subsidized housing in West Side neighborhoods. She talked to techies in vests and ragged people in socks, continuing steadily in the direction of the building with the annoying siren, where she resumed her pledge to end the screeching. Later, as the sun dipped below the skyline, she took a short break to enjoy positive energy and a free vodka grapefruit at a bar called Aunt Charlie's Lounge, which had Sonja for Supervisor coasters and a fan who asked for a selfie.

From there she walked to city hall. In the final hour before the polls closed, Sonja positioned herself in the center of the sidewalk, about a hundred yards away, per state law, from the line of people waiting to vote. "I'm running to legalize affordable housing." "It doesn't matter if you're a felon, if you're on probation you can vote." "When I moved here, I was thirty, I worked two jobs, made $10.50 an hour, and it was horrible, but things get better." As the night got colder, she started skipping to keep warm and talked about how San Francisco City Hall needed a clock tower because not everyone had a cell phone, so maybe she'd work on that. And then finally it was eight o'clock and the polls were closed, and she headed toward YIMBY HQ and a dive bar called Club 93, where a Soviet-style portrait of Sonja looking sternly to the distance was being projected on a back wall above a pool table.

At the office she was greeted by chants of "Son-JA! Son-JA!" Drinks were had. Vapes were toked. Someone brought a YIMBY cake. A less drunk collection of poll watchers had stationed themselves at the far end of the room, where they waited for the first results. Among them was a software engineer named Roan Kattouw, who stood with his laptop open. Being an engineer, Kattouw had figured out how to make the near-instantaneous process of collecting returns from a website even more efficient, by writing a short program that automatically refreshed the department of elections page every second so that he could spare himself the inconvenience of having to continuously press the return button. Despite the presence of a nearby chair, Kattouw, restless, stood with the laptop cradled on his right forearm and used his left hand to type. The screen was black with a descending twenty-four-hour clock that counted off as it refreshed the page.

20:47:48

20:47:49

20:47:50

The department of elections was running late, so Kattouw stood there, staring at the screen, as the clock continued to tick, 20:51:48, 20:51:49, and finally, at 20:51:50, they posted. And they were . . . bad. So bad. Matt Haney was in first, Christine Johnson was in second, and Sonja was a distant third. Emphasis on "distant." She had fifteen hundred votes or about 16 percent of the total.

"We've got a long way to go," Laura assured the room after the results had been called out, then came bounding toward Roan Kattouw and his computer to ask desperate questions. What about the polling? This was just the early-voter tallies, right? There really was a long way to go, *right*? Laura was looking for anyone to tell her that the numbers on the screen weren't as bad as they looked. "I think this means we lost," said Steven Buss, a YIMBY volunteer who worked at Google and believed in data. Laura stepped out of the party and into an office where she placed her face on a table top in despair. This wasn't just a loss. It was a complete and total thrashing.

"I, like, bought a party dress," Sonja told her campaign manager. "I guess I'm going to put it on."

It would at least be an early night. Matt Haney was cruising to a majority win and would end up crushing Sonja and Christine Johnson across the district, rendering their ranked-choice strategy moot. Laura started crying. Sonja did not. She walked over to a crowded couch and did what she always seemed to be doing in her spare moments during the campaign: Opened her shirt and fed her baby. Sonja never used a cover and for the past year had fed Anton during reporter interviews, at parties, while talking to voters, and now in a crowded room of people watching her experience one of her biggest failures and most embarrassing moments. But Sonja didn't do shame, and she lived free of people's judgment. She wasn't going to start being bashful now.

The hot and packed YIMBY headquarters thinned as people left for happier parties or to head around the corner to watch the rest of the returns at Club 93. Nationally, Democrats were taking back the house, which YIMBYs and their opponents were all celebrating equally. The rest of the housing ballot was mixed. The Proposition C homeless tax passed with more than 60 percent of the vote but was going to have years of legal challenges from business groups who argued it needed two-thirds. Proposition 10, the rent control initiative, was predictably crushed, losing by a margin of two to one and barely winning a majority in San Francisco, where everyone assumed it would do well. Michael Weinstein had already vowed to pay for another rent control initiative soon.

Over at what was becoming Matt Haney's victory party, David Campos stood onstage giving a warm-up speech while the man of the hour was drinking at the bar looking overwhelmed by the number of people cheering for him. Haney was finally introduced by a social justice activist who said "as a radical black woman, it's not an easy choice to lift up a cis white male" before calling him to the stage. Haney came out while a DJ played James Brown's "Get Up Offa That Thing" and did a mercifully brief and gangly jig before delivering a speech that slammed the imaginary pollsters in the room, slammed the other side for tweeting while his campaign was working, and slammed the independent expenditure committees that had supported Christine and

Sonja. He ended on a more positive note, asking the room, "Are you actually ready to solve problems now?" and left the stage for more photos, more interviews, more cheers.

Housing was the Bay Area's biggest issue, but that didn't mean you could be a single-issue candidate. That seemed like the most generous conclusion you could come to. There were other explanations, and they were probably right too. Matt Haney had the establishment endorsements. Sonja was too divisive and her campaign too amateurish. Even YIMBY allies started whispering that the smackdown was a needed lesson.

That analysis found its supporting evidence across the bay, where East Bay for Everyone had a string of wins. Lori Droste was re-elected to the Berkeley City Council and was primed to introduce new pro-density reforms. Buffy Wicks won and would go on to become an ally in the assembly and to co-sponsor Scott Wiener's next statewide upzoning bill. These women were YIMBY friendly, but they weren't exactly YIMBYs. YIMBYism did better, it seemed, when it plugged into well-rounded candidates whose identities went beyond housing, as had happened with Scott Wiener's senate campaign and repeated itself that night in Berkeley and Oakland.

Years earlier, in the months after that first YIMBYtown gathering in Boulder, when housing advocates from around the country were struggling to figure out what sort of message they wanted to send, an organizer from Seattle wrote an email to the entire conference asking if there should be some standards for when a YIMBY group could disavow someone whose tone and tactics they disagreed with. She was very obviously talking about Sonja, and, Sonja being Sonja, she posted the first reply. It was around a thousand words long and veered from philosophical ramblings on the nature of power to the success of Christianity being in its many sects. Sonja talked about how people can only really control themselves and her belief that life is a "do-ocracy." Finally, she ended: "If you have a group in your city that you think is too extremely YIMBY, lucky for you, they've created a very cushy role for you called 'good cop.'"

That seemed just about right. She'd blown a hole in the public conversation and in doing so had created the space for gentler voices to help fill it. Nobody was going to thank her for the service, but it was necessary dirty work, and now it was done. The day after the election she called Matt Haney to congratulate him on winning and reverted to her advocate role by pressing him to introduce her affordable housing everywhere proposal. She would go back to her day job suing suburbs, which was more her style anyway.

After the election, a young man named Ernest Brown, who worked with Victoria Fierce at East Bay for Everyone, started traveling around Berkeley and Oakland conducting house party housing forums. The first meeting was at Buffy Wicks's house, which sat on a quiet single-family street and that morning had a half-dozen bikes parked outside. Inside the house were tenants and landlords, tech engineers and non-profit employees, single-family-house owners and tall-building dwellers. They sat together on chairs and couches picking at little brunch cakes.

Ernest was a twenty-eight-year-old from Atlanta who spoke in a soothing drawl. He began the discussion with a short biography about how he'd grown up in a black neighborhood and gone to all black schools and all black churches and had never had a white peer before college. In 2016, he moved to the Bay Area and loved it. The opportunity, the diversity, he loved it all and wanted to stay. This was a segue into the punishing rents and doubled-up apartments and three-hour-long supercommutes that had come to cloud the California dream.

His speech wasn't about some new law or candidate. The room was all talk, no argument. Just a space for people to consider what sort of cities they wanted to live in, what it really meant to be progressive, where their kids would live if there wasn't any new housing, how that housing would get built if people were always against it, the terrors of being a tenant, the realities of being a landlord, and the precious gift of knowing that your region's biggest problem was that it attracted so many hopeful people who believed it could be better, and needed a little space.

NEIGHBORS FOR MORE NEIGHBORS

A DECADE OR SO EARLIER, when he started writing op-eds on America's growing housing problem, Ed Glaeser figured that if he had any influence on the public conversation, that influence would be with think tanks and people in elected office. Glaeser was an important person who worked in a columned building. When he thought about how problems got solved, he thought of other important people in other columned buildings. But instead of a city hall or statehouse or seated behind a microphone and a glass of water in front of Congress, he was onstage at the third annual YIMBYtown conference, running a laser pointer over data while the two hundred or so casually dressed attendees sat slouched in the rows of auditorium chairs in front of him.

Sonja was back in San Francisco running for office, but a strong Bay Area contingent that included Brian, Laura, and Victoria sat somewhere in the crowd. The conference was put on by a Boston-area group called A Better Cambridge, and people had flown in from New York, Los

Angeles, and Washington, from Portland, Seattle, Salt Lake City, Denver, and Minneapolis, from Austin, Tampa, and Charlotte, from Vancouver, London, Paris, and Melbourne. The cities were different, their symptoms the same: a shortage of housing and growth in high-paying jobs leads to rising rents and home prices, leads to outrage about displacement, leads to hatred of developers and calls for more rent control, leads to a countermovement from some sort of YIMBY group, leads to class and race conflict as people huddle to their sides. Schools were building affordable housing for teachers. Long-range-commuting cops were sleeping in their cars. Restaurants were switching to counter service because they couldn't find enough waiters. Entrepreneurs were building modern-day dorms for yuppies while resentful arsonists burned new developments down.

Glaeser was clearly with his people. He chided the "manufactured equality of suburbs," called the housing shortage a "catastrophe," and declared that the fight for urban space was a "fight for the future of humanity." Applause, applause, applause. After the address, he was mobbed by a semicircle of admirers who requested selfies and book signatures and asked him questions like which city he liked the most ("That's like asking which of my children I like the most").

YIMBY world was full of victories in 2018, and there would be many more in the months ahead. The housing crisis had turned the Bay Area from the booming place every city wanted to emulate to a cautionary tale of exactly what not to do, so most of the action was actually outside of California. Minneapolis was on the verge of becoming the first major city in America to eliminate single-family zoning, and shortly after Oregon would become the first state to do the same thing. Housing would also make its way into the 2020 presidential race, with several Democratic candidates explicitly calling for zoning reforms.

Back in Sacramento, Scott Wiener would introduce SB 50, a new version of his controversial upzoning bill, and unlike the first effort it would earn the support of several affordable housing and environmental groups and clear several state Senate committee hurdles, then get buried by a suburban legislator with an opaque and underhanded legislative tactic. It was as if people were scared this one might actually pass. Wiener's bill was technically still alive and he promised to continue pushing in 2020. Scott Wiener would always promise more work. But whatever happened with SB 50, it was clear that the philosophy of more housing was slowly starting to win, and, at least among younger voters, becoming a tenet of urban liberalism. Assuming the generational trends held and millennials remained mired in a housing wealth gap, it was now just a matter of time.

Still there was a brutal eviction crisis, and in cities around the country lower-income tenants continued to regard YIMBY groups as suspicious at best and the enemy at worst. This was a frequent topic of discussion at the conference, as it always was at YIMBYtown. During one session, an organizer named Janne Flisrand, from Minneapolis, suggested that the very term "YIMBY," with all the asymmetrical power dynamics it now connoted, should be dropped for something fresher. Her group was called Neighbors for More Neighbors. Another seminar was called "Anti-Gentrification Activists Aren't NIMBYs: Building Nuance for YIMBY Housing Policy in Gentrifying Neighborhoods." It was led by a Bay Area YIMBY named Joe Rivano Barros and was one of the better-attended sessions. About sixty people stood, sat, and huddled cross-legged on the floor of a hot and muggy classroom and gave a round of approving finger snaps when Rivano Barros began his presentation with the declaration: "So my central thesis today is that YIMBYs should basically full-stop not advocate for housing in gentrifying communities."

Unbeknownst to Barros, one of the people stuffed into the doorway during his presentation was a twenty-seven-year-old named Kai Palmer-Dunning. Palmer-Dunning was from Boston's historically black neighborhood of Roxbury, and he was involved with an anti-gentrification group called Reclaim Roxbury. He'd read that the YIMBYtown conference was coming to his neighborhood—the conference was held at Roxbury Community College—and upon googling the term "YIMBY" found lots of not-kind articles ("The Darlings of the Real Estate

Industry") that confirmed all his worst suspicions of what a pro-housing movement meant. But the gathering sounded interesting enough, so he decided to check it out for himself.

As it happened, the very next day Palmer-Dunning was going to a local assembly that had been organized by a racial justice group called Right to the City, which had started a national renters' rights campaign called Homes for All. That event was just a few blocks from the YIMBYtown Conference and was held in an old-timey church topped with a bell and wind vane, and was attended by a different set of two hundred or so people who sat on dusty cushions in creaky pews. Whereas the YIMBY event was young, in English, and followed by heavy nighttime drinking, this event was older, multilingual, and had a side room with free child care. The church's altar had been outfitted with a projector screen that said "Welcome" in English, Spanish, and Cantonese, and the periphery was lined with protest signs—"Luxury Housing Is Not the Answer"—for some unspecified future action.

Tenants' groups were also flush with victories that year, and they would also have more in the months ahead. New York would go on to expand local rent control laws. Oregon would become the first state to enact statewide rent control, and, shortly after, David Chiu would write and pass a bill that made California the second. In the space of five years, the Homes for All campaign had grown from a handful of groups in a dozen cities to seventy-eight organizations in forty-one cities and about half of U.S. states.

Boston had all the same problems as every other prosperous city. Rising rents. Investors buying old buildings and clearing out low-income tenants. The point of the church event, which was billed as the "Boston People's Plan Assembly," was to collect neighborhood-level proposals to build more affordable housing and stem displacement. It was a low-tech affair. The YIMBY meeting was heavy on Twitter and Slack discussions. The People's Plan Assembly began with a call-and-response session ("Whose city?" "Our city!") before the church broke into groups of a dozen or so people that gathered around leaders like Kai Palmer-

Dunning, who stood on a pew organizing a discussion and writing group ideas in large text on a sheet of butcher paper.

Unbeknownst to Palmer-Dunning, one of the people milling around the church while he was standing on the pew taking suggestions was Joe Rivano Barros. Rivano Barros had heard about the church event on Twitter and wasn't sure what to expect but left the YIMBY conference to check it out for himself.

Soon the two very separate gatherings would meet. Toward the end of the People's Plan Assembly, volunteers started moving the protest banners outside, where a crowd was gathering behind a marching band. Lisa Owens, the executive director of a Boston housing organization called City Life/Vida Urbana, who was also from Roxbury, went to the altar to explain what came next. "It's not a surprise that we are not the only gathering of people who are meeting around housing today," she said to the crowd. "We have something to say, and a bunch of us are going to march down there right now. We want all of you to come and march with us."

Following some cheers and claps, the assembly stood up in their pews and headed outside to form a wobbly line behind the band, which was warming up the drums. Right at the very front, next to a shopping cart with an amplifier, was a banner that read "Displacement Is the Crisis . . . We Are the Answer."

And they marched. Out of the churchyard, down a hill, and disjointedly around a street corner toward Roxbury Community College. A city bus honked. Curious pedestrians pulled out their cell cameras. Soon there was a flashing police escort driving slowly behind the crowd. Kai Palmer-Dunning ran ahead of the march to the YIMBY event, curious to see how it would all go down when two hundred people and a marching band dropped in to say hello.

HOUSING IS A SUBJECT that attracts extreme emotions and ideologies. It makes sense because land defines our existence and can't be reduced to purely economic terms. You can only sort of move land, and you can only sort of make it, so unlike basic commodities like food, clothing, and oil, a shortage of land or housing in one place can't really be rectified by bringing in a surplus from another. Other commodities can also be enjoyed somewhat independently; it doesn't affect our hunger to have someone else eating food at the same time we are. Contrast that with land, whose sustenance and enjoyment are closely tied to how many other people are using it. We inherently want to share space—up to the point we feel it's too crowded, a perspective that varies from person to person and is shaped heavily by when they arrived.

All this makes land schizophrenically capitalist and socialist, creating a vacuum that allows people to see whatever system they want to see. Developers claim to buy and sell land in a "free market," even though the prices they pay and charge are dictated by how close a piece of land is to socially constructed goods and community institutions, and of course other people. Marxists talk about commoditization and market failures but are rarely so brave as to declare what sort of list or quota system should replace money as the price of admission to thriving places.

It's complicated stuff, and once you get into the details and peel back the history and ask what sorts of policies will actually lead to a world that is more stable and more equitable, it's hard to walk away with a belief that any sort of rigidity is the answer. It's a fraught leap from "the government is responsible for redlining and redevelopment" to "therefore socialism." It seems equally fraught to believe that a capitalism that creates a business model on eviction and homelessness would make us all better off if it were allowed to fully run its course.

If there is a rhyme to postwar history, it's that whatever system we use, and whatever level of government is orchestrating it, when we think of cities as buildings and markets, and not collections of people, we are doomed to make the same mistakes. The sins of redevelopment came from a mistaken belief that social problems brought on by centuries of inequity and systemic racism could be cured not by investing in people but by starting with a clean slate of new buildings. Affordable housing shortages brought on by NIMBYism are the result of a mistaken belief that a society can grow even as its neighborhoods look exactly the same. The displacement that accompanies gentrification comes from a mistaken belief that markets will always lift all boats. Mixed solutions can feel like a cop-out, especially in polarized times. And yet, over and over, in city after city, it's always where people end up and what seems most likely to work. There's no way to rectify a housing shortage other than to build housing, and there's no way to take care of people whom the private market won't take care of other than subsidies or rent control, or both. The details are democracy.

Human beings have for all history had an extreme tendency to categorize themselves into tribes, and for all history this tendency has led to extreme difficulty in solving the so-called collective action problems, things like education, roads, transportation, and housing, that define a progressive society and require large-scale cooperation to solve. This is why countries with exemplary public systems are usually homogeneous. In place after place and culture after culture, social scientists have time and again documented how our deepest tribal tendencies, and the mistrust that comes with them, become most acute not when we are segregated by vast distances but when we are segregated block by block, as we are in cities and suburbs. This tendency gets further exacerbated by walls, freeways, railroad tracks, and the invisible lines of government that tell us what sorts of people live where and serve to harden our views of who is and isn't on our side.

According to this story, things like secluded suburbs and private tech buses don't just ignore local challenges or put off assimilation; they actually make tribal tensions worse, by insulating one group from problems that are in everyone's best interest to solve, while demonstrating to the other that the first group's interests are not the same. That mistrust filters widely through the public arena, and is very easily manipulated, until each side is convinced that any solution the other is offering cannot possibly be the same as theirs, and collective action fails. There's no easy remedy or off-the-shelf ism for solving problems that cut to the very nature of being human. And yet we see through the lens of our biggest and most complicated cities that a lot of things get worked out, messily and imperfectly, once we accept that the hardest problems are everyone's to solve, and actually decide to try.

TWO MONTHS BEFORE the YIMBYtown conference, Joey Lindstrom was at a Homes for All gathering in Atlanta. Lindstrom is the dapper lead organizer for the National Low Income Housing Coalition and a fixture of affordable housing conferences who is almost always dressed in some version of a suit and bow tie topped by either a flat cap or a fedora. The urban Left has a particular skill at finding new and creative ways of eating itself, so Lindstrom, hoping to be a connector, immediately answered yes when he was asked to attend YIMBYtown as well. He'd spent the weekend dipping in and out of classrooms to hear sessions with titles like "Building Alliances Between YIMBYs and Equity Groups," while fine-tuning a forty-seven-slide PowerPoint that he presented in a gym during the conference's final session.

The first slide read "Two Crucial Solutions: Robust Housing Subsidies and Expanded Market Rate Development." The presentation continued through various grisly statistics about lagging wages and rising rents and the 7 million affordable apartments we don't have for low-income households who need them. It was just a little past the halfway point, at a slide that read "The Legacy of Reduced Federal Support for Housing," that somewhere down the hall people started to hear what sounded like a very large group. There was a woman yelling, "We're here! Why won't you listen?" and the faint sound of, a band?

Lindstrom stopped talking, and the collection of YIMBYs in foldout chairs turned around in apprehension as the sound of two hundred people and a marching band got progressively louder as the Boston People's Plan Assembly made its way down a narrow hallway. The protestors burst through makeshift curtains and gathered at the front of the room under a basketball hoop. Kai Palmer-Dunning stood back filming while Lisa Owens from City Life welcomed everyone to Boston.

"There are some people that are part of the YIMBY movement that truly care about affordable housing," she said. "I want to invite those people who are here who care about affordable housing and who care about displacement protection, who care about the people who live in the city of Boston who've been living and working and fighting to stay in their homes. I invite you to learn from those of us who are already working on the front lines. I invite you to not put forward housing proposals without talking to us. I invite you to follow our lead."

Lisa Owens went through some finer points of zoning policy about which there would have almost certainly been some quibbles. And the days and months ahead would feature lots of disagreement and unproductive tweeting. But now, for the people who were in the room, face-to-face, it was healthy tension and a lot of clapping. Clapping followed by handshakes and Joey Lindstrom from the National Low Income Housing Coalition noting the weirdness of being the subject of a protest that included several people he considered friends and was organized by a coalition he worked with closely and whose conference he had just been to. Then the band revved back up and the People's Plan Assembly marched out.

"Usually the way it works when I'm doing a speech or talk is I quit halfway through to go join a protest," Lindstrom said when the gym was finally quiet. People laughed, and Lidstrom resumed his presentation. He had five minutes left and nineteen slides to get through.

ACKNOWLEDGMENTS

Unofficially, I began this book in 2013 when I moved home to the Bay Area after a decade in New York. I'd returned because my mom was dying of Alzheimer's, and I began my third run as a San Franciscan living a dozen blocks from my parents and childhood home in a Mission District apartment that had "Yuppie Scum" written on the stoop. For the next few years I wrestled with personal loss and the torture of memory while covering one of the most extraordinary periods in California history.

Which is to say this project was personal, and nobody was in it with me more than my family. My first official day of writing was the day after my mother's funeral, though I didn't get much done. My last official day of writing was the morning my son was born, though I didn't make the deadline. Somewhere in the middle my wife took a picture of me staring at my laptop while my daughter tried to get my attention. Add in late nights, worked weekends, canceled dinners, ruined vacations, and fits of stress. I pulled back from everyone during this project, but nobody saw this more than my wife Candace, whose constant support and encouragement made the work possible. She's a partner in every way, and our unit, C^4 (Conor, Candy, Callie, and Cole), is everything to me.

The Bay Area has been through quite a time these past years, and many of the things I loved about it have died. It's sad, and I have some private angry thoughts about it. But it would have been all too easy, and cheap, to allow the priority of my own experience to act as a substitute for reporting on the complicated forces and long arc of decisions that allowed the housing crisis to happen, and what sorts of actions might realistically help solve it. Besides, it was impossible for me to tell the stories of recent Bay Area transplants without thinking about my parents' decision to leave Philadelphia for San Francisco on a permanent honeymoon in 1967, or how my life might have turned out if a couple of newlyweds with $500 hadn't been able to find their first apartment and make the city and Bay Area their home.

I am obligated to note that, in addition to a lot of luck and two loving parents that filled the house with books and always encouraged my curiosity, I have richly benefited from many of the systems and land use policies that I've critiqued in this book, particularly Proposition 13. I should also note my father was a legislative assistant to Jerry Brown in the 1970s, though he never worked on housing and I'd never covered, met, or spoken to Brown before interviewing him once, over the phone, for this book. My father is also a San Francisco landlord, which is something of a double-edged sword, giving me insight into how difficult the business can be, but also showing me that rent control is far from the profit suck it is often portrayed as. In any case, I'd like to think that I am professionally trained to follow the data and the story and ignore whatever biases my family background might be expected to produce, and at every juncture I have tried. Still, a little disclosure never hurts.

Bringing a journalistic lens to a story you've lived through is hard, and my agent, Melissa Flashman, was a great collaborator who helped me turn a bunch of very raw ideas into the outline of a book. Then along came my editor, Virginia Smith, at Penguin Press, who got what I wanted to do and had enough faith in me to buy into the idea of a fluidly reported story that would begin half formed and go wherever it went. When it was time to sit down and write, Virginia and her assistant, Caroline Sydney, provided crucial advice that spanned the broadest strokes of reporting and high-level outlining to the tiniest and most precise line edits. It was a special opportunity to work with them and a partnership that I've come to learn very few authors have. I'll spend the rest of my life being grateful for it. My subsequent meetings with the marketing and publicity teams, who get up each day trying to turn more people into readers, reminded me that publishing, like journalism, is far from a solitary effort.

Toward the beginning of this project I went looking for a fluent Spanish speaker to help me translate a few interviews. When I found Lauren Hepler, I realized I had so much more. Over the next year she became my assistant and friend, doing interviews and filing notes on a range of topics. There's a handful of reporters who you can just instantly tell have it. Lauren has it, and the fun I had working with her has been surpassed only by the fun I've had watching her do her own stories and ascend in her career.

Doris Burke and Susan Beachy, who helped with research, always knew how to find stuff. Ben Phelan was my primary fact-checker, which wasn't always fun but definitely always worth it. Liliana Michelena and Cole Louison supplemented Ben's work, helping me get that much closer to the impossibility of perfection. Spencer Gondorf helped me with the hellish task of assembling citations, and Jose Fermoso read and critiqued a late draft.

So many different people agreed to participate in this book, and outside a few exceptions, they all bought into my desire to tell an up-close story where almost everything was on the record. This required a lot of courage, and the fact that I got pretty much unfettered access to so many different subjects from so many different backgrounds only confirmed my belief that a large range of people continue to believe in the power of journalism to illuminate important problems and get us all closer to the truth. I laid out the bulk of my process and interviews in the section on source notes, but it's worth noting that nobody has to talk to a reporter, so it's always appreciated when they do.

History is tricky, and I'm not trained a historian, so I relied on the guidance of several California experts. The late Kevin Starr, the dean of California historians, talked to me very early in this story, and the results of that one conversation made me realize how much California lost with his passing. Jim Newton, a journalist turned historian in his own right, was generous to read a draft, as did Robert O. Self. Eli Broad made some of that history, building lots of middle-class housing and two Fortune 500 companies through much of the period I wrote about, and I appreciate him lending me his precious time and insights.

To live your life as a reporter is to live in the awkward state of making audacious requests of strangers, and over the course of this book I started aiming that stuff at friends. The generosity of Caille Millner, who read a very early draft of the book and gave me advice that was tough, brilliant, and needed, is something I'll never forget. David Wessel and Timothy Aeppel, two of my former bosses at *The Wall Street Journal*, provided great feedback on startlingly short turnarounds. I've been trading ideas and story drafts with Ben Casselman since we became cubicle mates in 2006, so it was only fitting that I call him once a week for help. Emily Badger, who I sat next to in San Francisco for a good deal of this project, always had good ideas for getting around the toughest reporting and writing corners. She is also living proof that you can become dear friends with someone while being uncomfortably jealous of their talents. My cousin Polly Brewster is my long-running writing coach, so was always with me at the desk.

I've been newspapering for twenty years, but it wasn't until I started book leave that I realized just how much my daily rhythms are tied up in the hive brilliance of a newsroom. From my training ground at the *Los Angeles Business Journal* to the *San Diego Union-Tribune*, *The Wall Street Journal*, and now *The New York Times*, journalists have always been my people. The news is supposed to be competitive but is really a shared enterprise, so I want to offer a broad thanks to the many journalists around the world who are also picking away at the housing story and whose work inspires me daily, and particular thanks to Joe Eskenazi, my favorite San Francisco political reporter, who was my de facto consultant on the workings of San Francisco City Hall.

On that note, I spent a good deal of my book leave at my desk in San Francisco, for no reason other than to draft off the brilliance of the *Times*'s tech team during a run of utter dominance. It seems not remotely hyperbolic to say that the past decade of Silicon Valley news will form the historical document of one of the most consequential moments for democracy and the economy, the implications of which will likely take the rest of my lifetime or longer to fully reconcile with. It's been an honor to watch them cover it.

The New York Times has been the greatest professional home I've had. My greatest thanks goes to the entire institution for the values it espouses and the investment it maintains in journalism. Everyday some colleague I've never met publishes a great story, photo, video, chart, interactive, podcast, or TV episode that makes me proud to have a byline there and juiced to go to work. People whose names I'll never read print the paper daily and create hidden technologies that I don't understand but wouldn't have an audience without. In the manner of great cities, the joy of my five years on the staff has been less about any particular colleague or moment than the series of constant and casual interactions, many in the throes of deadline, with people up and down the editing and production process.

The stories that inspired this book rotated through several editors in the technology, economics, and national teams—some still there, others that have moved on—and in various instances were guided by visual journalists instead of a traditional "words editor." So it really would be impossible to find a way to thank everyone. Still I have to single out Dean Murphy for hiring me and creating my beat, Kevin McKenna for being a tireless advocate for me and my work, and Ellen Pollock, who is the same and allowed me to go on leave during a busy news period. Ashwin Seshagiri is the person who turns wild ideas into reality, and Julie Bloom on the National Desk has made those of us in California feel that much more loved.

I also worked closely with several photographers and photo editors whose visual vocabularies continue to open up new pathways for how to think about stories: Jim Wilson and Andrew Burton, who shot a number of my *Times* housing stories, and Whitney Richardson and Brent Lewis, photo editors who have pushed me to think more precisely about how to picture each scene of a story and in doing so have helped me add velocity to the often dry topic of housing policy.

Finally, I'd like to thank Dean Baquet, who is always game for a big California story, and gave final approval for the leave that allowed me to write this one. He also offered a bit of counsel for how to make this book complementary to the *Times*'s daily mission instead of having my time away detract from it. And it was good advice, because the housing story is far from over, and there's always more to do.

NOTES ON SOURCES

—

A note on fact-checking: An independent fact-checker contacted, whenever possible, the sources interviewed by the writer, sought the opinions of experts in various fields, reviewed all reporting gathered by the writer, and generated additional sourcing to confirm or correct the writer's conclusions.

CHAPTER 1

My account of Sonja Trauss's early life was based primarily on interviews with her, her parents, her brother Milo, and a visit to her childhood home in Philadelphia and the surrounding Germantown neighborhood, along with news clippings and property records listed in the endnotes. I also interviewed several of her old Philly friends, including Rose Luardo, Adam Leeds, Tip Flannery, and Andrew Jeffrey Wright of Space 1026.

My account of the early days of SF BARF was based on interviews with Sonja, elected officials, and several SF BARF members including Max Gasner and Micah Catlin. I supplemented that with letters, emails, social media, and video of public meetings.

CHAPTER 2

The history of how land use became an issue of growing economic importance and study was based on the books, news clippings and academic papers listed in the endnotes, combined with interviews with about a dozen academics, notably Kenneth Rosen, Jennifer Wolch, and Enrico Moretti at UC Berkeley; Edward

Glaeser, Lawrence Katz, Jason Furman, and Daniel Shoag at Harvard; Peter Ganong at the University of Chicago; and Michael Storper at UCLA.

The early history of the YIMBY movement was based on first-hand reporting and interviews with several policy writers including Matthew Yglesias, Ryan Avent, and Kim-Mai Cutler, as well as dozens of early YIMBYs, notably David Alpert of Greater Greater Washington, Will Toor of Better Boulder, Laura Loe Bernstein of Share the Cities, Madeline Kovacs of Portland for Everyone, Alan Durning of the Sightline Institute, Janne Flisrand of Neighbors for More Neighbors, Susan Somers of AURA, Alexander Berger of the Open Philanthopy Project, John Myers of London YIMBY, and Anders Gardebring of YIMBY Stockholm.

I attended the first YIMBYtown conference in Boulder. All accounts of the conference were witnessed firsthand and captured with a digital recorder.

CHAPTER 3

From late 2017 to early 2019 I interviewed dozens of tenants, nonprofit leaders, community organizers, clergy, residents, and business owners in the North Fair Oaks area. Much of the neighborhood's early history came from interviews with Linda Lopez, of the North Fair Oaks Community Council, Gregorio Mora-Torres at San Jose State University, and Roger Rouse at the University of Pittsburgh. Lauren Hepler, a bilingual journalist who has done extensive reporting in Mexico and California's Central Valley, aided me in many of my interviews with tenants and academics, and conducted several on her own.

The account of Trion's purchase of the Buckingham Apartments was based on interviews with local residents and clergy, investor materials that Trion distributed after the purchase and became the subject of a federal court case, and newspaper articles listed in the endnotes. Trion refused to make executives available for comment, but in a written correspondence disputed Sister Christina's account of their phone call after the purchase, saying their executives did not recall saying they wanted to be a "good neighbor," and that the call was primarily "to understand the nonprofit."

From December 2017 to March 2018 I followed Sandy Hernandez and other residents of the Hopkins Avenue and Regent Street apartments as they battled their landlord over the rent increase. I was present for every tenant meeting and the protest. All quotes were captured with a digital recorder and translated when necessary. I also conducted numerous follow-ups with several of the tenants as well as Sister Christina Heltsley, Rafael Avendano, and Daniel Saver.

I interviewed Jesshill Love in Redwood City and conducted several follow-ups over the phone before he stopped responding. He did not respond to numerous calls for comment from me and my fact-checker, as well as an office visit by Lauren Hepler. The account was based on his early interviews and supplemented with public investor materials, property records and voicemails I obtained.

Lauren Hepler and I also conducted numerous follow-up interviews with Sandy and Stephanie after they moved out. Stephanie was never interviewed without her mother present.

In 2018, after Sandy and Stephanie moved out, Lauren Hepler and I interviewed Ismael Pineda and his family as they were moving into their old apartment. We explained the story and their role in it, and they allowed us to come in and see the apartment and take pictures so we could document what had changed since Sandy and Stephanie had moved out. The Pinedas' housing history was based on interviews with the family and augmented with property records.

Though not directly applicable to the reporting, several books deepened my understanding of the economics and sociology of gentrification and displacement, including *The Near Northwest Side* by Gina Pérez, *There Goes the 'Hood* by Lance Freeman, and *Back to the City* edited by Shirley Bradway Laska and Daphne Spain. I was also aided by interviews with Matthew Desmond of Princeton, Japonica Brown-Saracino at Boston University, and Miriam Zuk, Karen Chapple and Justine Marcus of the Urban Displacement Project at UC Berkeley.

CHAPTER 4

The history of California's post–World War II growth spurt and subsequent battles over land use is based on the books and newspaper articles listed in the endnotes, combined with interviews with several historians, politicians and business leaders, notably Matthew Lasner at Hunter College, Ocean Howell at the University of Oregon, Christopher Sellers at Stony Brook University, William Fischel at Dartmouth, and Robert Ellickson at Yale. I also interviewed the honorable Jerry Brown, Eli Broad, co-founder of Kaufman & Broad and the Eli and Edythe Broad Foundation, and the late Kevin Starr, the California historian and former state librarian whose Americans and the California Dream series was (and remains) crucial to my understanding of California's sociopolitical history.

In addition to books and newspaper stories, my account of the Rumford Act and Proposition 14 was augmented by interviews with William Byron Rumford III, Robert O. Self of Brown University, and Albert S. Broussard, a professor of history at Texas A&M. I am further indebted to the many authors and administrators who run BlackPast.org, which is a great resource on many things, but a particularly great resource on the under-told story of African Americans in the West.

My account of Rick Holliday's career is based on interviews with him along with the articles listed in the endnotes. Although I didn't use the book directly, *Freedom to Build*, edited by John F.C. Turner and Robert Fichter, was helpful. Garrett Shields, a librarian at the California State Library, was also helpful in providing me with the brief legislative history of the Housing Accountability Act.

CHAPTER 5

My accounts of Tony Lagiss's land and the ensuing saga over the Terraces of Lafayette/Homes at Deer Hill projects was based on interviews with Steve Falk, Dennis O'Brien, Guy Atwood, Michael Griffiths, Sonja Trauss, Brian Hanlon, and Ryan Patterson, along with newspaper articles, property records, public meeting transcripts, the two lawsuits, and a review of the six-thousand-plus pages of planning documents, historical assessments, environmental impact reports, and resident letters contained in the city's administrative record. I also attended several Lafayette City Council meetings, including the one where Steve Falk resigned.

I was present at the 2015 "Sue the Suburbs" panel discussion. All observations were firsthand and quotes were captured with a digital recorder.

The history of Lakewood was assembled with the books and newspaper articles in the endnotes as well as interviews with Steve Falk and Michan Connor, an independent scholar and expert in urban fragmentation who was instrumental to my understanding of how city incorporation works. Coleman Alexander Allums, at the University of Georgia, was also helpful.

CHAPTER 6

My account of Scott Wiener's time on the San Francisco Board of Supervisors and subsequent run for state senate was based on interviews with Wiener as well as aides, notably Jeff Cretan and Annie Fryman, and a range of political partners and rivals including Calvin Welch and Peter Cohen of the Council of Community Housing Organizations, David Campos, Jane Kim, and David Chiu. I also reviewed video of Board of Supervisors meetings and the newspaper articles in the endnotes. Jason McDaniel of San Francisco State University and Joe Eskenazi, of Mission Local, were both helpful to my understanding of the history of San Francisco politics since 2000.

I was present for the first YIMBY Congress, so all observations were firsthand and all quotes came from a digital recorder.

The story of the 2017 housing package was based on interviews with various legislators, aides, and activists, including Senator Scott Wiener and Senator Nancy Skinner, Ben Metcalf, director of the California Department of Housing and Community Development, along with Laura Foote, Brian Hanlon, and Sonja Trauss.

I attended the YIMBY victory party, the 2017 housing package bill signing ceremony, and the 2017 YIMBY Gala. All quotes were captured with a digital recorder.

CHAPTER 7

I visited Factory_OS several times between 2018 to 2019 and conducted several interviews with Rick Holliday, Larry Pace, and various workers, along with several venture capitalists, historians, real estate developers, and rival modular housing companies including Blokable in Seattle and RAD Urban in Oakland.

The backstory of Rick Holliday's career and the founding of BRIDGE Housing was based on the various books and newspaper articles mentioned in the endnotes, along with interviews with Rick Holliday and Carol Galante from the Terner Center for Housing Innovation at UC Berkeley. I was also aided by David J. Erickson, manager of Center for Community Development at the Federal Reserve Bank of San Francisco, who walked me through the housing policies of the Nixon, Carter, and Reagan Administrations, and the history of the Low-Income Housing Tax Credit. Don Falk, chief executive officer of Tenderloin Neighborhood Development Corporation, and Michael Novogradac, of the accounting firm Novogradac & Company LLP in San Francisco, also helped me understand how the Low-Income Housing Tax Credit works.

The accounts of homelessness were collected from the various books and articles listed in the endnotes, firsthand reporting across Northern and Southern California, and interviews with dozens of homeless advocates, researchers, and city/county employees, notably Bob McElroy, chief executive of the Alpha Project; Dr. Wilma J. Wooten, the public health officer in San Diego County; Dr. Margot Kushel of UC San Francisco; and Dennis Culhane of the University of Pennsylvania.

The accounts of the homeless encampment near Rick Holliday's office were gathered firsthand over the course of four days of interviews with the people who live there and several (housed) neighbors nearby.

CHAPTER 8

The accounts of economic stress along the Middlefield Road retail strip were based on interviews with clerks and shoppers in 2018 and early 2019. The accounts of the Buckingham Apartments were based on interviews with neighbors and several of the building's tenants. After talking to me about the Buckingham Apartments once, in early 2018, Sister Christina refused to talk about the building, in accordance with a nondisclosure agreement that she signed as part of the St. Francis Center's purchase agreement with Trion. The re-opening celebration for the complex was open to the public, however, and Lauren Hepler attended and captured all accounts firsthand.

The account of Trion's founding and business practices were based on property records, social media, and interviews with former tenants and tenant organizers in California and Oregon, along with several past interviews with Max Sharkansky cited in the endnotes, and a brief written correspondence Trion sent back during fact-checking.

CHAPTER 9

I followed Sonja Trauss's Supervisor campaign from late 2017 to Election Day 2018 and over that time attended dozens of fundraisers, speeches, debates, voter sessions, and canvassing events, in addition to spending dozens of hours at the office and accompanying her and others to restaurants and bars after work. I also interviewed dozens of supporters, opponents, and donors, as well as Matt Haney and Christine Johnson. Scenes from the campaign trail were witnessed firsthand and all quotes were collected with a digital recorder.

The account of SB 827 comes from the material listed in the endnotes along with interviews with Brian Hanlon, Scott Wiener, and numerous members of Wiener's staff, along with dozens of supporters and opponents, notably Damien Goodmon, whom I have interviewed dozens of times over the phone and in in-person meetings in Sacramento, Oakland, and Leimert Park. The accounts of the YIMBY rally for SB 827 at City Hall were collected from news sources, social media, and interviews with participants on both sides, notably Laura Foote and Shanti Singh of Tenants Together.

CHAPTER 10

The accounts of Proposition 10 and the growth of the tenants' rights movement and rent control drives were based on interviews with dozens of tenants, organizers, and clergy, who I accompanied on signature gathering sessions in Northern

California, notably Cindy Cornell of the Burlingame Advocates for Renter Protections in Burlingame, Reyna Gonzalez of Faith in Action in San Mateo, and Volma Volcy and Yong Her of the Sacramento Central Labor Council, AFL-CIO. I also interviewed Damien Goodmon and Michael Weinstein from AHF/Housing Is a Human Right, Amy Schur of the Alliance of Californians for Community Empowerment, Daniel Saver of Community Legal Services in East Palo Alto, Tony Roshan Samara of Urban Habitat, and Tom Bannon of the California Apartment Association.

The accounts of the YIMBY endorsements meeting, the last days of Sonja Trauss's Campaign, and Ernest Brown's house party events were all witnessed firsthand and all quotes were captured with a digital recorder.

EPILOGUE

I attended the 2018 YIMBYtown conference as well as the Boston People's Plan Assembly and extensively interviewed participants on both sides, as well as a few who went to both events. All scenes were witnessed firsthand and quotes captured with a digital recorder.

I also interviewed Ryan D. Enos at Harvard University about group dynamics in cities. My conclusions about how tribal behaviors affect collective action problems were drawn largely from that conversation and his 2017 book, *The Space Between Us*.

PREFACE

xi   **the homeownership rate:** *Locked Out? Are Rising Housing Costs Barring Young Adults from Buying Their First Homes?* (McLean, VA: Freddie Mac, June 2018).

xi   **quarter of tenant:** *The State of the Nation's Housing 2019* (Cambridge, MA: Joint Center for Housing Studies of Harvard University, 2019).

xii   **about a million:** "National Estimates: Eviction in America," Eviction Lab, May 11, 2018, https://evictionlab.org/national-estimates/.

xii   **about four million:** "Sex of Workers by Travel Time to Work," U.S. Census Bureau, 2017, https://censusreporter.org/data/table/?table=B08012&geo_ids=01000US&primary_geo_id=01000US#valueType%7Cestimate.

xiii   **Transportation accounts for:** "Sources of Greenhous Gas Emissions," United States Environmental Protection Agency, https://www.epa.gov/ghgemissions/sources-greenhouse-gas-emissions.

xiii **In October 1945:** Nina Leen, "The California Way of Life," *Life*, October 22, 1945, 105.

CHAPTER 1: MEMBERS OF THE PUBLIC

2 **exist yet as:** City and County of San Francisco, San Francisco Planning Commission, Public Meeting (SFGovTV, May 1, 2014), sanfrancisco.granicus .com/player/clip/19987?view_id=20.

6 **nicely stenciled lettering:** "G.E.T. OUT: Faux Tech Contingent Brings the Gentrification of SF OUT of the Closet at PRIDE," Heart of the City, www .heart-of-the-city.org/get-out--sf-pride.html.

6 **a human blockade:** "December 9, 2013," *Heart of the City*, www.heart-of-the-city .org/google-bus-block---dec-9.html.

6 **chronicled on Twitter:** Nick Wingfield, "Seattle Gets Its Own Tech Bus Protest," *New York Times,* February 10, 2014, bits.blogs.nytimes.com/2014/02/10 /seattle-gets-its-own-tech-bus-protest/?_php=true&_type=blogs&_php=true& _type=blogs&_r=1.

9 **dividing up housing:** Sonia Hirt, *Zoned in the USA: The Origins and Implications of American Land-Use Regulation* (London: Cornell University Press, 2014), 153.

9 **ad described Germantown:** "Fairfax Apartments," *Evening Public Ledger*, September 14, 1914.

CHAPTER 2: ORGANIZING THE UNORGANIZABLE

16 **oppose exurban housing:** Bernard J. Frieden, *The Environmental Protection Hustle* (Cambridge, MA: MIT Press, 1979), 9, 18.

16 **entire chapter bashing:** Bernard J. Frieden, "Better Living Through Environmentalism," in *The Environmental Protection Hustle.*

16 **Frieden was no zealot:** Frieden, *Environmental Protection Hustle,* 5, 38.

17 **dog looking upward:** "Sky-High Housing: Building Up, Prices Up," *Time,* September 12, 1977.

17 **"and probably unorganizable":** Bernard J. Frieden, *Environmental Protection Hustle,* 6.

18 **headline in 1981:** Wayne King, "Changing San Francisco Is Foreseen as a Haven for Wealthy and Childless," *The New York Times,* June 9, 1981, www.nytimes.com /1981/06/09/us/changing-san-francisco-is-foreseen-as-a-haven-for-wealthy-and -childless.html.

18 **"and I contend":** Larry Katz, "Housing and the Political Economy of 'Social Schizophrenia,'" Department of Economics Graduation Ceremony, University of California at Berkeley, June 12, 1981.

23 **cracked stucco house:** Edward Glaeser and Joseph Gyourko, "Urban Decline and Durable Housing," *Journal of Political Economy* 113, no. 2 (April 2005): 345–75; Edward Glaeser and Joseph Gyourko, "The Economic Implications of Housing Supply," *Journal of Economic Perspectives* 32, no. 1 (Winter 2018): 3–30.

24 **writer named Kim-Mai:** Kim-Mai Cutler, "How Burrowing Owls Lead to Vomiting Anarchists (or SF's Housing Crisis Explained)," TechCrunch, 2014, https://techcrunch.com/2014/04/14/sf-housing/.

30 **stunting American migration:** Peter Ganog and Daniel Shoag, "Why Has Regional Income Convergence Declined?," *Journal of Urban Economics* 102 (November 2017): 76–90.

30 **tallied across all:** "Obama Administration Releases Housing Development Toolkit," National Low Income Housing Coalition, October 3, 2016, http://nlihc .org/resource/obama-administration-releases-housing-development-toolkit.

30 **These studies all:** Richard Florida, "How Housing Supply Became the Most Controversial Issue in Urbanism," City Lab, May 23, 2019, https://www.citylab .com/design/2019/05/residential-zoning-code-density-storper-rodriguez-pose -data/590050/; "Blanket Upzoning—A Blunt Instrument—Won't Solve the Affordable Housing Crisis," The Planning Report, March 15, 2019, https://www .planningreport.com/2019/03/15/blanket-upzoning-blunt-instrument-wont-solve -affordable-housing-crisis.

31 **"We can work together":** "Remarks by the President at U.S. Conference of Mayors," Obama White House, January 21, 2016, http://obamawhitehouse .archives.gov/the-press-office/2016/01/21/remarks-president-us-conference -mayors.

CHAPTER 3: *NO HAY PEOR LUCHA QUE LA QUE NO SE HACE*

41 **mostly male laborers:** Roger Christopher Rouse, "Mexican Migration to the United States: Family Relations in the Development of a Transnational Migrant Circuit" (PhD diss., Stanford University, 1989).

54 **Daniel could tell:** Daniel Saver, email to author.

59 **America's largest metro:** "The State of the Nation's Housing 2018," Joint Center for Housing Studies of Harvard University, www.jchs.harvard.edu/state-nations -housing-2018.

59 **within a mile:** "Rising Housing Costs and Re-segregation in San Francisco," Urban Displacement Project, www.urbandisplacement.org/sites/default/files /images/sf_final.pdf.

59 **Given the choice:** Karen Chapple and Anastasia Loukaitou-Sideris, *Transit- Oriented Displacement or Community Dividends? Understanding the Effects of Smarter Growth on Communities* (Cambridge, MA: The MIT Press, 2019), 2010.

CHAPTER 4: PLANS OF OPPRESSION

64 **goodbye war babies:** Kenneth T. Jackson, *Crabgrass Frontier: The Suburbanization of the United States* (New York: Oxford University Press, 1985), 232; Kevin Starr, *Golden Dreams: California in an Age of Abundance, 1950–1963* (New York: Oxford University Press, 2009), 6.

65 **alleviate the shortage:** Ethan Rarick, *California Rising: The Life and Times of Pat Brown* (Berkeley: University of California Press, 2005), 25, 52, 53.

65 **The only possible:** Rarick, *California Rising*, 53.

66 **five million new:** Jackson, *Crabgrass Frontier*, 233.

66 **1.7 million in:** Jackson, *Crabgrass Frontier*, 233.

67 **Cape Cod had:** Jackson, *Crabgrass Frontier*, 11.

67 **during a walk:** Starr, *Golden Dreams*, 18.

67 **telling Khrushchev that:** Robert J. Gordon, *The Rise and Fall of American Growth: The U.S. Standard of Living Since the Civil War* (Princeton, NJ: Princeton University Press, 2016), 357.

68 **"cannot combine the two":** Jackson, *Crabgrass Frontier*, 241.

69 **had to stare:** D. J. Waldie, *Holy Land: A Suburban Memoir* (New York: W. W. Norton, 2005).

69 **a consummate booster:** Rarick, *California Rising*, 13.

69 **approve $1.75 billion:** Rarick, *California Rising*, 217.

70 **"Build barriers around":** Rarick, *California Rising*, 210.

70 **party to commemorate:** "We're Top Banana Now," *Oakland Tribune*, December 23, 1962.

70 **men on horseback:** Rarick, *California Rising*, 1.

71 **"station wagon crowded":** Eugene Burdick, "From Gold Rush to Sun Rush," *The New York Times*, April 14, 1963.

72 **demolish homes in:** Matthew Lasner, interview by author, 2018.

74 **black assemblyman from:** Lawrence P. Crouchett, *William Byron Rumford, the Life and Public Services of a California Legislator: A Biography* (El Cerrito, CA: Downey Place, 1984), xv, 43.

74 **Of the 350,000:** Rarick, *California Rising*, 259.

76 **victory was sweet:** Rarick, *California Rising*, 263–67; Crouchett, *William Byron Rumford*, 264–69.

76 **a liberal Republican:** Starr, *Golden Dreams*, 254.

76 **could be enshrined:** Rarick, *California Rising*, 273, 289.

76 **Republican state senator:** Robert O. Self, *American Babylon: Race and the Struggle for Postwar Oakland* (Princeton, NJ: Princeton University Press, 2003), 167.

77 **Majority-black districts:** Self, *American Babylon*, 263.

77 **draw but one:** Rarick, *California Rising*, 289.

78 **combining the fear:** Rarick, *California Rising*, 338, 356, 359.

78 **"today the blunt":** "Freeways: U.S. Gold Turned Down in S.F.," *Los Angeles Times*, March 27, 1966.

79 **didn't start building:** "Politics: A Rash of New Candidates," *Los Angeles Daily Times*, March 27, 1966.

79 **Save the Bay:** Starr, *Golden Dreams*, 421, 428.

79 **wrote Harold Gilliam:** Starr, *Golden Dreams*, 417.

80 **predominantly focused on:** Raymond Dasmann, *The Destruction of California* (New York: Collier Books, 1966), 190.

81 **dogs to quadruple:** Christopher C. Sellers, *Crabgrass Crucible: Suburban Nature and the Rise of Environmentalism in Twentieth-Century America* (Chapel Hill: University of North Carolina Press, 2012), 3, 83, 168.

83 **"era of limits":** Edmund G. Brown Jr., State of the State Address, January 7, 1976, Governors' Gallery, http://governors.library.ca.gov/addresses/s_34-JBrown1.html.

83 **living that Schumacher:** Arthur I. Blaustein, "California Still Dreaming," *Harper's Magazine*, June 1, 1977.

84 **committed to passivity:** Blaustein, "California Still Dreaming."

86 **"concert and execute":** Robert C. Ellickson, "Suburban Growth Controls: An Economic and Legal Analysis," *Yale Law Journal* 86, no. 3 (January 1977): 389.

86 **common usage over:** William A. Fischel, "The Rise of the Homevoters: How the Growth Machine Was Subverted by OPEC and Earth Day," in *Evidence and Innovation in Housing Law and Policy*, ed. Lee Anne Fennell and Benjamin J. Keys (Cambridge, UK: Cambridge University Press, 2017), 11, 15.

91 **"were a Communist":** Howard Jarvis, *I'm Mad as Hell: The Exclusive Story of the Tax Revolt and Its Leader*, with Robert Pack (New York: Times Books, 1979), 53–54.

91 **Brown said in:** Edmund G. Brown Jr., State of the State Address, January 16, 1979, Governors' Gallery, accessed 2017, governors.library.ca.gov/addresses/s_34-JBrown4.html.

92 **tackle the crisis:** Henry Weinstein, "Task Force to Study High Housing Costs," *Los Angeles Times*, February 13, 1980.

CHAPTER 5: SUE THE SUBURBS

95 **founded in 1983:** "Our History," BRIDGE Housing, https://bridgehousing.com /about/history/.

100 **during his windup:** City of Lafayette, Lafayette Planning Commission, Public Meeting, October 15, 2013, http://lafayette.granicus.com/MediaPlayer.php?view _id=19&clip_id=916.

102 **the word "cancer":** Susan Candell, Documents for Lafayette City Council meeting, August 8, 2015, https://lafayette.granicus.com/MetaViewer.php?view _id=3&clip_id=2482&meta_id=46371.

103 **"adding people instead":** City of Lafayette, City Council Meeting, Public Meeting, August 10, 2015, http://lafayette.granicus.com/MediaPlayer.php?view _id=3&clip_id=2482.

106 **"success drawing attention":** "California Renters Legal Advocacy and Education Fund—General Support," Open Philanthropy Project, June 2016, www .openphilanthropy.org/focus/us-policy/land-use-reform/california-renters-legal -advocacy-and-education-fund-general-support.

107 **holding a textbook:** Patrick Clark, "The Activist Group Suing the Suburbs for Bigger Buildings," Bloomberg, December 9, 2015, www.bloomberg.com/news /articles/2015-12-09/the-activist-group-suing-the-suburbs-for-bigger-buildings.

108 **constellation of new:** Michan Andrew Connor, "'Public Benefits from Public Choice': Producing Decentralization in Metropolitan Los Angeles, 1954–1973," *Journal of Urban History* 39, no. 1 (2012): 79–100.

108 **first "contract city":** John Wentz, "Should Lakewood Annex to Long Beach," *Western City*, January 1952, www.lakewoodcity.org/civicax/filebank/blobdload .aspx?BlobID=22686.

109 **total of 700,000 residents:** Connor, "'Public Benefits from Public Choice.'"

109 **named Charles Tiebout:** Charles Tiebout, "A Pure Theory of Local Expenditures," *Journal of Political Economy* 64, no. 5 (October 1956): 416–24.

110 **"Lakewood Plan cities":** Gary J. Miller, *Cities by Contract: The Politics of Municipal Incorporation* (Cambridge, MA: MIT Press, 1981).

110 **Compton's poor population:** Ryan Reft, "Educating Compton: Race, Taxes, and Schools in Southern California's Most Notorious Suburb," KCET, August 7, 2014, www.kcet.org/history-society/educating-compton-race-taxes-and-schools-in -southern-californias-most-notorious.

112 **without cities' approval:** "City of Lafayette Staff Report," http://lafayette .granicus.com/MetaViewer.php?view_id=3&clip_id=2951&meta_id=58509.

114 **"not bring lawsuits":** City of Lafayette, City Council Meeting, Public Meeting, August 10, 2015, http://lafayette.granicus.com/MediaPlayer.php?view_id=3&clip _id=2482.

116 **"My conscience won't"**: Steven Falk (@Steven_B_Falk), "My letter of resignation," Twitter, September 27, 2018, 6:56 a.m., http://twitter.com/steven_b_falk/status/1045311105365504000?lang=en.

CHAPTER 6: THE SECOND HOUSING PACKAGE

118 **"the monotone of"**: Joe Eskenazi, "Body Politic: Scott Wiener Strips Down City Bureaucracy," *SF Weekly*, February 13, 2013, www.sfweekly.com/news/body-politic-scott-wiener-strips-down-city-bureaucracy/.

119 **The progressive label**: Benjamin Wachs and Joe Eskenazi, "Progressively Worse: The Tumultuous Rise and Acrimonious Fall of the City's Left," *SF Weekly*, November 23, 2011, https://archives.sfweekly.com/sanfrancisco/progressively-worse-the-tumultuous-rise-and-acrimonious-fall-of-the-citys-left/Content?oid=2183264&showFullText=true.

120 **San Francisco politicians**: Jason A. McDaniel, "The Progressive Ideological Coalition and the Crisis of Housing Affordability in San Francisco," *The New West*, August 9, 2015, https://thewpsa.wordpress.com/2015/08/09/the-progressive-ideological-coalition-and-the-crisis-of-housing-affordability-in-san-francisco/.

120 **local BDSM festival**: Scott Wiener (@Scott_Wiener), "#UpYourAlley fair! #DoreAlley #leather #BDSM #LGBT @FolsomStEvents," Twitter, July 31, 2016, 3:03 p.m., https://twitter.com/scott_wiener/status/759872134365663232?lang=en.

121 **permit amounted to**: J. K. Dineen, "Supervisor Wiener to Introduce Affordable Housing Legislation," *San Francisco Chronicle*, September 14, 2015, www.sfchronicle.com/bayarea/article/Affordable-housing-legislation-goes-to-Supes-6504387.php?psid=2ESrd.

121 **According to local**: David Talbot, *Season of the Witch: Enchantment, Terror, and Deliverance in the City of Love* (New York, NY: Free Press, 2012), 248–49.

122 **testified in favor**: City and County of San Francisco Planning Commission, Public Meeting, December 3, 2015, https://sanfrancisco.granicus.com/player/clip/24255?view_id=20&meta_id=470365.

125 **would have shut**: "City of San Francisco Mission District Housing Moratorium Initiative, Proposition I (November 2015)," Ballotpedia, https://ballotpedia.org/City_of_San_Francisco_Mission_District_Housing_Moratorium_Initiative,_Proposition_I_(November_2015).

125 **year getting yelled**: David-Elijah Nahmod, "Affordable Housing Activists Take Their Battle to Supervisor Wiener's Home," *Hoodline*, May 31, 2015, http://hoodline.com/2015/05/affordable-housing-activists-take-their-battle-to-supervisor-s-home.

126 **"threat of displacement"**: Michael Hankinson, "When Do Renters Behave Like Homeowners? High Rent, Price Anxiety, and NIMBYism," *American Political Science Review* 112, no. 3 (2018): 473–93.

129 **just begun surging:** Joe Garofoli and Lizze Johnson, "Bernie Sanders to Campaign for Jane Kim in SF," *San Francisco Chronicle*, October 14, 2016, www.sfchronicle.com/bayarea/article/Bernie-Sanders-to-campaign-for-Jane-Kim-in-SF-9972390.php.

131 **a 157-unit project:** Joe Rivano Barros, "In Stunner, City Strikes Down Major Mission Project," *Mission Local*, November 16, 2016, https://missionlocal.org/2016/11/in-stunner-city-strikes-down-major-mission-project/.

132 **audible gasps in:** City and County of San Francisco Board of Supervisors, Public Meeting, November 14, 2016, http://sanfrancisco.granicus.com/player/clip/26569?view_id=10&meta_id=526895.

134 **photo on Thiel's:** Anna Wiener, "Why Protestors Gathered Outside Peter Thiel's Mansion This Weekend," *New Yorker*, March 14, 2017, www.newyorker.com/news/news-desk/why-protesters-gathered-outside-peter-thiels-mansion-this-weekend.

142 **full of headlines:** Erika D. Smith, "Out with California's NIMBYs and in with the YIMBYs," *Sacramento Bee*, July 20, 2017, www.sacbee.com/opinion/opn-columns-blogs/erika-d-smith/article162699668.html.

142 **new day described:** Peter Kremer, "State Sends a Signal in the Housing Crisis," *Los Angeles Times*, October 20, 1980.

143 **"Plenty of paradox":** Associated Press, "Gov. Brown Signs Bills Aimed at Fixing California Housing Crunch," September 29, 2017, https://sanfrancisco.cbslocal.com/2017/09/29/gov-jerry-brown-california-affordable-housing-bills/.

CHAPTER 7: THE OLD WAYS

149 **"literally without shelter":** National Academies of Sciences, Engineering, and Medicine, *Permanent Supportive Housing: Evaluating the Evidence for Improving Health Outcomes Among People Experiencing Chronic Homelessness* (Washington, DC: National Academies Press, 2018), doi.org/10.17226/25133.

149 **skid row–style poverty:** Marian Moser Jones, "Creating a Science of Homelessness During the Reagan Era," *Milbank Quarterly* 93, no. 1 (March 2015): 138–78.

149 **initial explanation was:** Martha Burt, *Over the Edge: The Growth of Homelessness in the 1980s* (New York: Russell Sage Foundation, 1992), 4.

149 **subsequent recovery failed:** Christopher Jencks, *The Homeless* (Cambridge, MA: Harvard University Press, 1994), 49.

149 **as "starving time":** David Erickson, *The Housing Policy Revolution: Networks and Neighborhoods* (Washington, DC.: Urban Institute Press, 2009), 35.

150 **hit of crack:** "The United States Drug Enforcement Administration 1985–1990," The Way Back Machine, updated August 23, 2006, https://web.archive.org/web/20060823024931/http:/www.usdoj.gov/dea/pubs/history/1985-1990.html.

151 **Columbia University graduate:** Jones, "Creating a Science of Homelessness During the Reagan Era."

152 **crushed to death:** Erin Tracy, "Homeless Woman Killed in Caltrans Accident Was 'Flower Child' with a Roller-Coaster Life," *Modesto Bee*, April 17, 2019, www .modbee.com/news/article229325389.html.

153 **a remarkable statistic:** Jay Bainbridge, Thomas Byrne, Dennis P. Culhane, Stephen Metraux, and Magdi Stino, "The Age of Contemporary Homelessness: Evidence and Implications for Public Policy," *Analyses of Social Issues and Public Policy* 13, No. 1 (2013): 1–17.

153 **becoming senior citizens:** Thomas Byrne, Dennis P. Culhane, Kelly Doran, Eileen Johns, Stephen Metraux, and Dan Treglia, "The Emerging Crisis of Aged Homelessness: Could Housing Solutions Be Funded from Avoidance of Excess Shelter, Hospital and Nursing Home Costs?" University of Pennsylvania, January 20, 2019, https://works.bepress.com/dennis_culhane/223/; David Bangsberg, Judith A. Hahn, Margot B. Kushel, and Elise Riley, "The Aging of the Homeless Population: Fourteen-Year Trends in San Francisco," *Journal of General Internal Medicine* 21, No. 7 (2006): 775–78.

154 **$20 billion a year:** Matthew Desmond, "How Homeownership Became the Engine of American Inequality," *The New York Times Magazine*, May 9, 2017, www.nytimes.com/2017/05/09/magazine/how-homeownership-became-the -engine-of-american-inequality.html.

155 **bleaching the sidewalks:** "The San Diego Hepatitis A Epidemic: (Mis)handling a Public Health Crisis," San Diego County Superior Court Grand Jury, May 17, 2018, www.sandiegocounty.gov/content/dam/sdc/grandjury/reports/2017-2018 /HepAReport.pdf.

156 **$425,000 per unit:** Jonathan Woetzel et al., "Closing California's Housing Gap," McKinsey & Company, October 2016, www.mckinsey.com/featured-insights /urbanization/closing-californias-housing-gap.

159 **in 1948 *Harper's*:** Kenneth T. Jackson, *Crabgrass Frontier: The Suburbanization of the United States* (New York: Oxford University Press, 1985), 236.

159 **construction industry's productivity:** Filipe Barbosa et al., "Reinventing Construction Through a Productivity Revolution," McKinsey & Company, February 2017, www.mckinsey.com/industries/capital-projects-and-infrastructure /our-insights/reinventing-construction-through-a-productivity-revolution.

CHAPTER 8: THE VALUE-ADD INVESTOR

170 **the least profiting:** John Logan and Harvey Molotch, *Urban Fortunes: The Political Economy of Place* (Berkeley: University of California Press, 1987), 104.

171 **"efforts at urban":** Logan and Molotch, *Urban Fortunes*, 113.

175 **Trion bought it:** Sam Levin, "Low-Income Families Face Eviction as Building 'Rebrands' for Facebook Workers," *Guardian*, September 21, 2016, www .theguardian.com/technology/2016/sep/21/silicon-valley-eviction-facebook-trion -properties.

176 **Trion fortuitously unloaded:** Tyler Stewart, "An In-Depth Look at Multifamily on the West Coast," May 29, 2018, RealCrowd podcast, 16th episode.

177 **double the rent:** Curt Lanning, "Low-Rent Apartments in Tigard Kicking Residents Out," KOIN, last updated September 22, 2016, www.koin.com/news /low-rent-apartments-in-tigard-kicking-residents-out/870144355.

177 **"We've been able":** Stewart, "An In-Depth Look at Multifamily on the West Coast."

178 **anesthesiologist who gave:** Stewart, "An In-Depth Look at Multifamily on the West Coast."

179 **RealCrowd raised $1.6 million:** Lora Kolodny, "RealCrowd Raises $1.6M to Bring Crowdfunding to Real Estate," *Wall Street Journal*, March 26, 2014, https://blogs.wsj.com/venturecapital/2014/03/26/realcrowd-raises-1-6m-to-bring -crowdfunding-to-real-estate/.

179 **"thermostat that costs":** "Trion Properties: How an Ex-investment Sales Broker Built a $100M Portfolio," *A Student of the Real Estate Game*, January 20, 2016, http://astudentoftherealestategame.com/trion-properties-how-an-ex-investment -sales-broker-built-a-100m-portfolio/.

180 **"sit so well":** Stewart, "An In-Depth Look at Multifamily on the West Coast."

CHAPTER 9: SONJA FOR SUPERVISOR

189 **support climate action:** Conor Dougherty and Brad Plumer, "A Bold, Divisive Plan to Wean Californians from Cars," *New York Times*, March 16, 2018, www .nytimes.com/2018/03/16/business/energy-environment/climate-density.html.

189 **politely hated 827:** Rachel Swan, "SF Supervisors Opposed to Wiener's Housing-Transit Bill Soften Stance a Bit," *San Francisco Chronicle*, March 12, 2018, www .sfchronicle.com/politics/article/SF-supervisors-opposed-to-Wiener-s-12748029.php.

189 **"look like Dubai":** Alissa Walker, "Sen. Scott Wiener Will Introduce New Version of Transit Density Bill," Curbed Los Angeles, October 9, 2018, https://la.curbed .com/2018/10/9/17943490/scott-wiener-interview-density-transit-sb-827.

189 **mayor of Berkeley:** Janis Mara, "Berkeley Mayor on Wiener-Skinner Housing Bill: 'A Declaration of War Against Our Neighborhoods,'" *Berkeleyside*, January 22, 2018, www.berkeleyside.com/2018/01/22/berkeley-mayor-wiener-skinner-housing -bill-declaration-war-neighborhoods.

190 **anti-827 rally:** Rachel Swan, "Kim Runs Against Wiener Housing Bill in Her Race for Mayor," *San Francisco Chronicle*, April 6, 2018, www.sfchronicle.com /politics/article/Kim-runs-against-Wiener-housing-bill-in-her-race-12810672.php

?psid=2ESrd; SupeJaneKim, "Jane Kim on Senate Bill 827," YouTube, April 16, 2018, www.youtube.com/watch?v=pD2Dby4GOPg.

191 **Which was the:** Ethan Rarick, *California Rising: The Life and Times of Pat Brown* (Berkeley, CA: University of California Press, 2005), 320.

191 **In the 1950s:** Josh Sides, *L.A. City Limits: African American Los Angeles from the Great Depression to the Present* (Berkeley, CA: University of California Press, 2004), 120–23.

195 **signed a letter:** "National Fair Housing and Civil Rights Experts Announce Support for Senator Wiener's Transit Housing Bill," Senate.ca.gov, April 5, 2018, https://sd11.senate.ca.gov/news/20180405-national-fair-housing-and-civil-rights -experts-announce-support-senator-wiener%E2%80%99s.

195 **Then they killed:** Conor Dougherty, "California Lawmakers Kill Housing Bill After Fierce Debate," *The New York Times*, April 17, 2018, www.nytimes.com /2018/04/17/business/economy/california-housing.html.

CHAPTER 10: THE RENT IS TOO DAMN HIGH

205 **"We'll fight very hard":** Liam Dillon, "How California Has Become a National Battleground for Rent Control as Money Flows In from Landlords," *Los Angeles Times*, October 31, 2018, www.latimes.com/politics/la-pol-ca-rent-control -campaign-spending-20181031-story.html??dssReturn=true.

207 **largest AIDS nonprofit:** Christopher Glazek, "The C.E.O. of H.I.V.," *The New York Times*, April 27, 2017, www.nytimes.com/2017/04/26/magazine/the-ceo-of-hiv.html.

207 **He described himself:** Christine Mai-Duc and Javier Panzar, "'Thug,' 'Bully,' 'Satan': This L.A. Activist Has Never Shied from Controversy While Building an AIDS Political Powerhouse," *Los Angeles Times*, October 19, 2016, www.latimes .com/politics/la-pol-ca-aids-healthcare-foundation-propositions-20161019-snap -story.html.

208 **an "egotistical billionaire":** Joe Eskenazi, "Prop. 10: Californians Like Rent Control, Hate Ballot Measure That Would Expand Rent Control," Mission Local, October 29, 2018, https://missionlocal.org/2018/10/prop-10-californians-like -rent-control-hate-ballot-measure-that-would-expand-rent-control/.

209 **about $22 million:** "California Proposition 10, Local Rent Control Initiative (2018)," Ballotpedia, https://ballotpedia.org/California_Proposition_10,_Local _Rent_Control_Initiative_(2018).

210 **big homeless tax:** "San Francisco, California, Proposition C, Gross Receipts Tax for Homeless Services (November 2018)," Ballotpedia, https://ballotpedia.org /San_Francisco,_California,_Proposition_C,_Gross_Receipts_Tax_for _Homelessness_Services_(November_2018).

212 **The total tab:** "California Proposition 10, Local Rent Control Initiative (2018)."

218 **YIMBY-supported measures:** J. K. Dineen, "Housing, by Any Means Necessary," *San Francisco Chronicle*, November 1, 2018, www.sfchronicle.com/politics/article /How-powerful-is-Bay-Area-s-pro-housing-13352047.php?psid=2ESrd.

223 **fifteen hundred votes:** "November 6, 2018 Election Results—Summary," City and County of San Francisco Department of Elections, https://sfelections.sfgov .org/november-6-2018-election-results-summary.

233 **Social scientists have:** Ryan D. Enos, *The Space Between Us* (Cambridge: Cambridge University Press, 2017), 174–75.

INDEX

———